THE CAREER
GAME LOOP

THE CAREER GAME LOOP

LEARN TO EARN IN THE NEW ECONOMY

JESSICA LINDL

WILEY

Published by John Wiley & Sons, Inc., Hoboken, New Jersey.
Published simultaneously in Canada.

For general information on our other products and services or for technical support, please contact
our Customer Care Department within the United States at (800) 762-2974, outside the United
States at (317) 572-3993 or fax (317) 572-4002.

Wiley also publishes its books in a variety of electronic formats. Some content that appears in print
may not be available in electronic formats. For more information about Wiley products, visit our web
site at www.wiley.com.

Library of Congress Cataloging-in-Publication Data is Available:

ISBN 9781394217663 (Cloth)
ISBN 9781394217670 (ePub)
ISBN 9781394217687 (ePDF)

COVER DESIGN: PAUL MCCARTHY
COVER ART: © GETTY IMAGES | KLAUS VEDFELT

SKY10099586_030725

Contents

About the Author

Jessica Lindl is the vice president of Ecosystem Growth at Unity Technologies, where she leads initiatives that empower millions of learners worldwide to succeed in the new economy. With over two decades of experience at the intersection of technology, education, and workforce development, Lindl has been a pioneer in leveraging game skills to unlock new career pathways for learners of all ages. She frequently speaks at global conferences and advocates for inclusive, accessible pathways to success in the tech industry.

In addition to her work at Unity Technologies, Lindl shapes public education practice as a Pahara-Aspen Institute Fellow. She influences education technology investments as an advisory board member for GSV Ventures, and she advocates for equitable career opportunities nationwide with the Corporate Council at Jobs for the Future.

Acknowledgments

Thank you to the entire Unity Community for embracing me as a life-long apprentice of your brilliance, and to my close partners in this book—Aaron, Anuja, Aurore, Ellen, Joy, Kayla, Kevin, Lucy, Neal, and Rachel.

Foreword

When I was first asked to write this foreword, I couldn't help but feel a bit excited—and also a little reflective—about my own journey in the world of gaming and careers. You see, my career, much like yours probably has been (or will be), wasn't always a straight path. It's been more like an epic quest with unexpected twists, some challenging boss battles, and, let's be real, more than a few respawns along the way. And that's why *The Career Game Loop* feels so important right now. It captures how we can navigate today's fast-changing, unpredictable job market by tapping into something many of us are already familiar with: the mindset of a gamer.

For those of you who might not know me, I've spent over 35-years in the entertainment industry, from my early days in radio to my two decades at Xbox, where I connected with millions of gamers and developers through podcasts, live shows, and events. Along the way, I've had the incredible opportunity to witness firsthand how gaming can change lives—not just through entertainment but also through the valuable skills we develop by playing. What I love about this book is that it taps directly into that idea: the notion that the skills we build in gaming aren't just for fun; they're actually tools that can help us thrive in our careers and in life.

Let me give you a little story to start things off—one that speaks to how gaming has shaped my own career in ways I couldn't have imagined. When I first started out, I had no idea that my path would eventually lead me to Microsoft, much less to a long career helping build the Xbox brand. Back then, I was just a guy who loved radio and video games, figuring out how to turn my passions into something meaningful. It wasn't like I had this grand career plan all laid out—far from it! But here's the thing: gaming taught me the value of perseverance, problem-solving, and strategic thinking.

I remember one day when I was working in radio, I got a call from a friend who was at Microsoft. He told me they were working on this exciting new project in music streaming (this was the year 2000). I jumped at it! A few years later I heard about this other project called "Xbox," and next thing I knew, I was helping shape what would become one of the biggest platforms in gaming. I didn't land that opportunity by knowing exactly where I was headed. Instead, I got there by being flexible, learning new things, and approaching challenges with the kind of mindset I'd developed through years of gaming—curious, adaptive, and unafraid to take risks.

That's exactly what *The Career Game Loop* is about. It's not just a book for gamers (though if you are one, you're going to love how it connects those dots). It's for anyone who's trying to navigate the ups and downs of today's job market—a world where industries are changing rapidly, technology is disrupting everything, and the old rules of career progression don't seem to apply anymore. Whether you're just starting out, trying to make a career pivot, or leveling up in your current role, this book offers you a road map. And what's brilliant about it is that it breaks down career building in a way that will feel familiar to anyone who's ever played a video game.

Jessica has done something special here by taking the concept of the "game loop" and using it as a framework for career growth. Now, if you're not familiar with game loops, let me explain quickly. A game loop is the repetitive process that defines the core of what you do in a game. Think about the games you love—whether it's *Call of Duty*, *Minecraft*, or *The Witcher*. In each one, you have this loop of tasks: you pick a quest or a goal, you gather resources or skills, you fight your battles, and then you reap your rewards before heading out on the next adventure. You keep leveling up, learning new strategies, and unlocking new achievements. It's a process of constant growth and improvement.

And here's the thing: your career works the exact same way.

In this book, Jessica lays out what she calls *The Career Game Loop*. It's a career framework that breaks down into four main phases: first, you choose your quest—that's deciding what kind of work you want to pursue or what problem you want to solve. Next, you level up by learning new skills, acquiring knowledge, and growing in your role. Then, you go into the job hunt—seeking out new opportunities, whether it's a promotion, a new company, or even a career pivot. And finally, you get to job craft—this is where you customize your role, adapt to new challenges, and continue to grow within your field. Once you've completed the loop, you start over, stronger and wiser from the experience.

It's such a brilliant analogy because it shows how careers, like games, are not linear. The days of having a single career path that you follow from college until retirement are over for most people. Today's world requires us to be adaptable, to expect change, and to continually evolve our skills. That might sound daunting, but gamers know that this is part of the fun. We don't shy away from a tough boss fight or a tricky level—we lean into the challenge. And when we fail, we learn from it and try again. That's exactly how we need to approach our careers.

Let's talk for a second about failure. I know it's a word that makes a lot of people uncomfortable, but it really shouldn't. One of the most valuable things gaming has taught me is that failure isn't the end—it's part of the process. Whether you've been crushed in a multiplayer match or wiped out in a raid, you know that feeling of wanting to throw the controller across the room. But you also know that you can always respawn, rethink your strategy, and try again. And when you finally succeed? Man, that victory feels so much sweeter because of the struggle. That's how it works in careers, too. You're going to face setbacks. You're going to take wrong turns. You might even fail spectacularly. But if you view those failures as opportunities to learn and grow, you'll come out of it stronger and more resilient.

Jessica captures this perfectly in her book. She doesn't sugarcoat the challenges of today's job market, but she offers a way forward that feels empowering. She reminds us that, like in gaming, careers are about learning, experimenting, and adapting. The key is to stay flexible, embrace the process, and see each challenge as an opportunity to level up.

One of my favorite sections of the book is where she talks about community. In gaming, we know the value of teaming up with others. Whether you're in a co-op campaign or part of a massive multiplayer guild, you know that the people you play with can make all the difference. The same goes for your career. Having a strong network of mentors, peers, and supporters can be a game changer. In my own career, I've been lucky enough to work with some incredibly talented and generous people—mentors who helped me see opportunities I might have missed, peers who pushed me to be better, and a community that has supported me every step of the way.

Jessica emphasizes that building this community is an essential part of your career game loop. It's not just about what you know, but who you know and how you collaborate. Just like in multiplayer games, we don't get anywhere without a little help from others. Whether it's a mentor offering guidance or a colleague sharing their expertise, the people around us can help us grow in ways we can't do alone.

Another point I love in this book is how it encourages us to think of our careers as dynamic and evolving. Remember when you started a game and thought you were heading in one direction, only to discover halfway through that the real challenge was somewhere else? That happens in real life too. Sometimes we think we know what we want in our careers, but as we explore new opportunities and learn new skills, we realize our true passion lies in a different direction. That's okay! In fact, that's one of the most exciting parts of the career game loop—you get to pivot, try new things, and discover paths you didn't even know existed.

I can tell you from personal experience that the willingness to adapt and try new things is crucial. When I first joined Xbox, the gaming landscape was nothing like it is today. We've seen the rise of digital distribution, cloud gaming, cross-platform play, and so much more. The industry is constantly evolving, and to keep up, we've had to evolve right along with it. That same mindset applies to any career. The world is changing fast, and the skills that were in demand a decade ago might not be as valuable today. But if you're willing to keep learning, keep leveling up, and stay curious, you'll always find new opportunities.

In *The Career Game Loop*, Jessica gives you the tools to do just that. She breaks down the process into actionable steps, helping you see your career as a series of challenges and opportunities—just like a great game. And whether you're a gamer or not, this approach will resonate with you because it's grounded in real-world experiences and practical advice. She's not just talking theory here. She's giving you a playbook for how to navigate the complexities of today's job market and come out on top.

So, whether you're a gamer looking to turn your hobby into a career advantage, or someone who's trying to figure out how to thrive in this unpredictable world of work, this book has something for you. It's packed with insights, strategies, and most important, a sense of empowerment. You've got what it takes to succeed—you just need the right tools, the right mindset, and a willingness to embrace the loop.

Alright, I think I've said enough. Now it's time for you to dive into the book and start your own career game loop. Choose your quest, level up your skills, and get ready to craft a career that's as dynamic and exciting as any game you've ever played.

Good luck. I know you can do it!

—Larry Hryb, aka "Major Nelson"
Director of Community at Unity

Introduction

Think this job market is tough? Try life as a witcher.

If you've played *The Witcher*, or seen the show, or read the books, you'll know: witching is a scary business. If you've never heard of *The Witcher*, you'll just have to take my word for it.

On a good day, you'll fight a frothing horde of sludge zombies whose greatest ambition is to claw you to death, pickle you in swamp muck, then consume you bit by tender bit. On a bad day, you might get tangled up with a rotting corpse who's got a bone to pick with the living and an army of plague-infested rats at her command.

The wild thing about witchers—and the gamers who control them—is that they don't just fight one of these horrors and call it a day. They go looking for these fights, one after another, again and again and again.

Werewolf down? Let's get ourselves a vampire. Vampire slain? Let's move on to the demonic, faceless gravedigger and his violent mob of undead spirits.

Players of *The Witcher* aren't trapped in a revolving door of vicious nightmares. They're making an intentional effort to find these creatures and battle them, repeating an elaborate procedure every time.

I want to break down that procedure for a moment. (Stick with me—I've got a point here.)

First, the player goes looking for a quest. Maybe they pick up a contract to help a struggling town. Maybe they pity someone who's desperately searching for their wife. One way or another, there's a monster out there, and the player volunteers to slay it.

Next comes the prep. The player interrogates locals about the monster, then does some forensic probing at the scene of the crime. They get their potions brewed and their gear packed.

And then they chase down their leads. Find the monster. Fight it. Kill it.

On the other side of victory are rewards. Bags of gold. Shiny new gear. The player levels up their character, improves their gadgets, grabs new equipment, and seeks out their next quest.

Then the cycle begins again.

In the world of game design, this repeating procedure is called a *core game loop*. And, as far as I'm concerned, it's the key to unlocking career growth in the new economy.

Big Bad Uncertainty

Previous generations entered the working world knowing, from the start, what they would do and how they would do it. Where you grew up, who your parents were, what you looked like, how much money you had, what school you went to—these things determined what kind of career you'd have. And once you had that career, there was usually just one way to do things: the way they've always been done.

Then came the digital revolution and everything changed. Free software. Free information. Digital social networks. Rapid communication breeds rapid innovation, and rapid innovation breeds rapid disruption.

Every time technology steps forward, businesses rise and fall. Jobs disappear. Jobs spring up. Jobs transform. Value shifts. To stay nimble, more employers recruit a disposable contract-based workforce. So you get remote work. The gig economy. Where will I live? What will I be doing a year from now? The more we learn about technology, the more uncertain our own lives become.

Today, things like race, gender, class, geography, and sexuality continue to influence our futures dramatically, in big and bigoted ways. But most of us have lost the algorithmic certainty that dominated our parents' and grandparents' careers. There are just too many variables. Technology transforms too quickly. News travels too fast. Disruptors upend whole industries overnight. In the new economy, nothing about our careers is certain.

Everyone's a Witcher

I've spent the entirety of my own career chasing this storm of uncertainty. As a college junior, I interned at the FCC, the federal agency that regulates communications. It was 1994, and the FCC had their hands full with radio, phones, cable, and TV. A new form of communication was emerging—the internet—and the question was whether they should regulate that, too. The FCC took this matter so seriously that they assigned it to an intern (me) and locked her in a windowless room to figure it out.

The following years sent me down a winding road through tech, education, and workforce development. Where would the internet take us? How would work evolve? How would education evolve? To me, the answers to these questions all seemed interdependent.

For years, I ping-ponged around the worlds of tech, work, and learning. I became the CEO of an educational gaming company. The COO of a career-training venture. I worked with the White House to promote the use of games for education.

Everywhere I went, I built teams, and those teams surprised me. I found that, as among all my employees, the contributors who grew up gaming seemed most equipped to triumph in the face of 21st-century challenges. They learned new skills quickly, solved unsolvable problems, made fast friends with folks from very different backgrounds, and communicated clearly even when the way forward felt unclear.

Eventually, this discovery led me to Unity.

You might not have heard of Unity, but if you play video games, then you've seen our work. We design one of the world's most popular "game engines," which is what it sounds like: a super-powered digital machine that makes games go. Like the engine of a car, you won't see the Unity Engine unless you pop open the hood of your game. But whether you see it or not, it's there, whirling the wheels and racing things forward.

At Unity, I lead our efforts in education and workforce development. I'm privileged to work with a team of dedicated designers, educators, creators, and organizers—many of whom helped write this book. Together, we educate people to work in games, and we use games to educate people to work in anything.

In my role, I've interfaced with every kind of professional under the sun—people from every socioeconomic background, in every sort of industry, at every stage of their careers. Ivy league grads. Community college students. Mid-career pivoters. Job seekers from emerging countries. And what I hear everywhere is the same: Worry. Stress. Terror in the face of uncertainty.

In a landscape of short-term contracts, frequent layoffs, and the menacing forward-march of artificial intelligence, we all feel like witchers—scrounging for contracts, surrounded by monsters.

But here's the thing . . .

There's a reason why people love playing *The Witcher*.

Chaos Is a Ladder

It's certainly true that the economy is changing, and that our careers are changing with it. But I don't think that's bad news. In fact, I think it's terrific news. There has never been a more exciting time to work.

Previous generations experienced more career certainty precisely because so little was possible. Things were the way they were, they worked the way they worked, and there was nothing you could do to change that.

But today, *anything is possible*. Our futures are no longer solely determined by whether we got the right degree from the right school or took the right job in the right city with the right title. And the environment around us is constantly shifting.

Today, the average person spends just four years in any given job.[1] Experts estimate that 85% of the next decade's jobs haven't been invented yet.[2] And of the jobs that do already exist, an estimated 1.1 billion of them will be radically transformed by new tech.[3] Bottom line: 40%—nearly *half*—of the skills that define career success are about to change.[4]

If all that uncertainty sounds like chaos, that's because it is. But chaos is good for us. Great even. Because, as anyone who's seen *Game of Thrones* knows, "chaos is a ladder." If you're open to adapting, it's a clear climb to the top.

That's what we'll need to do if we want to flourish in the new economy: adapt. It used to be that career growth was rigid and linear (see Figure I.1). First you went to school, then you started your career.

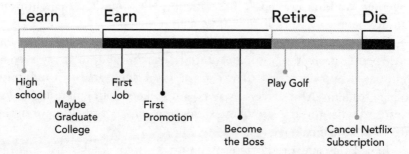

Figure I.1 Linear Career

Figure I.2 Looping Career (learn-earn-advance loop)

First you learned, then you earned. But now, and in the decades to come, we will learn and earn continuously, always developing new skills and applying them. Always adapting (see Figure I.2).

Learn, earn, advance. Learn, earn, advance. If we can repeat that cycle, we'll thrive.

Reinventing the Wheel

This new, cyclical approach to career crafting is actually quite natural. But it seems strange because it differs from what came before. Our education system was fashioned to prepare us for one lifelong profession. It wasn't built to support continuous upskilling.

When our schools were first developed, they were designed for an industrial economy, not a knowledge economy. They were designed to staff assembly lines, not to incubate disruptive startups. They taught us to follow directions, not to solve unforeseen problems.

You might say that our current system was built to ensure that you would never have to "reinvent the wheel." But today, the most lucrative, most rewarding work you can find is precisely in reinventing wheels. We're rethinking everything that's taken for granted. We're tossing out our instruction manuals, taking things apart, and building them back better.

If we want to reinvent the world around us, and if we want to thrive in a world that's constantly *being* reinvented, we need to know how to reinvent ourselves.

Which raises the question—who's going to teach us how?

Spending my career at the intersection of technology, work, and education, I've seen technology reinvented. I've seen work reinvented. And through it all, I've seen education stay almost entirely the same. This despite the fact that the numbers are clear: our education system isn't working.

More than one-third of undergrads don't complete a degree within eight years.[5] When evaluated about five years after launch, one-third of new higher-ed degree programs graduate 0 students, and two-thirds graduate fewer than 10.[6]

Then, even when students do graduate with four-year degrees, more than half find themselves underemployed a year after they graduate—trapped in jobs that didn't require four-year degrees to begin with. Nearly half of all grads will remain underemployed for another decade after that.[7]

So if our education system isn't prepared to support us, and our elders don't know how to navigate this new economy any better than we do, where can we go for help?

After a few decades of working on this question, I discovered an unlikely answer: video games.

Game Loops

Just a moment ago, I talked about the cyclical nature of contemporary work. We learn, earn, advance; learn, earn, advance. To old-timers, this learning-earning cycle seems daunting. They expect linearity. First you go to school, then you have a career. Learn, then earn, then retire, then die. For these folks, returning to the start of that cycle can feel like failure—like you had to give up and start again.

But gamers see things differently. To gamers, learning-earning cycles aren't demoralizing, and they aren't scary. Just the contrary: they're wild, addictive fun. In fact, learning-earning cycles are *the whole point*. You couldn't have video games without them! At every level, we're introduced to a new challenge, a new puzzle, a new enemy. We learn to overcome it. We earn our reward. We advance. Learn, earn, advance. Learn, earn, advance—continuously accumulating more and more skill every time.

Of course, this progression isn't always smooth. Sometimes we face an unusually tough challenge or struggle with a particularly tricky mechanic.

We take two steps forward, one step back. But gamers know that even these learning curves are all just part of the fun, making play more riveting and victory more rewarding. This too is a natural dimension of learning-earning cycles (see Figure I.3).

Game designers have a term for cycles like this. They call them *core game loops*.

We saw one of those loops at the beginning of this Introduction. In *The Witcher 3*, you choose a monster-hunting quest, prepare for it, find the monster, slay it, collect your reward, and then begin the loop again with a new quest.

There are all kinds of game loops out there. The term describes any repeating sequence of action that you might perform in a game. But the "core" loop is the one that *defines* the game. Without it, the game wouldn't *be*.

So in a side-scrolling platformer, you might run, jump, collect a coin, then repeat. Similar deal in a first-person shooter: aim, shoot, advance, repeat. And this isn't just true of video games.

Monopoly: Roll dice. Move piece. Buy/build/rent. Repeat.

Hide-and-go-seek: Count, seek, find. Then hide, be found. Repeat.

Tag: Run, tag. Then run, be tagged. Repeat.

If you're a gamer, then you're a master of game loops. The learning-earning cycle of contemporary careers is just another one of those loops, and you'll master this one in exactly the same way you've mastered all the others.

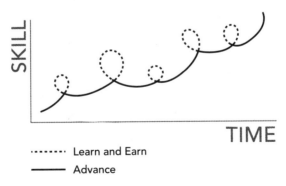

········ Learn and Earn

——— Advance

Figure I.3 Learn-Earn-Advance Graph

If you take nothing else away from this book, take away this: skills learned gaming are relevant. Careers are changing, yes. But for gamers, that change isn't something to fear. It's something to celebrate. More is possible than ever before. More is within reach. And the skills you need to win in this new world are the same skills you've been building your whole life.

The Core Career Loop

To prove that point, this book will lay out the four phases of what I call the *Core Career Loop*.

Phase 1: You choose a profession to pursue.

Phase 2: You learn the skills necessary to work in that profession.

Phase 3: You hunt down a job in that profession.

Phase 4: You use that job as a springboard toward further growth, beginning the cycle again.

Or, put more briefly (see Figure I.4):

1. Choose Quest
2. Level Up

Figure I.4 Core Career Loop

3. Job Hunt

4. Job Craft (repeat)

At the heart of this book are four parts, one for each phase. In each phase, we'll take a closer look at the challenges ahead of you and the strategies you can use to win.

Along the way, we'll discover that building a strong career also requires building a strong community. And we'll see that community building follows its own four-phase cycle. So, after discussing each phase of the Core Career Loop, we'll look at a parallel phase in the Community Loop. Those four Community Loop phases will be as follows (see Figure I.5)

1. Mentors

2. Coaches

3. Sponsors

4. Bosses (repeat)

Finally, before closing out the book, we'll take a one-part look "Beyond the Loop," exploring how hiring, managing, and promoting practices must evolve with contemporary careers. This final part will, of course, speak to managers. And it will also speak to career loopers,

Figure I.5 The Community Loop

revealing what employers look for during hiring, what makes a good boss, and what kinds of help you should be asking for.

This Book Is for You

This book will explore how the Core Career Loop works, how to master it, and why gamers are uniquely adept at navigating it. Ultimately, we'll learn to love the chaos of the contemporary economy, enjoying extraordinary growth and unparalleled possibility.

To be clear, this is not a book about *gamifying* careers. It's a book about crafting careers while using the transferable skills that you've built up over years of gaming. So if you're a gamer, this book's for you. It can help you find your first job, pivot to a new profession, reenter the working world, or imagine your work for the first time.

One exception: this book will not address professions that require extensive licensing. Think law and medicine. But if you're from one of those fields, I encourage you to stick with us anyway. Technology touches every industry. Disruption happens everywhere. Many of this book's fundamental principles will still apply.

This book is also for managers and institutional leaders who want to understand what contemporary careers will look like, and how their own institutions must change to match them. Managers will learn to evolve their hiring, managing, and promoting processes. And it's my hope that institutional leaders will adapt and transform their organizations in response to this new landscape.

There are far-reaching implications here for global employers, as well as nonprofits in education access and workforce development. The same goes for educational institutions of all kinds—from primary school to higher ed, from bootcamps to certification programs, and beyond.

Game On

There's another word for uncertainty: *opportunity*. We have never been so free to choose our own paths, so at liberty to pivot, or so empowered to adapt. The same internet that unleashes unparalleled chaos also unleashes unparalleled possibilities. With that internet's help, we can knock on more doors, learn about more industries, join more communities, and self-teach nearly any skill.

This book will show that gamers are uniquely well-equipped to seize these opportunities and meet the challenges of this moment.

We don't need special social or economic privileges, and we don't need inherited family networks to thrive. Like the witchers who came before us, all we need are the right tools, a good map, and a keen sense of adventure.

Let the hunt begin.

Notes

1. "Employee Tenure in 2022." Bureau of Labor Statistics, September 22, 2022. https://www.bls.gov/news.release/pdf/tenure.pdf.
2. "Realizing 2030: A Divided Vision of the Future." Dell Technologies, June 8, 2023. https://www.delltechnologies.com/content/dam/delltechnologies/assets/perspectives/2030/pdf/Realizing-2030-A-Divided-Vision-of-the-Future-Summary.pdf.
3. Cann, Oliver. "The Reskilling Revolution: Better Skills, Better Jobs, Better Education for a Billion People by 2030." World Economic Forum, January 22, 2020. https://www.weforum.org/press/2020/01/the-reskilling-revolution-better-skills-better-jobs-better-education-for-a-billion-people-by-2030/.
4. "Reskilling Revolution: Preparing 1 Billion People for Tomorrow's Economy." *World Economic Forum*, January 9, 2023. https://www.weforum.org/impact/reskilling-revolution/.
5. Hanson, Melanie. "College Dropout Rates" EducationData.org, August 16, 2024. https://educationdata.org/college-dropout-rates
6. McKenzie, Lindsay. "Newly Launched Degree Programs Struggle to Produce Graduates at Scale." *Inside Higher Ed*, December 8, 2020. https://www.insidehighered.com/news/2020/12/08/newly-launched-degree-programs-struggle-produce-graduates-scale.
7. Weissman, Sara. "More Than Half of Recent Four-year College Grads Underemployed." *Inside Higher Ed*, February 22, 2024. https://www.insidehighered.com/news/students/academics/2024/02/22/more-half-recent-four-year-college-grads-underemployed.

Part I

Choose Quest

For the last 100 years, there was little choice at the start of our careers, and even less choice once they began. Career decisions were made early—and often were made for us. Once begun, most professional paths were linear and predictable.

Today, options abound. We can learn about more professions, access more professions, and change professions more often than ever before. That explosion of opportunity is exciting, but it can also be daunting.

How do you choose the right professional path?

1

How Gamers Learned to Choose

1.1 No Choice

Today, video games train us to make challenging career choices. But it wasn't always that way. It's taken a long journey for the video game to become a medium of choice making. Long enough, in fact, that nobody can quite agree when that journey began. Pull out a calendar and pick any year you like, from the 1960s to the 1970s to the 1980s, and there's probably a case to be made. Me? I choose 1983, at the Westown Cinema.

If you wanted to paint a portrait of my childhood in Waukesha, Wisconsin, you'd only need one color: gray. Winter began around November and lasted all year long. When I wasn't at home, bundled up from the cold, I was at school, bundled up from the nuns. With an hour a day of bland bible recitation and a dress code that made Mother Theresa look like a flapper, life indoors was just as gray as life outdoors.

And then, in 1983, the Westown Cinema arrived and lit my life with color.

Looking back today, I suppose the cinema's arcade was dark and dingy and unimpressive, with soda-stained carpet and only six or so games. But, to us tweens, that arcade was a neon heaven, blinking and beeping and blaring with fun.

At its glorious center was *Donkey Kong*.

Released in 1981, many cite *Donkey Kong* as the first "platformer" game. In it, you became "Jumpman," a heroic carpenter who jumped over barrels and ran past gaps, climbed ladders, and smashed obstacles, in an effort to rescue his girlfriend, Pauline, from her captor—a giant, sinister gorilla.

Donkey Kong impressed the heck out of us. We didn't know to want anything more. Of course, we do now.

In *Donkey Kong*, the goal was to defeat all your enemies and then progress to the next level, where you'd do the same thing again. When you failed, the game would reset, and you'd have to repeat the process. The idea was to get so good that you could reproduce the same successful outcome every time. You'd memorize each level, tune yourself to its rhythms, and nail down the best possible route for victory.

This was the norm for games in the early 1980s. They were all repetitive or linear or both. In the unlikely event that a game had a story, that story would be predetermined. Fixed. "On rails," as the saying goes, referring to a train that can only go where the tracks lead it. There was no deviating. No choosing.

This was especially true of early coin-operated (coin-op) games. From the manufacturer's perspective, the point of the game was to separate people from their quarters. The game had to be short, delivering a game over quickly. And that short game had to be rewarding enough to keep you feeding the machine.

Given these objectives, little story was required. And there was certainly no time for choice or consequence. Instead, games would focus on simple, addictive mechanics, ratcheting up difficulty with every level.

Donkey Kong was just such a game. And, for that reason, it's not at all the sort of game that prepares players for decision-making in today's job market. But in 1983, *Donkey Kong's* hero, Jumpman, was preparing for a career change, and the industry was going to change with him. There wouldn't be a choice. Shigeru Miyamoto would see to that.

1.2 Jumpman

Donkey Kong was Shigeru Miyamoto's first major success. It had been his brain child, and it catapulted him into a legendary game design career. But when Miyamoto first entered the workforce, he didn't want to make video games at all.

Growing up in a rural Japanese village during the 1950s and 1960s, Miyamoto spent his childhood exploring forests and mountains and caves. When he wasn't out adventuring, he was building his own toys from wood and string. Slingshots. Puppets.[1] So when he grew up and got a degree, he got one in industrial design. His plan: to become a toy maker.[2]

Nintendo was a natural first stop. By the 1970s, Nintendo had been making playthings for about a hundred years. They were Japan's leading manufacturer of playing cards, and, in the last few decades, had begun branching out to other kinds of games and gizmos. It was the perfect place for a budding toy maker.[3]

But by the time Miyamoto joined in 1976, Nintendo had begun down a new path—one that would lead them *away* from toys. They'd begun creating video games. Three years after Miyamoto joined up, Nintendo launched their first dedicated coin-op division.[4] And a year after that, they ran into a crisis.

One of Nintendo's first arcade games, *Radar Scope*, had flopped in the United States. The game was supposed to capitalize on the success of a popular shooter by another publisher. But by the time Nintendo shipped *Radar Scope* to America, nobody was interested in shooters anymore. Maze games had become all the rage. *Pac-Man* had upended the market.[5]

Now Nintendo of America was sitting on two thousand arcade cabinets that it couldn't sell. These were six-foot units that, together, accounted for most of Nintendo America's budget. Plus, these cabinets were racking up a fortune in storage fees.

Nintendo's CEO turned to his team for help, and Miyamoto offered up an idea: Nintendo could retool the existing cabinets with new art and a new game. He suggested that this new game could feature three characters—Jumpman, Pauline, and a felonious gorilla.

1.3   Nintendo's Favorite Plumber

By 1983, *Donkey Kong* was already a hit with me and my friends and the rest of the planet. Now Nintendo was releasing Miyamoto's sequel, *Mario Bros.* In this new game, "Jumpman" was redubbed "Mario." He changed careers, from carpenter to plumber, and moved to the sewers under New York City. Here, he and his brother Luigi began a new rescue mission. And it was a smash hit.

In fact, it was such a big hit that Nintendo ported the arcade game straight over to their brand-new home console. That journey from arcade to home would start Nintendo on a path toward a new kind of play experience—one that would forever alter games and the skills they teach us.

By this time, home consoles had been on the market for more than a decade, and they were seriously challenging the value proposition of coin-ops. From a business perspective, home consoles eliminated the intermediaries between publishers and players. Now publishers could pocket more money on every transaction. And from my perspective, it was a lot easier to play games at home than to brave the Wisconsin winter, trudging out to the Westown Cinema arcade.

But more important than either of those considerations was the simple fact that console games promised to be *better*. Initially, publishers tried to duplicate and port arcade games, but the most successful console games took the medium somewhere new.

Because players could return to their home consoles as often as their parents allowed, these games could introduce more depth. Games might still be "on rails," telling one fixed story without any deviations from playthrough to playthrough, but now in-game events could accumulate to deliver a more sophisticated experience.

Nintendo's leadership understood that they couldn't rely on ported arcade games forever. If a game was moving to the home console, it needed to offer something more. So, in fall 1984, a little less than one year after the Westown Cinema opened, they directed Shigeru Miyamoto to begin production on a sequel to *Mario Bros.* This new game would introduce larger levels and more complex mechanics. It would take advantage of the home console format to level up the game, from *Mario Bros.* to *Super Mario Bros.*

As if the pressure to create one stellar, super-seller, all-time classic wasn't enough, Nintendo approached Miyamoto with a second ask during that same year. Nintendo planned to release a hardware add-on for their console that would enable players to save progress at a much larger scale. The executives wondered: while working on *Super Mario*, could Miyamoto simultaneously create an entirely new game that would demonstrate the value of this second device?

This was no small request. Whole studios have collapsed under the pressure of creating just one game at a time. Now one small team (five people!) was supposed to create two flagship games simultaneously?[6] For this to work, Miyamoto insisted that the two games would have to be utterly dissimilar. "We tried to separate the different ideas," he recalls, adding that the second game would have to be "Mario's total opposite."[7]

But what on earth would that be?

Nobody knew yet. When the team finally did find their answer, it would revolutionize the industry and lay the groundwork for a host of new player skills—skills that have become essential in today's job market.

That's why I'm telling you all this, by the way. As I said in this book's Introduction, all games teach skills—even just-for-fun, noneducational games. And those skills have broad applications outside of games. In particular, those skills position gamers to build uniquely successful careers in today's exciting, challenging job market.

Understanding what gamers can become and what they can achieve requires understanding the games themselves and where those games came from. We'll return to Miyamoto in a minute, but first, I want to clarify this link between games and careers.

1.4   Branching Out

My own career was deeply influenced by games. Their relentless demand for quarters motivated me to get my first job—I was a 10-year-old with a paper route. Later, I'd go on to work for the Westown Cinema arcade directly. But I also missed out on much of what games had to offer.

In my teen years, gender norms pulled me away from arcades. I was a girl, and girls didn't game. I missed out on 20 years of play, 20 years of learning, 20 years of skill building. Only as an adult would I return to the medium and discover how much it had to offer.

Today, I mourn that missed opportunity for learning. And I'm writing this book partly in the hope that others won't miss out like I did. I hope that this book will encourage gamers of all sorts to keep playing and to take advantage of their *very particular set of skills*. I also hope that it will inspire big-time decision-makers to take gamers and games more seriously.

I see the incredible impact of the medium all around me: on my sons, on my nieces and nephews, on their peers, on job seekers and entrepreneurs and wildly successful business owners, in the United States and around the world, inside the games industry and outside of it.

I see the impact every day in the people who work with me at Unity, an organization devoted to making game creation more accessible. Many of these folks don't really do anything related to games at all—they just happen to work at a games company, accounting, lawyering, marketing, and so on. But their careers are nevertheless entirely different, and entirely better, for having spent so much time at play.

Take, for instance, James Stone. Today he's our director of product management, which means that it's his job to envision the future of the Unity game engine, evolving it to better serve our users. Although it certainly helps that James is a game development (dev) wiz (he ran his own indie company, NerdRage Studios), game dev isn't really part of his job here. His role is about strategic thinking, people management, and business sense. It's about identifying what people need, and how the product can evolve to give it to them. You'd find a similar role at any tech company. But you won't find a similar person.

James is uniquely capable and charismatic. And, more to my point, his one-of-a-kind career is the sort that only a gamer could create.

1.5 Detective Stone

The first bits of the James Stone backstory won't surprise you. Like so many tech-industry geniuses, he was allergic to school but loved electronics and games. When his friends were going to college, he dropped out and got a job fixing computers. So far, so familiar.

But then the game went off the rails.

"You know," James says, "I've had moments where I've been sat in a boma surrounded by spearmen who were, like, protecting me, and I'm like, what am I doing here? Why am I here? What led me to this point?"

What indeed, James. What indeed.

James's parents had been famous musicians. Worried about the dangers of raising two Black boys in 1970s America, they'd moved the family to a tiny village in Hampshire, England, where the boys' grandparents would raise them.

After James dropped out of his college, his grandmother yanked him away from his video games, stuck him in a suit, and sent him off to an interview.

That first job wasn't particularly glorious, working in a small town at a small electronics store. Sometimes he'd build tables, sometimes he'd fix computers. But he learned quickly. And in the early 1990s, anyone who knew anything about computers was a hot commodity.

What followed was a meteoric career in information technology (IT). Before he knew it, James was the boss. And he loved managing teams. But moving from corporate office to corporate office, the work eventually got stale.

As it happened, two of James's poker buddies were cops, and they'd been hearing about his dissatisfaction for some time. One night at the pub, they proposed a solution while James dealt a hand. "The police are always looking for cybersecurity experts," James remembers them saying. "You could become a detective! You could take down hacking rings!"

James liked the idea of "doing some good in this world," as he puts it. Plus he thought the name Detective Stone sounded pretty badass. So he checked out a career day, and that was that. Detective Stone went and got his badge.

But it turned out that the police *weren't* always looking for cybersecurity experts—they already had plenty. Instead, they put him on patrol, where he mostly dealt with conflicts about alcohol and drugs. "As an officer on the street, you're fighting all the time," James explains. "And that's not me."

"I look back now, and it was a ridiculous career move in many ways," James adds. "But it taught me so much. That I was capable of so much more than I thought I was."

Did I mention that James was also a photographer?

James was also a photographer.

He'd been snapping photos since he was a kid. Now he was an adult, looking for a way out of his misfit job, and his camera seemed like the answer.

This realization came, in large part, thanks to a 19-year-old whose photography adventures James followed online. "He used to go off to the Hamer tribe in Ethiopia," James remembers. "And he would go to these incredible places all around the world. His photographs were incredible, and he'd video himself taking them."

More than anything else, James cites one particular video as having jump-started the rest of his life:

> At the end of this video, this kid just sat down, and he was talking to the camera, and he just said, "Many people ask me how I do these things." And he said, "I just get up and do it."
>
> He was like, "If you need to go to a country, you go buy a plane ticket, and you get on a plane. The only thing that holds anyone back is themselves. If you want to do something, just do it."
>
> So I did.

James turned in his badge, began an IT role for one of the world's largest children's charities, and started a photography school. Soon, he was working with UN agencies and humanitarian groups, traveling the world to photograph kids in peril, raising awareness for human rights causes around the globe.

This wasn't easy to do. Travel isn't cheap, so James had to juggle three simultaneous jobs to follow the path he'd chosen. But, for James, the struggle was worth it.

Recalling his days in documentary photography, he rattles off some of his most memorable subjects. There was the Tanzanian girl whose daily, nine-mile walk to school sent her winding through prison yards, down train lines, across vast dangerous stretches of Tanzanian bush. There was the nomadic African tribe that was being forced to settle for the sake of a census, with lethal ramifications. There were the Cambodian river tribes, and the efforts to create education access for girls in remote regions of Guatemala. And there was that night in the boma shelter, surrounded by spearmen.

James's photography work scored him big pieces in major news outlets. It won him awards. It thrilled him, and it filled his life with a sense of purpose. But it also propelled him toward greater and greater risks. So when he found himself the father of two children, it became clear that something had to change.

James continued his IT management work, but he knew it wasn't a fit anymore. He became listless and dispirited, uncertain about what he ought to do next. Until his partner pointed out the obvious. "The one thing I see you do every day is play video games," she said. "So why don't you make video games?"

James took her insight to heart and taught himself Unity. After his first mobile game release, he went all in. He made games in the United Kingdom, in China, in Thailand, and then, reasoning that he had this Unity thing pretty much figured out, he came and got a job with us.

At every twist and turn of his career path, friends and family would give James a hard time. *Why do you keep swapping professions? Why can't you settle down?*

Inspired by his father, James arrived at an easy answer: "I want to follow what drives me, what I'm passionate about. And if it means a complete change, then so be it. I'm not afraid to take the chance and see where life leads."

James's career path has been driven by passion. Curiosity. A relentless thirst to explore. To discover. And those are precisely the forces that contemporary video games encourage us to follow.

Here—let me show you what I mean.

1.6   The First Choice Makers

In 1974, while Shigeru Miyamoto was still in school and James Stone was waiting to be born, Gary Gygax and Dave Arneson were launching a game that would change play forever. Ultimately, this game would help Miyamoto craft *Mario*'s opposite, and it would become the foundation for the career-building skills that would someday propel James Stone around the world, from IT specialist to detective to photographer to Unity leader.

Gygax and Arneson's game was called *Dungeons & Dragons (D&D)*, and it was unlike anything that had come before. In *D&D*'s fantasy world of wizards and elves, a player could do anything. Truly anything. Most players explored dungeons and hunted down dragons. But if you wanted to hang around a medieval pub all day, you could do that, too. Or you could run for mayor. Or become a blacksmith's apprentice. Anything!

This was the first "role-playing game" or RPG, and it wasn't a video game. Instead, it was played with pen and paper and conversation. As a player, you would control a hero in the story. Your friend would control the world around that hero. You'd say what the hero does, and your friend would tell you how the world responds.

This, of course, was a far cry from what gamers were seeing in arcades. Arcade games were tightly controlled experiences, carefully designed for maximum efficiency and profitability. There was only one path to take and only one way to take it. Even on PC and console, there was no equivalent to *D&D*'s freedom of choice and expanse of possibility.

So, for many video game designers, *D&D* became a sort of holy grail. How could we experience that same breadth of choice and possibility when we were alone in front of a computer or console? And someday, when computer graphics caught up, how might they bring worlds like *D&D* to life visually?

The first major step in this direction didn't involve visuals at all. In *Colossal Cave Adventure*, you played a hero diving into dungeons, solving puzzles, and collecting treasure. Unlike computer games that had come before, this one was text-based: you would type commands, describing your character's actions. Then the computer would reply with prose, describing how the world responds.

(If this sounds a lot like contemporary AI chatbots, that's no coincidence. Much of *Colossal Cave Adventure*'s development took place in Stanford's AI Lab during the 1970s. When the game made its way over to MIT's AI Lab in 1977, "no one got any work done for a week."[8])

In addition to pioneering the text adventure genre, *Colossal Cave Adventure* offered a sense of possibility and freedom never before seen in electronic games. It introduced a vast world and invited you to explore it at will. "Go east," you'd tell the computer, and then it would. You could move in any direction. You could bypass, backtrack, and skip, moving through the game's adventures in your own sequence.

And this wasn't just about navigation either. If you saw a lantern, you could grab it, drop it, light it, extinguish it, and even break it. (If you tried to eat it, the game would call your bluff, replying, "Don't be ridiculous!"[9])

And when it came to solving puzzles, there was freedom to invent novel solutions. You could bribe the troll to let you cross the bridge unharmed, or you could tame a bear and have it chase the troll away for you.[10]

Now, for the first time, we had something like *D&D* on computers. But we hadn't yet captured the holy grail. Games like this needed to make the jump from prose to graphics.

Atari made that jump first, and gave their console game a shortened version of the same name—*Adventure*. This new release placed players on a colorful, pixelated map with simple object icons. Players viewed this map from the top down, and explored it with the same freedom that they'd had in *Colossal Cave Adventure*.

Two years later, the game *Ultima* expanded on this concept. It too offered players a vast world, and gave them unprecedented freedom to explore that world. But it also went a step further, giving players more control over the story's hero and their quest. Players created their own characters, with different strengths and weaknesses. Then they navigated the world freely, choosing which quests to go on and in what sequence.

A new genre had emerged: the "Open World RPG." Players were free to explore a game's immersive world at will. They were free to choose their own paths and their own activities. And their choices often influenced how the story turned out.

A revolution was afoot in American video games. RPGs were reimagining what gaming could be. The holy grail was closer than ever.

But the search was still local. The magic of video game open worlds hadn't yet spread across our own, real open world.

1.7 RPGs Go Global

By the end of the 1970s, RPGs had become hugely popular in the United States, but they were still relatively unknown elsewhere. You might say that if *D&D* was the holy grail, only a small portion of the game design population was looking for it.

That's where Henk Rogers came in—the man who would ultimately become a king of game globalization. A few years after our story, he would get mixed up with Russian spies while pursuing the Soviet-owned game *Tetris*, bringing it out from behind the Iron Curtain. But for now, he was merely a lover of games.

Rogers was born in Holland, to a Dutch Indonesian family. His studies took him west, to New York and then to Hawaii, before his heart eventually took him east, to Japan, where the woman he loved was headed. Fortunately, his father lived there, too.[11]

When Henk Rogers arrived in Japan, his career path was already carved out for him: he would work in his father's gem business. He'd contribute what he could, working his way up. And he did contribute meaningfully for some time. In fact, he stayed long enough to invent an entirely new process for cutting and preparing gems. But his heart wasn't in it. His heart was in games.

While studying computer science back at the University of Hawaii, Rogers had fallen in love with *Dungeons & Dragons*. Deeply, almost pathologically, in love. "We played constantly, using photocopies of the three original *Dungeons & Dragons* books," he remembers. "Some weekends we'd start playing on a Friday evening, and we wouldn't stop till Monday morning."[12]

Unfortunately, following one love of his life had meant abandoning another. Here in late-1970s/early 1980s Japan, Rogers got the impression that nobody was playing *D&D*. (The game wouldn't receive its Japanese translation until 1985.[13]) Nor did it seem to him like anybody was playing the video games inspired by it.[14] In fact, Japan had produced a few video game RPGs, but they hadn't been successful, and, true to Rogers's impression, the genre remained relatively unknown.[15]

This, Rogers decided, would be his next career move. He'd break away from the linear path set out for him and create the first major RPG in Japan.

He began work in 1983, determined to release the game by Christmas of that year. And indeed, by the end of the year, he had created his first RPG. In homage to his abandoned career in gemstones, he named the game *The Black Onyx*.[16]

Today, RPGs are huge in Japan. Just four years after *The Black Onyx* hit the market, Japan's police force would arrest nearly three hundred schoolchildren for ditching class to buy another RPG, *Dragon Quest III*.[17]

Today, 5 out of every 10 Japanese men and 3 out of 10 Japanese women consider themselves fans of the genre.[18] But back in 1984, the genre had only just been born, and nobody cared. *The Black Onyx* seemed destined to flop.

"During the first month of the game's release, we received just one phone call," Henk Rogers recalls. "The second month, we sold four copies." When money ran short and things got desperate, Rogers adopted a new Hail Mary strategy. He went to the office of every computer magazine in Japan, and demoed the game personally.

His efforts paid off. Every one of those magazines ran a review of the game the next month. And sales turned around instantly. April 1984: ten thousand copies sold. May 1984: ten thousand copies sold. June 1984: ten thousand copies sold.[19]

But *The Black Onyx* wasn't the only gaming breakthrough of 1984. Back at Nintendo headquarters, executives were celebrating the success of *Mario Bros.*, and creators were hard at work developing its successor, *Super Mario*. In the midst of all that, Shigeru Miyamoto was looking for *Mario's* polar opposite. And, fortunately for gamers everywhere, he was also playing *The Black Onyx*.

1.8   Mario's Opposite

When Nintendo executives told Shigeru Miyamoto that they needed a second game—one that would demonstrate the value of expanded data storage and saved progress—Miyamoto began looking for *Super Mario's* opposite. This new game would need to present an entirely different world, as well as an entirely different gameplay experience.

For that entirely different world, Miyamoto didn't have to look far. *Super Mario* took place in the sewers beneath New York City. Its opposite was intimately familiar to Miyamoto, who'd grown up in rural Japan, climbing mountains, wading through woods, and exploring caves. The protagonist of this game would do the same, navigating a medieval kingdom that teemed with nature. They'd begin as an ordinary villager and ultimately become a national hero.

And then there was *Super Mario's* mechanical opposite. When Miyamoto began work on the *Mario Bros.* sequel, he knew that "*Super Mario Bros* should be linear," never leaving players any doubt about what action they should take next.[20] And there was a good reason for this.

In his *Mario* sequel, Miyamoto wanted to take advantage of the home console's capacity to deliver more than an arcade game: players would return to *Super Mario* again and again, reinforcing and expanding their skills, encountering new levels and mechanics of increasing complexity. Each moment of skill growth would be carefully designed, building on what came before, and preparing players for what came next. The game's linearity would empower Miyamoto to control how these skills were taught and implemented.

To achieve that game's opposite, Miyamoto would have to abandon linearity for a nonlinear experience. He'd have to embrace player choice, empowering gamers to decide their own sequence of events. And he'd have to shift the focus away from skill growth, emphasizing exploration instead. Miyamoto recalls, "we were trying to create worlds that people would want to immerse themselves in. . . ."[21]

To achieve this, Miyamoto did some exploring of his own, discovering inspiration outside of his own personal experience. His central influences became *Ultima* and its spiritual sequel, *The Black Onyx*.[22]

1.9   The Legend of Zelda

In 1986, three years after the Westown Cinema opened its doors, and three years after *Mario Bros.* jumped into the world, Nintendo released *Super Mario's* opposite: *The Legend of Zelda*.

Here was a truly beautiful game, brought to life with vivid color and an all-time great, ear worming underscore. Players went on heroic journeys across a magical kingdom of forests and caves. They leveled up, geared up, uncovered a rich story full of mythic lore and valiant derring-do, and most important of all, they made unilateral choices.

There were no fixed paths. No "rails" to follow. In *Zelda*, you could explore the world freely, from the very start. You could wander and investigate, going anywhere you wanted, burning through vegetation and blowing down walls. You could discover hidden caves and secret items. You could choose from different weapons and overcome challenges any way you liked.

Miyamoto's new game was a revelation—one that would forever change the medium. It opened up new vistas in open worlds, offering revolutionary freedom to explore in your own way, and at your own pace. It might not have been the first of its kind, but the game's aesthetic beauty, wondrous adventures, thrilling action, and delightful puzzles would make it an unparalleled messenger for the power of nonlinear games.

In years to come, others would build on its contributions—at Nintendo and beyond. In the nearly half-century since *Zelda's* adventures began, video games have ventured out to larger and more detailed worlds, explored the moral dimensions of player choices, and delivered deep and lasting in-game consequences for those choices with branching narratives and multiple endings.

In 2023, the journey to radical player choice came full circle with *Baldur's Gate 3*—a video game full of rich story, extraordinary graphics, and apparently limitless choice. Here was the holy grail at last, fittingly delivered as an officially licensed adaptation of *Dungeons & Dragons.*[23]

And that game builds not just on *The Legend of Zelda*, but on so many other games for which *Zelda* paved the way. In 2003, *Star Wars: Knights of the Old Republic* introduced a dynamic morality system that tracked every choice players made, determining whether they were moving toward good or evil, and recalibrating the world around them to respond accordingly in real time.

In 2001, *Grand Theft Auto III* likewise made huge strides in these domains. The game featured realistic traffic patterns, day/night cycles, and a population of computer-controlled characters who seemed to lead full lives, going about their own business in the background. More important, players moved freely through the city, reinventing their own professional identities again and again. They could become taxi drivers, racing around town in pursuit of fares. They could become firefighters, putting out flames and saving lives. They could even become police officers, chasing down law breakers and bringing them to justice.

Sound familiar?

1.10 The Free Roamers

It takes no stretch of the imagination to see how games like these might have influenced people like James Stone—the Unity product director who went from computer fix-it person to police officer to documentary photographer to game designer to tech leader. James and his fellow gamers are uncommonly comfortable with exploring the world around them, making big choices, and changing their minds. They're relentlessly curious and unflinchingly flexible.

Games have never stopped growing. From the day the Westown Cinema lit up my life to the day you read this, games will have kept innovating and evolving—just like the players they serve. Along the way, gamers have become explorers, iterative experimenters, and choice makers. In the language of game design, they have become "free roamers."

They explore worlds, interrogate characters around them, and discover hidden opportunities. They try out side quests, experiment with play styles, and seek out the approach that suits them best. When it comes time to make hard choices in ambiguous contexts, they choose boldly and commit. And when their paths twist and turn, diverge and digress, gamers adapt. They embrace nonlinear, unblazed trails. They become heroes—each in their own way.

I know very few parents who actively encourage their children to play video games. And I think that's a darn shame. Me? I regret that I stopped playing games so young, and I delight in gifting new games to my kids. In fact, I'll often play with them.

That's because titles like *Zelda* make gamers some of the most capable, intuitive career crafters out there. And that's what I want for all of us.

There was a time when, like our video games, our careers were on rails. Today, that's no longer the case. The job market is an open world that we're free to roam. And nobody's better prepared for it than gamers.

1.11   The Trail Ahead

In this book's Introduction, I explained that contemporary careers are cyclical. We learn, earn, advance; learn earn, advance. I called that cycle the *Core Career Loop* and broke it down into four phases:

1. Choose Quest
2. Level Up
3. Job Hunt
4. Job Craft (repeat)

In this first part of the book, we'll talk about Phase 1: the choice.

Every person's loop begins with a choice. And every time we cycle the loop, we must make that choice again. Whether I'm just beginning my career or I'm making a mid-career pivot, I must select a specific profession or field that I want to pursue. Game design? Finance? Politics? I begin by choosing where to direct my efforts.

But how do I make that choice?

Throughout the rest of Part I, we'll explore precisely how gamers can draw on their deeply trained, open-world, free-roaming skills to choose well, choose well again, and adapt when the outcomes of their own choices surprise them.

We'll begin in Chapter 2 with an examination of how gamers cultivate many options, looking beyond the obvious opportunities at home to the infinite opportunities *out there.*

Then, once we appreciate the full scope of our options, Chapter 3 will explore how gamers make definitive choices, listening both to their hearts and to their minds as they select a profession to pursue.

Chapter 4 will reflect on the surprises that inevitably arise throughout this journey, and how gamers adapt to meet those surprises.

Chapter 5 will go on to discuss the worries that hold us back—worries about disadvantages and failures—and we'll look at the gamer's well-earned confidence that they can thrive even in the most unfamiliar professional fields.

And finally, in Chapter 6, we'll take our first of many dives into the Community Loop, exploring the essential means by which mentors influence our choices. Because, as *The Legend of Zelda* famously taught us, it's dangerous to go alone.

But that dive into the Community Loop is a little ways away. First, let's begin by looking up and out, to what I call the *opportunity horizon.*

Notes

1. Paumgarten, Nick. "Master of Play." *The New Yorker*, December 12, 2010. https://www.newyorker.com/magazinc/2010/12/20/master-of-play.
2. NPR Staff. "Q&A: Shigeru Miyamoto on the Origins of Nintendo's Famous Characters." NPR, June 19, 2015. https://www.npr.org/sections/alltechconsidered/2015/06/19/415568892/q-a-shigeru-miyamoto-on-the-origins-of-nintendos-famous-characters.

3. Paumgarten, "Master of Play."
4. "Nintendo History." Nintendo.com. Accessed September 17, 2024. https://www.nintendo.com/en-gb/Hardware/Nintendo-History/Nintendo-History-625945.html.
5. Parish, Jeremy. "35 Years Ago, Nintendo's First Brush with Video Disaster." USgamer.net, January 20, 2014. https://web.archive.org/web/2019050205 1532/https://www.usgamer.net/articles/35-years-ago-nintendo-had-its-first-brush-with-video-game-disaster.
6. Schmitz, Tobias. "Inside Nintendo 47: Das Super Mario-Entwicklerteam Unter Der Lupe." Nintendo-Online.de, August 24, 2014. https://nintendo-online.de/artikel/report/18111/inside-nintendo-47-das-super-mario-entwicklerteam-unter-der-lupe.
7. SuperSectionX. "The Adventure of Hyrule - Interviews - Superplay Interview with Miyamoto." Accessed September 17, 2024. https://www.angelfire.com/games5/makzelda/interviews/superplay.html.
8. Robinett, Warren. "Chapter 2: The First Text-Based Adventure Game: Colossal Cave." Inventing the Adventure Game: The Design of Adventure and Rocky's Boots, n.d. http://www.warrenrobinett.com/inventing_adventure/inventing_ch2.htm.
9. "The Colossal Cave Adventure Page." Accessed September 17, 2024. https://rickadams.org/adventure/.
10. Dyer, Jason. "Adventure (350 Points): Puzzles and Concluding Remarks." Renga in Blue, March 27, 2011. https://bluerenga.blog/2011/03/27/adventure-350-points-puzzles-and-concluding-remarks/.
11. Sramana Mitra. "The Story of Tetris: Henk Rogers (Part 1)," September 16, 2009. https://www.sramanamitra.com/2009/09/16/the-story-of-tetris-henk-rogers-part-1/.
12. Parkin, Simon. "The Making of: The Black Onyx, the Game That Hooked Japan on RPGs." *Time Extension*, December 29, 2023. https://www.time extension.com/features/the-making-of-the-black-onyx-the-game-that-hooked-japan-on-rpgs.
13. Yanagida, Masaki. "The Rise and Fall of D&D in Japan." TokyoDev. Accessed September 17, 2024. https://www.tokyodev.com/articles/the-rise-and-fall-of-dnd-in-japan.
14. Parkin, Simon. "The Making of: The Black Onyx, the Game That Hooked Japan on RPGs."
15. Messner, Steven. "The Forgotten Origins of JRPGs on the PC." Pcgamer, April 15, 2017. https://www.pcgamer.com/the-forgotten-origins-of-jrpgs-on-the-pc/.
16. Parkin, Simon. "The Making of: The Black Onyx, the Game That Hooked Japan on RPGs."
17. GK. "One Million Sold in One Day." *Compute!*, June 1988. https://archive.org/details/1988-JUn-compute-magazine/page/6/mode/2up?view=theater.

18. Statista Research Department. "Popularity of Role-Playing Video Games (RPGs) Among Men in Japan 2020, by Age Group." *Statista*, November 24, 2022. https://www.statista.com/statistics/1116176/japan-popularity-video-game-genre-role-playing-games-men-by-age-group/.

19. Parkin, Simon. "The Making of: The Black Onyx, the Game That Hooked Japan on RPGs."

20. SuperSectionX. "The Adventure of Hyrule - Interviews - Superplay Interview with Miyamoto."

21. Staff, "Q&A: Shigeru Miyamoto on the Origins of Nintendo's Famous Characters."

22. Altice, Nathan. *I Am Error: The Nintendo Family Computer / Entertainment System Platform* (MIT Press, 2015), 172.

23. Reuben, Nic. "Baldur's Gate 3 Review – Awe-inspiring D&D Rendition Is a Towering Landmark." *The Guardian*, August 9, 2023. https://www.theguardian.com/games/2023/aug/09/baldurs-gate-3-review-pc-mac-ps5-larian.

2

Five Tactics for Expanding Horizons

2.1 Seeking Influence

Here we are, at the start of the Core Career Loop. We're on Phase 1, and it's time to make a choice. What sort of profession will we pursue?

For about half of the US's adult population, the answer is an easy one: *influencer.* And that number goes up if you just ask Gen Z: 57% would go full-time as paid social media celebrities if they could.[1] But that's probably not because it's the best job in America. "It's because people want what they hear about," says Mona Mourshed.

For 20 years, Mona's been building bridges between education and employment worldwide. For a decade now, she's led Generation, a global nonprofit that works with folks of all ages, connecting them to careers that previously felt out of reach.

In her work, Mona often talks about four gaps that separate people from the work that will serve them best: (1) the gap between the known and the unknown, (2) the gap between job interest and job placement, (3) the gap between a regular workplace and a great workplace, and (4) the gap between technical skills and behavioral skills.

"The very first gap is exposure to different professions," Mona says. And it's not just about knowing what's out there. Mona points out that you also have to know what those professions are really like: "What's great about that job? What's not great about that job? What kind of income and career path does that job give you?"

I like to call the thing that we're trying to improve here our "opportunity horizon." It's the landscape of possibilities that we see when we look out at the world. By default, these horizons look pretty small.

Mona says that people want to become social media influencers because that's what they're exposed to. Sure, influencer jobs look cushy, but so do plenty of other jobs that most of us haven't heard about.

Meanwhile, the influencer life has a lot of downsides, and there's so much more out there. "You don't hear as much about robotic process automation, or being a retrofit advisor, or being a solar panel installer," she observes. "But these other professions are growing massively. And they have very solid incomes that can literally alter your life trajectory."

One recent study looked at half-a-million middle school and high school students, quantifying the gap between fields they'd be great for (based on proven aptitude) and fields they'd actually thought of pursuing. Out of all the students who'd thrive in a given field, how many hadn't even considered it?

- Tech: 75%
- Manufacturing: 66%
- Health care: 43%[2]

All of these industries are on the brink of stratospheric growth, and yet all of them are also anticipating giant employment shortfalls. That's bad news for the industries, but great news for us. Projections suggest that the American manufacturing industry will have more than two million unfilled job postings by the next decade.[3] And when it comes to the tech industry, forecasters expect that its workforce will grow twice as fast as the overall US workforce.[4]

There's so much opportunity out there. And yet our professional choices are limited by our imaginations of what might be possible. Before we choose what to pursue, we must first seek out new influences, expanding our opportunity horizons. We need exposure to more professions, a better understanding of what those professions have to offer, and a better understanding of what they demand.

And that's where our gaming skills are going to begin serving us.

2.2   Horizon Expanders

It's a post-apocalyptic landscape, but not the gray, grimy, hideous sort we're used to. The apocalypse has rewilded the world. Autumnal vegetation blankets everything in gold and crimson. Flora and fauna roam untamed. There are a few machines left, here and there, and even they've gone wild. It's our job to reign them in.

We're playing *Horizon: Zero Dawn*, a game celebrated for its gorgeous open world. Our heroine, Aloy, grew up in one small corner of that world, nursing one small ambition: to win an auspicious tribal contest. She's trained relentlessly, becoming an unparalleled climber, runner, and hunter. But when she ventures out of her tribe's territory, she discovers that the world has so much more to offer her, and so much more to ask of her.

When asked about the game's title, lead writer Ben McCaw had a simple explanation, "For us, 'Horizon' represents a boundless new world. . . ."[5]

That's what gamers face today: a boundless new world. Ours bursts with expanding industries, advancing tech, and new opportunities. And like Aloy, gamers have learned extraordinary tools for exploring that world.

Gamers know that some of the most exciting opportunities aren't the ones you're first exposed to by your tribe. They're the ones you discover far, far away. Gamers venture out, into the beyond. They peak around corners. Turn over rocks. Socialize with strange characters who've seen things they haven't and know things they don't. They search in the dark. Eavesdrop. Experiment.

From *Zelda* to *The Witcher* to *Horizon* and beyond, games have taught us to look for opportunities everywhere.

In open world games, there are usually a few key tactics you can use to discover new opportunities. The big two are exploration and conversation. You roam cities, climb mountains, cross galaxies, searching for quests. And along the way, you strike up chats with the characters you encounter. Many of them need help from someone just like you.

In our own world, the principle's the same. But we use different methods to broaden our opportunity horizons. I like to boil these down to five key tactics.

2.3   The Five Tactics

2.3.1   *Community*

The people around us do stuff. We should ask them about it.

For most people, the number-one most common influence on their career choices will be their parents.[6] And that's a great start. The better we know people, the better we can understand what they do. The same goes for friends and other family members.

But like Aloy, we can't limit ourselves to our own tribes. If we want expanded horizons, we need to look further. Reach out to extended family. Friends of friends. Friends of friends of friends. Mona recommends asking, "Who likes their job? Is it a fit for you? And can they help you pursue it?"

This is, without a doubt, the most powerful of all the tactics. For that reason, we'll be returning to it many times throughout this book, as we explore the Community Loop.

I'll say more about this at the end of Part I. But for now, let's move on to tactic two.

2.3.2   *Online Research*

The next best place to look is the easiest: the internet.

Benefits abound here. It's fast of course. And it's convenient. You can do it anytime, and you can find anything. But what really sets the internet apart for our purposes is the sheer vastness of perspective.

When learning about professional paths through community channels, tactic 1, we usually go narrow and deep. By *deep*, I mean that we're connecting directly and personally with people, which creates an opportunity to get a fuller, more honest sense of how people feel about their work. But our breadth is "narrow": we might get input from just 1, or 2, or 10 people. Hardly enough data points to judge an entire profession or industry.

On the internet, though, we can hear from everyone. We can hear from people who love a profession and people who hate it. We can hear from the people who do the job and the people who manage them. We can hear what journalists think of the industry, what insiders think of the industry, what newbies think of it, even what retirees think of it. We can go as wide as we want to.

And there are so many channels for learning. First, you've got websites specifically designed to expose you to professions that you might not have thought of. There are plenty of mission-driven organizations that offer these, including universities, nonprofits, and government bodies like the Department of Labor and the military.

Those websites often feature assessments. Answer a few questions about yourself, and you'll get back a big report. *Here are some of your natural strengths. Here are some of your natural predilections. Here are a bunch of professions that you'd be great for.*

You can also start with the internet's infinite encyclopedia of lists. The top 50 most profitable professions. The top 40 most creative professions. The top 30 professions for people who love STEM. The top 20 professions for people who love mountains. The top 10 for people who love people. The top 5 for people who love cats.

Then, in the wider world of the web, you can start envisioning yourself in those professions, figuring out whether they're good fits. Social media influencers will talk you through professions that they're working in. Blog articles will break down the pros and cons of different roles. Search for videos, and you'll usually find people telling you how it feels to do their job. They'll show you what their work actually looks like, and perhaps even let you tag along for a virtual day-in-the-life.

Meanwhile, on discussion forums and social media, you can connect with digital communities for just about any profession. You can post with a question, or you can just lurk and see what people talk about.

Look at industry sites and job postings, and you'll learn about specific jobs in a field, what skills you'll need for those jobs, what growth looks like in those jobs, and how much you can expect to earn.

Then, once you've got your eyes on a specific industry or profession, it comes time to consider the third tactic.

2.3.3 *Conferences*

Lianna Johnstone used to recruit for Meta. Now she's a technical recruiter at Niantic, the augmented reality developer behind *Pokemon Go.* It's

Lianna's job to connect great talent to great opportunities, often offering her own insights on perfect-fit roles that job applicants might not have considered.

When I asked her for tips to expand opportunity horizons, her first suggestion was surprisingly old-school. "Industry conferences," she said, without missing a beat. "Even if you're just going to observe."

Once you've got an industry or profession in mind, head for the belly of the beast if you can. Conferences can be pricey and a hassle to get to, so, by design, they specifically attract the most passionate, most curious, most open-minded folks in the field. That's where you want to be.

Conferences are often thought of as networking hubs—and for good reason. If you're game to wave to strangers and shake some hands, you'll make great connections. But even if you aren't, Lianna says that conferences expose us to new professions and teach us what those professions are really like.

"Speakers talk about different aspects of what they're working on," says Lianna. "At booths, people will talk about different aspects of their roles, or what their companies do." Lianna adds that simply reading speaker bios can give you a masterclass in an industry's landscape.

Even if you hide in a corner and speak to no one, you'll learn what companies are up to, what people in this field are up to, what kinds of issues they think about, what kinds of problems they solve. And if you do make some conversation, you might even leave with a job. (More on these conversations in Part III.)

2.3.4 *Career Guidance Organizations*

A moment ago, I mentioned that many mission-driven organizations (orgs) host websites where you can learn about different professions. Well, Mona Mourshed points out that these orgs do more than just web hosting. Many will work with you one-on-one, in person or online.

Mona runs one such org herself. Her nonprofit, Generation, works to prepare, place, and support people as they move into life-changing careers that would otherwise have been inaccessible to them.

Her team begins with employers to understand what job vacancies exist and at what volume. Then her team identifies job seekers who are interested in exploring those roles.

"We'll put the whole thing in front of you and tell you what's great about this job, not great about this job, and so on," Mona says. "And then you pick a path from there." If job seekers are interested, Generation provides training to get them into those open roles, and then continues to support them for their first six months on the job. Generation then goes on to track their progress for five years post-program.

Although Mona and her nonprofit are awesome, they aren't the only ones who do this kind of work. She recommends looking for orgs like hers, that will train and place you in a role. She also adds that there are plenty of organizations that exist to inform you about professional options. And those can be helpful for horizon expansion, too, even if they don't train and place you.

These initiatives are especially easy to access if one's provided through a school you attended. High schools and universities often run career offices, which work with students and alumni, helping them dis-cover unknown professions and pursue opportunities in those fields.

Which brings us to the fifth and most divisive tactic.

2.3.5   College

At college, you can quickly check out a wide variety of disciplines, both through classes and through your campus community. The course catalog is a mini-map of career options just waiting to be explored. Most colleges make it easy to take an intro class in just about any field. Try a 101 class on architecture, on business, on software engineering. Worst-case scenario, you take one semester of econ that you'll never use. Best case scenario, you find your calling.

And it's not just classes that make college an incredible expander of horizons. It's also the school's community. Your fellow students are exploring the mini-map, too. They can tell you where they've been and what they've seen.

Plus, you've got a roster full of industry experts—your professors— who are paid to tell you about their work and answer any questions you throw at them. In so many ways, college is an explorer's heaven.

Later in this book, we'll hear from Joy Horvath, a program manager here at Unity. Joy leads an initiative that's making it easier for new talent to enter the games industry. And when she isn't working on that, she designs games of her own.

When Joy began undergrad, she intended to work in fashion. It's only through her college community that she discovered her love of game design. If it hadn't been for those design nerd friends, we never would've had the privilege to work with Joy, and the worlds of games would be so much the worse for it.

So there's plenty of good to say about college's capacity for expanding our horizons. But I also think it's important to issue words of warning here. College isn't everything it's made out to be.

For many of us, college has become a must-do. It seems like a given that anyone who's serious about their professional future ought to enroll. And we imagine that our college diplomas will grant us access to the professions of our dreams. But that isn't true at all. And the costs of college can far outweigh its benefits.

College costs have increased by 169% since 1980, while pay for young workers is up by just 19%.[7] And tuition costs keep inflating by 12% every year.[8] Meanwhile, these upfront tuition costs don't even account for the income that college grads lose by delaying their entrance into the workforce for four years.

Then, once we complete a four-year degree, it takes about 15 years to see a positive ROI (return on investment).[9] And some degrees never see a positive ROI at all.[10]

So before choosing to enroll in college, I recommend asking these four questions:

1. Do I have the money?
2. Do I have the time?
3. Do I know what I want to get out of college?
4. Are my wants well aligned with what college is actually able to deliver?

2.4   The Choice Ahead

At the start of Part I, I talked up the enormous importance of choice making. We spent a whole bunch of time looking at how arcades and consoles evolved to train gamers for the career decisions that they'll make today. But to choose well, we first need to cultivate great options. Before we point a finger and say, *That's the one*, we need to be sure that we're well-informed.

No matter what circles we run in—no matter how urbane or worldly—we're only ever glimpsing a sliver of what the world has to offer. We have to begin with exploration, trekking across the map, diving down through the entire dialog tree, before we choose.

Then, once we've got the lay of the land, that's when we pick the quest that suits us best. Which is what we'll do in Chapter 3.

Notes

1. Garfinkle, Madeline. "Gen Z's Main Career Aspiration Is to Be an Influencer, According to a New Report." *Entrepreneur*, September 20, 2023. https://www.entrepreneur.com/business-news/what-is-gen-zs-no-1-career-choice-social-media-influencer/459387.
2. "State of the Future U.S. Workforce Report: Preparing Students for the Jobs of the Future." YouScience, 2024. https://resources.youscience.com/rs/806-BFU-539/images/2024_StateoftheFutureWorkforce_Report.pdf.
3. Wellener, Paul, Victor Reyes, Heather Ashton, and Chad Moutray. "Creating Pathways for Tomorrow's Workforce Today." *Deloitte Insights*, May 4, 2021. https://www2.deloitte.com/us/en/insights/industry/manufacturing/manufacturing-industry-diversity.html.
4. "State of the Tech Workforce 2024," CompTIA, March 2024, https://www.comptia.org/content/research/state-of-the-tech-workforce.
5. McCaw, Ben. "Join Our AMA with the Developers of Horizon Zero Dawn on March 16th, 4PM CET." Reddit, March 16, 2016. https://www.reddit.com/r/horizon/comments/5zidtl/comment/df0f20q/?context=3.
6. Flaherty, Colleen. "Students' Biggest Career Influences." *Inside Higher Ed*, January 12, 2024. https://www.insidehighered.com/news/student-success/life-after-college/2024/01/12/survey-college-students-talk-career-influences.
7. Hess, Abigail Johnson. "College Costs Have Increased by 169% Since 1980—but Pay for Young Workers Is up by Just 19%: Georgetown Report." CNBC, November 2, 2021. https://www.cnbc.com/2021/11/02/the-gap-in-college-costs-and-earnings-for-young-workers-since-1980.html#:~:text=According%20to%20the%20researchers'%20analysis,have%20increased%20by%20just%2019%25.
8. Hanson, Melanie. "College Tuition Inflation Rate" EducationData.org, September 9, 2024, https://educationdata.org/college-tuition-inflation-rate

9. Hanson, Melanie. "College Degree Return on Investment." EducationData .org, November 19, 2021. https://educationdata.org/college-degree-roi

10. Cooper, Preston. "Does College Pay Off? A Comprehensive Return on Investment Analysis." FREOPP, May 8, 2024. https://freopp.org/white papers/does-college-pay-off-a-comprehensive-return-on-investment-analysis/.

3

Professional Pathfinder and Job Feel

3.1 Tinker, Tailor, Soldier, Spy

Study magic at the College of Winterhold or poetry at the Bards College. Become a hitman for the Dark Brotherhood, or enlist in the Imperial Army. These are just a few of the professions you can pursue in the titanic, open-world game *Skyrim*.

When playing the game, some diehard completionists will chase down all 273 of its quests, but most players have scarce time. They pick and choose the missions that suit them best.

The real world magnifies both extremes of this experience. In life, there are even more professions available to us, and even fewer that we can realistically pursue before game over.

Using our five tactics for expanding opportunity horizons, we will have discovered many of these possible professions. Engineer, detective, photographer, manager. Automator, advisor, installer, influencer. Tinker, tailor, soldier, spy. Now the time comes to make hard choices. How do we choose the quest that suits us best?

In life, as in games, this will not be a single-factor decision. When choosing quests in open world RPGs, we might consider how fun the mission sounds, the number of experience points it yields, how the quest fits into the overall story, and how long it takes to complete.

Later in this book, we'll look at other kinds of role-playing games—massively multiplayer onlines (MMOs) and multiplayer online battle arena (MOBAs). In these team-based games, players assign themselves characters with different skills and then collaborate to win. That assignment process likewise requires multifactor decision-making. We consider which role we enjoy playing most, which we're best at, which abilities will be most useful to the team, and so on.

When selecting a profession to pursue, we will go through a similar, multidimensional decision-making process, this time weighing four key factors:

1. **Passion:** What do you love?
2. **Skill:** What can you be good at?
3. **Mission:** What does the world need?
4. **Sustainability:** What will pay you well?

It can be helpful to arrange these four factors in a Venn diagram, optimizing for maximum overlap (see Figure 3.1). We'll call this diagram the *Professional Pathfinder*.[1]

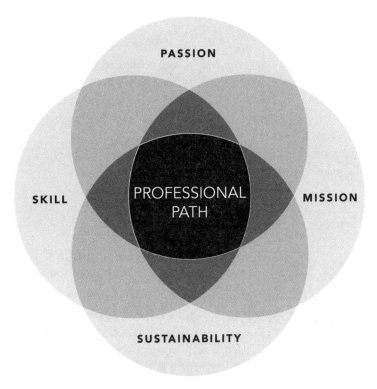

Figure 3.1 The Professional Pathfinder

3.2   Factor 1: Passion

"Do something you love," the saying goes, "and you'll never work a day in your life." That might not be true for everyone; many people find that hobbies feel more like work once they're monetized. But it's certainly true that loving your work requires working in a way you love.

Here's what I mean: as a gamer decides what profession to pursue, it's good for them to notice that they love gaming. This doesn't necessarily mean that they'd be happy working in the games industry. Some people will be. Others might feel that working in the industry sucks all the joy out of play.

But once a person notices that they love games, they can ask themselves *why*. What kind of games do they love? And what do they love about those games?

Maybe a person loves *Zelda* for its puzzles. Well, there are a bunch of great professions for puzzle-solvers: engineering, cybersecurity, forensics, architecture.

Or maybe a person loves *Skyrim* because they get to try out lots of professions and wear different hats. That person might enjoy event planning or project management—both fields that involve flexible roles and endless novelty.

By contrast, one of those 273-quest *Skyrim* completionists might do well as a compliance officer, supply chain manager, or database administrator, tracking to-do lists to ensure that every *i* gets its dot and every *t* gets its cross. Although someone who loves open-ended, do-anything sandbox games might enjoy the ambiguity of user experience design, lab science, and entrepreneurial startups.

Think broadly and abstractly about what you love. Then identify the fields and professions that align best.

3.3   Factor 2: Skill

When thinking about what you can be good at, there's a fair bit of nuance to consider.

First, it's common to assume that skill and passion go hand-in-hand, but there are often discrepancies. Not everyone loves the things they're good at, and not everyone's good at the things they love. You can be a great programmer but hate sitting in front of the computer all day. And you can love working construction but have terrible knees.

Next, it's important to note that we aren't asking what you *are* good at, we're asking what you *can* be good at.

If you're missing skills for a certain profession, don't let that deter you. It's a given that you'll need new skills for new professions. That's not a problem. In fact, it's great! Remember the cyclical motto for contemporary careers: *Learn, earn, advance; learn, earn, advance.*

You just need to be able to pick up any missing skills later—in Phase 2 of the Core Career Loop.

As a general rule, I'm a big believer that we can grow many of the skills we want to. But some skills present more challenges than others. The aspiring programmer who hates sitting at a computer is going to have an awfully hard time learning to code. And the aspiring construction laborer who has bad knees isn't going to fare so well during training.

Likewise, you can absolutely learn the violin at age 50, but if you want to become a professional soloist, you'll need lots and lots and lots of practice. Do your finances and personal life afford you the requisite time? If the answer is yes, then the violin is indeed something you *can* be good at.

Finally, when evaluating what we can be good at, it's important to account for both technical and durable skills.

Technical skills are trade-specific abilities. Which coding languages do you know? What software do you use? How do you fill in medical compliance forms?

Meanwhile, durable skills (commonly called *soft* skills or *behavioral* skills) are the abilities that fuel success across disciplines. How adaptable are you? How communicative? How decisive? Both of these are important skill types to consider in the Professional Pathfinder.

So ask yourself: What skills do I feel confident about? What skills do other people celebrate in me? What skills could I pick up with some study and practice? And which of the professions on my opportunity horizon most align with those skills?

3.4 Factor 3: Mission

Sarah Krasley is the CEO of Shimmy Technologies, a mission-driven organization that trains job seekers for work in the apparel industry. Shimmy's especially devoted to reaching women worldwide, empowering them to work in factories and earn equitable wages. For many of these women, training with Shimmy will create domino effects across their lives, improving their dignity, their income, and even their personal safety.

When asked for her advice on career decision-making, Sarah said that each of us must try to leave the world better than we found it. "Does the world really need someone to build another food delivery app?" she asked. "Probably not. Ask how you can help."

Doing a job you love, doing it well, and making oodles of cash definitely sounds like a good time. But ultimately, most people won't be satisfied with their work until they find some way to make a positive impact on the world around them.

I'm not saying that everybody needs to roll up their sleeves and clean the ocean. Or save the Amazon. Or deliver aid to under-resourced populations. Not all good looks like charity. There are many, many ways to improve the lives of others. I'm saying that each of us will ultimately need to find ours.

I'm going to use Unity as an example to illustrate what I mean. I want to be clear: I'm not doing this to sell you on Unity's brand. If you're reading this book, you probably already know about Unity, and you might even like us. So, mission accomplished. What I want to do now is share how I think about doing good in a corporate context that, on its surface, might look exclusively profit-driven and ethically neutral.

I think Unity's a helpful example because there's nothing especially altruistic-sounding about the work we do. We're a big, global tech company that makes software to build games and more. And we get paid to do it.

But, from where I sit in the company, I see the positive effects of our work every day. And those positive effects aren't only created by teams in education, workforce, development, and social impact. Every person who works here, from coding to accounting to sales, contributes to making Unity an effective, feasible, accessible engine that can be used for good.

First, there are all the things built with our technology. A blockbuster game like *Pokemon Go* might not be a work of charity, but it's brought joy to millions. And for many, its augmented-reality, played-in-the-world design has drawn people outdoors, encouraged neighborhood exploration, and created a stronger sense of social connectedness. *Pokemon Go* is powered by Unity.

So are many other games that give people joy and connection. Plus, a fair number of those games are, in fact, designed with social causes in mind. They tell stories of marginalized people, raise awareness about little-known issues, create new forms of play for people with disabilities, and even educate gamers about their own health.

Meanwhile, Unity isn't just a game engine—it's a platform for creating all kinds of immersive experiences. When Shimmy trains women to work in factories, they use software powered by Unity. Sandra Day O'Connor's education nonprofit, iCivics, has reached about nine million students using Unity. And the studio LevelEx has trained more than half a million health care professionals, including NASA astronauts and half of all medical students nationwide—all using Unity.

Then there's the impact that Unity has on creators themselves. Part of our ethos is that we want our tools to be accessible. That means making them easy to learn and easy to use.

We pursue that objective both through the user-centered design of our platform (guided by people like James Stone) and through the facilitation of free and low-cost learning opportunities. We host online learning content, fund in-person learning opportunities, and actively focus on supporting Unity communities worldwide.

And I can tell you without a doubt that learning to use Unity changes lives. Because so many different industries use Unity, mastering our software opens the door to tons of high-paying job opportunities. We're talking about the kinds of jobs that empower people to lift themselves out of poverty and improve the lives of their families for generations to come. (I'm not exaggerating here. Unity's social impact team works with folks like this all the time.)

And like I said before, it's not just the social impact team that's creating these opportunities. Every person who works at Unity helps make the platform an engine for good. Even the most businessy, profit-driven divisions of our company are essential to this effort. Without them, none of this would be financially feasible. The whole thing would crash and burn.

Again, I know it might sound like I'm trying to toot the Unity horn here. But that's not my goal. I'm not saying that Unity is the ultimate agent of altruism. Nor am I saying that Unity is special. In fact, what I'm saying is precisely the opposite. My point is that there are so many companies out there like Unity. There are so many ways to do good. And that can include working at for-profit organizations and corporate titans.

Games bring joy into people's lives. Tech tools democratize opportunity. Real estate developers create homes. Gyms and fitness centers enable healthy living. Airlines and hotels facilitate connection. The list goes on and on.

When choosing a profession to pursue, ask: What does the world need? Which of those needs do you connect to most? And where in your opportunity horizon do you see an opportunity to help?

3.5   Factor 4: Sustainability

You can love a profession. You can be great at it. You can feel connected to its mission. But if it won't pay you what you need to pay the bills, then, as far as I'm concerned, it can't be the right profession to choose.

There are a lot of factors that affect pay in a given industry or profession—regulations, unions, and more. But for our purposes, I'm going to focus on two in particular: supply and demand.

This is the principle of labor demand in a nutshell: if an employer needs more people to do a job than are willing and able to do it, then the employer has to give people an extra incentive to work for them. They do that by offering more pay. But if lots of people are willing and able to do the job, then the employer doesn't need to create more incentive. So they pay less.

Here are some scenarios where your employer might have to pay more because the labor supply is low:

- It's a job that few people want to do. *(Babysit my pet tiger.)*
- It's a job that few people know how to do. *(Train my pet tiger.)*
- It's a job that few people can access. *(Take my pet tiger for a walk in her favorite rainforest.)*

Here are some scenarios where your employer might pay less because the labor supply is high:

- It's a job that lots of people want to do. *(Play video games at home, and fill out short surveys about them.)*
- It's a job that lots of people know how to do. *(Play video games at home, and fill out short surveys about them.)*
- It's a job that lots of people can access. *(Play video games at home, and fill out short surveys about them.)*

And that's just the supply side. Demand can also vary. Ultimately, pay is determined not by either individual figure, but by the difference between the two.

- There are more poets than jobs for poets. Labor supply is higher than demand. So we can expect low pay for most poets.
- Construction firms need more master plumbers than they can find. Labor demand is higher than supply. So we can expect high pay for most master plumbers.

When considering your opportunity horizon, look for the options where demand exceeds supply. That's where you can make a sustainable living.

It's also important to consider the long term. We're not only interested in supply and demand *today*, we're also interested in what those things will look like tomorrow.

In a dying industry, demand is declining. Pay might be good today, but we anticipate that it will decrease in the coming years as businesses shut down or offer fewer jobs. By contrast, in a growing industry, demand is increasing. We expect pay to keep getting better as more jobs open up. Technological change often prompts these industry transformations.

A quick example: the printing press was invented about 1440. But a year later, if you were a handwriting scribe or copyist, your short-term job prospects still looked great.

Poll the patrons of your local alehouse, and you probably wouldn't find many folks who could write, let alone mass-produce a legible text for distribution. And it's not like anybody *had* a printing press. The press was invented in Germany and wouldn't make it to Italy until a quarter-century later in 1465. It would take another decade to land in Great Britain.

So when it came to writing things by hand, there was still a low supply of laborers and high demand. However, even if scribing was "a good job," you'd be right to call it a dying industry. In the long term, demand was sure to decline. By 1550, people would need scribes and copyists about as much as they'd need dinosaur tamers.

Meanwhile, print media was a growing industry. The world was about to need a whole bunch of press operators, maintenance technicians, typesetters, book binders, publishers, print shop owners, newspaper editors, and so on. That was the field to go into.

About 500 years later, the internet would shake things up all over again, killing off the print media industry while creating an entirely new media industry online. During both of those technological revolutions, the best pay went to those who looked ahead, assessing not just today's supply and demand but also tomorrow's.

As we make career decisions today, we have to think ahead too. Renewable energy will continue killing off fossil-fuel jobs while creating new jobs around solar panels, wind turbines, energy storage, and smart grids. Industrial robotics will continue killing off assembly line jobs while creating new ones in design, engineering, programming, integration, and maintenance. GPS-powered machinery will continue transforming job prospects in agriculture. 3D printing will continue transforming job prospects in construction.

When you look at the industries and professions on your opportunity horizon, ask, Where are vacancies increasing? Where are they decreasing? How will emerging technologies affect supply and demand? And how will those changes affect the financial prospects of my chosen career path?

3.6   Job Feel

That's it for the Professional Pathfinder, but there's one last decision-making consideration I want to discuss before we move on. I call this one *job feel*.

In 2008, Steve Swink released a landmark book for designers called *Game Feel*. In it, Swink argued that the most powerful influence on a game's qualitative success isn't merely its on-paper attributes like plot, sound, or graphics. The biggest influence is the game's "feel."

The factors that influence job feel can differ from those that influence game feel, but the general principle is the same: what ultimately makes or breaks a job is more nebulous and more complex than the on-paper job description. It has more to do with things like agency, environment, challenge, novelty, and so on.

As you consider your opportunity horizon and narrow in on a chosen profession or industry, ask these questions:

- **What does the work feel like?** Isolated? Collaborative? Fast-paced? Deep and deliberate?
- **What is the industry community like?** Casual or formal? Warm or cold? Rough or welcoming? Close or scattered?
- **What is the culture for feedback in this industry?** Are mentors and coaches common? Is feedback given to build you up or tear you down?

- **How much agency are you given?** Do leaders in this industry micromanage employees or empower them?
- **Are these interesting problems to solve?** How challenging is the work? How varied are the projects?
- **How is the work–life balance?** What kinds of hours do most people work? How often do they work weekends? How often do they take vacation?

There are all sorts of ways to learn about job feel. The easiest way is to ask professionals in the space, which we can do using many of the same tactics discussed in Chapter 2, when we expanded our opportunity horizons. We can meet industry insiders through our friends and family and communities, through the internet, and through conferences.

We can also go deeper by trying the work ourselves in time-limited, low-commitment ways. These include shadowing, volunteering, interning, side-gigging, and doing short-term contract work. All great ways to experience what a field is actually like.

Ultimately it's the way a job *feels* that will determine its fit for us.

3.7 The Paradox

Throughout this chapter and the one that preceded it, we've thought carefully about career choice making, diversifying our options, and selecting the professional paths that will serve us best. But if we think about Shigeru Miyamoto, we'll recall that he chose to become a toy maker, then somehow ended up a video game designer instead.

Our choices define our career paths, but we can't always control where those paths will take us.

In Chapter 5, we'll examine this paradox more closely, exploring how it works and what gamers do about it.

Note

1. Hat tip to Lyle Maxson, who recommended this approach, and whom we'll meet soon. (Also note that this system is commonly referred to by the misnomer *Ikigai*—a Japanese term meaning "reason for being.")

4

Gravitational Pull and Expecting the Unexpected

4.1 The Future

I wasn't supposed to work for Unity. I was supposed to work for the State Department.

I was born to a family of Midwesterners who, for generations, never moved more than a hundred miles from the place they were born. That streak went unbroken until the Vietnam War, when Uncle Sam drafted my dad into the military and shipped him out to Turkey. My mom and I went with him. And after a few years abroad, I knew: I was going to be the family globetrotter. I loved getting to see more of the world, and I wanted to see as much of it as I could.

When I enrolled in college, my plan was clear. Major in economics and international relations. Graduate. Join the Peace Corps. Then the State Department.

To get into the Peace Corps, I figured that I'd first need to establish my international bona fides. So when the summer of my junior year approached, I set my sites on flashy foreign policy internships. But I didn't have the grades to snag one. Instead, I landed at the FCC, the federal agency that regulates communications. And there was nothing foreign about it. A colossal bummer.

It was 1994, and the FCC hadn't quite figured out what to do about the internet. Was it just a fad? Was it here to stay? Would it need to be regulated? At the time, people were more concerned about phones and radio, TV and cable. Just give the internet to the intern, they figured. So there I sat all summer, in a little windowless room, reading about the future.

My future.

When I graduated, I turned down the Peace Corps, and I moved to San Francisco instead. The internet was going to change everything. I had to be a part of it.

4.2   Thrown for a Loop

From the very start of my career, nothing went as planned. I switched jobs, switched paths, switched missions before I even hit my mid-twenties.

Turns out, that's not so unusual.

Our most recent data on this dates back to 2008, when people reported moving on from their employers every four years.[1] In fact, younger workers, aged 25–34, reported moving on even faster—beating the norm by more than 25%.[2] And experts agree that this rate of change will keep quickening in coming years.[3]

In many ways, it's the internet that's responsible for all this change. It's the internet that opened the floodgates to a whole new era of transformation—what many now call *the fourth industrial revolution*. It's the internet that made rapid innovation and rapid disruption possible. And at a personal level, it's the internet that changed my own life.

The internet threw my career for a loop the very first time I touched it. In an instant, it yanked me off my path and pulled me into its orbit. And then, just as quickly, it spat me back out.

4.3   Unity at Last

As it turned out, being part of the internet revolution wasn't that great. It was 1997, and I was selling data pipes to Bay Area businesses. Not exactly changing the world. To be fair, I learned a ton. I learned how to sell. I learned how to hire talent. But most of all, I learned that I needed a stronger sense of purpose from my work.

I gathered all my savings, took out a bunch of loans, and paid for another shot at schooling, this time researching the link between education and economic opportunity. This was a total pivot. I spent the next decade working in technology and education trying to improve academic outcomes for underserved students. And it was tough.

These students were spending more time playing video games than doing schoolwork. How could their academic outcomes ever improve?

Eventually, I figured out what you already know: video games weren't the enemy. Since the invention of the blackboard, there has never been a better-designed tool for learning. Soon I was running an educational gaming company housed at the offices of EA and Zynga, creating games and building assessments to demonstrate the academic power of play.

We discovered that video games weren't just helping kids do math problems and learn scientific names for things. Games helped kids develop durable, transferable skills that would serve them not just at school but also later in life, at work. These games weren't only a means to improving learning outcomes, they were also a means to improving career outcomes.

And that's what led me to Unity. Now I get to connect all the dots, working at the intersection of games and education and economic opportunity. We teach creators to use game development software, which in turn creates economic opportunity by way of job access and entrepreneurial opportunities.

So much for the State Department. It's here at Unity that I've finally been able to connect games to learning to career opportunities to the internet, and do it all with a global perspective.

4.4   The Controller's Disconnected

My story is like so many others. We've already heard about famous game designers whose careers turned out differently than they intended. Shigeru Miyamoto wanted to make toys, but instead he ended up designing some of the world's most celebrated video games. Henk Rogers was supposed to work in gemstones, but instead he ended up popularizing role-playing games in Japan. And then there was James Stone, who went from IT specialist to police officer to photographer to game designer to tech leader.

When we're choosing our career paths, we often believe that we have more control than we do. We believe that the professions we choose will be the ones that we get and stick with. But that's rarely the case. In this chapter, we're going to talk about why we have so little control over our career outcomes and what to do about it.

But before we do, I think it's important to establish some ground rules for the language we'll use to talk about all this.

In this book, we'll use the term *career* to refer to the lifelong journey of work. Each of our careers will twist and turn, and we won't be able to control them nearly as much as we might imagine. That story we heard in Chapter 1 about James Stone was a "career" story—the entire history of his working life.

To frame this in terms of the Core Career Loop, you might visualize a single "career" as a long chain of loops linked together. We cycle the loop over and over and over again, and then we step back and look at everything that's happened over a lifetime of work, and we see a "career."

By contrast, for us, the term *profession* will refer to a single field of work that we intentionally choose here in Loop Phase 1. Information technology specialist is a profession. Police officer is a profession. Game designer is a profession. Like James, most of us will change professions many times throughout our careers, as we cycle through the Core Career Loop, returning to Phase 1 again and again.

And then, in Loop Phase 3, we'll start looking for "jobs." We'll define a *job* as a specific employment opportunity—a particular role at a particular company. Even if we stay in the same profession for a long time, we might move through many jobs. When James worked in the IT profession, he moved from company to company, rising up the corporate ladder. Each time his title or his company changed, he was starting a new "job."

Those are pretty much all of our key terms. But there's still one more I want to talk about. It's a subtype of "jobs" called *dream jobs*.

4.5   Dream Jobs

I want to animate characters for Riot. I want to design computers for Apple. I want to be president of the United States.

Sometimes a dream job is defined by its title ("starting quarterback"). Sometimes a dream job is defined by its description ("play sports for a living"). And sometimes it's defined by a particular company that we imagine will be the perfect employer ("The New England Patriots").

It was Andrew Connell who suggested we talk about dream jobs here. Andrew's a virtual reality (VR) developer, consultant, and game designer. He's created VR training experiences for the US Navy, multinational corporations, and little old us—Unity. Today he handles VR for a global consulting firm.

Andrew didn't really mean to become a hotshot VR expert. He stumbled into it by hitting a kind of rock-bottom: a moment when he was struggling to earn an income and had no promising professional prospects. "I just needed to get up and do something about it," he says. "I decided I would make something on a regular basis, put it on the internet, and share it with people."

Andrew knew a thing or two about VR, so he figured he'd make instructional videos about VR and stick them on YouTube. Andrew says that these videos weren't supposed to become part of his career story. He just wanted to get some kind of momentum going in his life, so that he could eventually yank himself out of the hole he was in. If there was a shadow of ambition, it "was just that I could make like a hundred bucks a month on ad revenue."

Instead, Andrew's YouTube work ended up earning him between $1,000 and $10,000 a month. A whole community formed around Andrew's YouTube channel. Then companies started contacting him for help, and his consulting practice was born.

For Andrew, his career's big, transformative opportunity wasn't a dream job he'd envisioned—it was a dream job he stumbled into. "We all ultimately don't know what our dream job entails," he says.

Andrew's been down the dream job rabbit hole before, and he's seen his friends go down it, too. He says that "you hear all those horror stories of people who were like, 'I got my dream job.'" Then you ask them how the job's going and they say, "Oh, it's awful. I quit after six months."

When we intentionally pursue dream jobs, Andrew argues, we're trying to exert more control over our careers than we really have. He says that this counterintuitively leads to worse outcomes. Dream jobs often turn out to be disappointing. And while we chase them, we close ourselves off to the other signals and opportunities that come our way.

That latter point is the one I find most concerning. The world around us is constantly changing. We, ourselves, are constantly changing.

As we're about to see, it's precisely this change that makes careers so unpredictable. And that's all fine. Change is good. In fact, this chapter will argue that the most reliable technique for professional success—in every sense of "success"—involves aligning ourselves with those forces of change and submitting to the chaos.

But when we relentlessly pursue a single dream job, we close ourselves off to other possibilities. In our efforts to control career outcomes that cannot be controlled, we lose our connection with how the world outside is evolving, how we ourselves are evolving, and how our opportunities are evolving too.

We need to tune into these signals, not drown them out. And in a minute, we'll explore what tuning into them looks like. We'll talk about the dream job's opposite—what I'll call *gravitational pull*.

But to understand gravitational pull, we first have to understand the lightning storm of chaos that it responds to.

4.6   Inside the Chaos

This is why our careers are so unpredictable: because we and the world around us are constantly changing. Let's start with the world around us.

Back in 1965, the engineer Gordon Moore predicted that every two years, we would double the number of transistors on an integrated circuit.[4] He turned out to be essentially right.

Since then, Moore's law has become an analogy for the fact that technological innovation keeps speeding up at exponential rates. The computer scientist Ray Kurzweil eventually reformulated this principle as "the law of accelerating returns."[5]

And there's no denying that it is indeed a *law*. For most of human history, technology remained entirely identical from the time you were born until the time you died. In fact, it usually stayed identical for thousands of generations afterward. It took us two and a half million years to figure out fire. Then eighty-eight thousand more years to figure out agriculture.

But things sped up afterward. It's only about five thousand years to get from agriculture to the wheel. And then it's about half that—two thousand years—from the wheel to bronze.

If you skip ahead to about 1800 when the locomotive's invented, innovation suddenly becomes . . . well . . . a runaway train. Twenty years to the first photograph. Then fifteen more years to the first telegraph.[6]

In my own lifetime so far, I've seen the invention of the home computer, the home video game console, the internet, the smartphone, and consumer-facing AI. (There was also the invention of email, which, I think we can all agree, was a huge mistake.)

The point is that technology keeps evolving faster. And every time it evolves, the working world around us evolves, too. New professions emerge. Old professions collapse. Whole industries rise and fall. And our best-laid career plans go sideways. Technology sends us careening off in directions that we couldn't predict. Like when you get an internship that exposes you to the future of human communication, and it changes your life's mission forever.

This is all to say nothing of the economic and political changes that reshape our market. Regulation, unionization, and the shake-up of capital can radically redirect our careers.

When the 2008 recession hit, and then again when COVID hit, businesses shut down, and people lost their jobs. Many of these people had plans. They had visions for their future. Now they had to reinvent themselves.[7]

And our careers don't only surprise us with hardships. Often, as Andrew Connell experienced, it's the opportunities that surprise us. When the COVID lockdowns came, they taught us just how much we could do online, just how much we could do from home, just how much we could do independently, and this too transformed careers. People switched to jobs at companies far, far away. They switched to jobs that let them work from home. They switched to professions that had never been accessible to them before.

And these events don't just catalyze changes to the workplace. They can also catalyze a change of personal priorities. The global pandemic gave lots of people their first sustained break from work in years. For many, it also delivered encounters with mortality and human fragility. This inspired many people to rethink their work and what they wanted from it. They rethought how much time they wanted to spend on the job, what they wanted to spend that time doing, what kind of role they wanted work to play in their lives.

Which brings us to an entirely different locus of career-altering chaos: the chaos within.

4.7   The Chaos Within

It's not just recessions and pandemics that inspire changes of priorities. Just the simple process of living and aging will do that.

Jonathan Stull is the president of Handshake, an organization devoted to ensuring that all college students have equal access to meaningful careers. He and his team have partnered with nearly two thousand colleges and universities, and nearly one million employers, to build stronger college-to-job pipelines.

Because he's often helping students enter their first profession, it's become especially important to Jonathan to educate early-career job seekers about the change that inevitably comes for us all. "What you want and value really changes throughout your lifetime and your career," he says. "We have to be prepared for that change."

There are all kinds of ways that values change. What we want from work changes. The way we like to work changes. The causes that matter to us change.

You might see a person who's worked in corporate their whole life take a pay cut to join a nonprofit. Or a person who's spent their whole life working for underfunded causes decide they need a more sustainable income.

You might see folks decide that they want to spend more time with family and less at work. Or, after years of focusing on the home front, decide that they want to invest more time in their careers.

And our work styles change, too. People who've done solo work realize they want more collaboration. People who've always worked on teams realize they want more solo time. People crave more novelty at work. Less novelty at work. A job where everyone's family. A job that's just a job.

And, thinking back to our Professional Pathfinder—*what does the world need*—people's personal missions change, too. A person loses a loved one and decides to pivot into grief counseling. A person experiences the delight of Disneyworld and asks how they can become part of the magic. Ecological turmoil inspires someone to become an activist. Or after years of pursuing large-scale change, a person decides to focus on little ways that they can help the people closest to them.

It might seem strange to describe these decisions and realizations as "chaos." They sound pretty voluntary. But, as Jonathan Stull points out, internal change can surprise us just as much as external change. There's no predicting when these changes will happen or how they'll affect us. The only thing that's certain is that these transformations of values will come, and when they do, they'll call on us to take our careers in new, surprising directions.

We can only build rewarding careers if we listen for these calls, and answer when they come. Or, to put it another way, we can only build rewarding careers by pursuing our "gravitational pull."

4.8   Embracing Gravitational Pull

Gravitational pull is about relentless inquiry. It's about staying tuned into changes happening around us and inside of us. When we embrace gravitational pull, we don't try to become expert controllers, forcing predetermined career outcomes. Instead, we become expert adapters, transforming our careers in conversation with an evolving world.

That's important because, as we've seen throughout this chapter, we can't possibly succeed at forcing outcomes. We can't control where our careers will take us. But we can choose to collaborate with the chaos.

I find that this collaboration generally makes careers more successful and lives more enjoyable. More successful because we're open and available to emerging opportunities. More enjoyable because we aren't trying to control the uncontrollable.

Again, *inquiry* is the operative idea here. When pursuing gravitational pull, we have to actively investigate all the modes of change that we've discussed so far in this chapter—both the change happening out in the world and the change happening inside of us.

Investigating external change looks a lot like expanding opportunity horizons. We use the same five tactics—chief among them, conversation. We ask people what they do, why, and how they feel about it. When we hear that someone's making a professional pivot, we ask why and to what.

In the process, we learn about the jobs around us. We learn about new professions that are emerging and old ones that are dying off. We learn how work is changing across different fields. We learn how the economy is evolving.

Along the way, we *notice*. What sounds exciting and what sounds boring? What sounds risky and what sounds secure? What's capturing our interest and exciting our imagination?

Simultaneously, we notice the emotions that arise in our own work. We monitor for when we feel excited and when we feel frustrated at work, when we feel resentful and when we feel grateful, when we feel bored and when we feel inspired.

It's through this noticing that we'll investigate *internal* change, discovering how our personal senses of passion, of skill, of mission, of sustainability are changing. In this way, we constantly recalibrate our internal Professional Pathfinder. Ultimately, this investigation reveals new "centers of gravity," where external opportunities and internal values align.

Pursuing gravitational pull doesn't exactly give us control over our careers' long arcs. We must still surrender to the chaos. But this pursuit of gravitational pull does give us some agency in the matter.

4.9 Agency and Surrender

This is what sets the embracer of gravitational pull apart from the dream jobber. When we pursue dream jobs, there's only ever one strong option at a time, and that option usually stays in our crosshairs for a long while. Even if that option really does qualify as a viable "professional path," the option is static. And its stasis traps us, often tying us to a super-precise vision of the future—one that we don't have the power to ensure.

By contrast, when we embrace gravitational pull, we discover many strong options, and these options evolve frequently. Our conception of viable professional paths evolves, too, as we notice our internal values transforming.

The upshot is that we look to our opportunity horizons and see many options that seem like potential fits. And our judgment about fit is stronger because our conception of our own values is more up-to-date.

Then, when life throws our careers for a loop—when innovation or economic turmoil or shifting values shake things up—we're better prepared to adapt. We can't control the chaos. Our careers will twist and turn and surprise us. But when we embrace our gravitational pull, we seize all the agency we can and surrender to everything else.

Because we do have *some* agency. We control the short-term decisions that we make, following our gravitational pull at every opportunity. Every time we cycle through the Core Career Loop—when we change jobs or make a professional pivot—we're not merely being tugged around by the economy or by old dreams or by new fears. We're making informed decisions, guided by our own centers of gravity.

And yet those centers of gravity are not of our own making. We discover them and surrender to them. In the long run, gravitational pull is going to take us to surprising places. Our interests and values and skills will change—the world around us will change—and gravity will change with them.

Either way, the outcome's going to surprise us. If we're willing to surrender, we'll adapt to those surprises better. And have more fun doing it.

4.10   Fun, Not Fear

My team and I have seen these career evolutions firsthand, over and over and over again. It's our job to train future creators on the Unity platform no matter their goals. For millions of these creators, their dream is to work in the games industry. And many do. But once they know the platform inside-out, many creators also go on to very successful careers in other industries.

In a recent study we conducted, we found that while about half of Unity creators work in gaming today, the other half have repurposed their skills for about two dozen other industries and professions across the economy. It'll come as no surprise to learn that many Unity creators go into engineering and animation. But they also go into transportation and automotive industries. They go into architecture and construction. Health, education, finance, defense. And the Unity-to-aerospace pipeline is huge!

In the modern marketplace this is the norm. The new skills we learn don't always draw us in closer. They often fling us out further.

Many of us were born to old-timers, who never worked in a profession more than a hundred miles from the field where they began. But today's economy calls for trailblazers—people who search for far-flung opportunities and want to experience all that they can.

We must ready ourselves to adapt. We must ready ourselves for surprise.

Don't let this scare you. The fact that you can't control career outcomes shouldn't create a sense of futility. For those who will eventually go on to other professions, time spent learning game development isn't wasted. The skills that they build as game developers serve these folks well when they move into other industries.

And the same principle will hold in any field. To go deep is to go broad. If you level up in any industry, you will develop durable skills that travel with you and make you successful throughout your career, no matter where that career takes you.

It's a wild ride, and a fun one at that. The best way to enjoy it is to let go of the safety bar, throw our hands in the air, and shriek through all those loop-de-loops.

In Chapter 5, we'll talk through the three kinds of fear we might face on that ride—and the joy of confronting each.

Notes

1. Bialik, Carl. "Seven Careers in a Lifetime? Think Twice, Researchers Say." *The Wall Street Journal*, September 4, 2010. https://www.wsj.com/articles/SB10001424052748704206804575468162805877990.
2. Fry, Richard. "For Today's Young Workers in the U.S., Job Tenure Is Similar to That of Young Workers in the Past." Pew Research Center, December 2, 2022. https://www.pewresearch.org/short-reads/2022/12/02/for-todays-young-workers-in-the-u-s-job-tenure-is-similar-to-that-of-young-workers-in-the-past/.
3. "Having Many Careers Will Be the Norm, Experts Say." World Economic Forum, May 2, 2023. https://www.weforum.org/agenda/2023/05/workers-multiple-careers-jobs-skills/.
4. Moore, Gordon E. "The Experts Look Ahead: Cramming More Components onto Integrated Circuits." *Electronics*, April 19, 1965. https://hasler.ece.gatech.edu/Published_papers/Technology_overview/gordon_moore_1965_article.pdf.
5. Kurzweil, Ray. *The Age of Spiritual Machines: When Computers Exceed Human Intelligence* (Penguin Books, 2000), 41.
6. Roser, Max. "This Timeline Charts the Fast Pace of Tech Transformation Across Centuries." World Economic Forum, February 27, 2023. https://www.weforum.org/agenda/2023/02/this-timeline-charts-the-fast-pace-of-tech-transformation-across-centuries/.
7. Janicki, Hubert. "From Great Resignation to Great Reshuffling: How The COVID-19 Pandemic Prompted More People to Change Jobs." United States Census Bureau, May 13, 2024. https://www.census.gov/library/stories/2024/05/great-reshuffling.html.

5

This Game Is Beatable

5.1 Calling an Audible

Steven Christian's football career had been going exactly as planned. After graduating high school, he'd been rated a three-star recruit, attracting scholarship offers from more than a dozen universities. He could have gone to teams like Villanova or Texas Christian University, which had near-perfect winning streaks. Or he could've chosen Stanford and stayed close to home. Ultimately, he chose the University of Hawaii.

For three years, he played cornerback and free safety, blocking passes, catching interceptions, and sacking QBs. But by his junior year, he'd been sidelined. "My second hip surgery was on my 21st birthday," he says. That meant a month in a wheelchair and three months more off his feet. "The eggs that I put into the football basket were not going to hatch."

Incredibly, he would still go on to play more college football at Oregon State University. But whatever pro-ball plans he'd had would have to change.

5.2 The Three Fears

It's a scary thing, choosing a new profession. Whether we're just starting out with no workplace experience or we're departing a familiar field for new frontiers, there's no guarantee that things will work out. Sometimes the search process can be rocky, and so can the early days in a new profession. We don't see the progress we expect in the time that we expect it. Funds run low. Confidence falters. Especially for those of us who don't have prestigious family connections, it can feel like we're on our own, lost at sea.

In this chapter, we're going to unpack all that, talking through three key fears that we're likely to face in Phase 1 of the Core Career Loop, as we choose a profession to pursue.

First, there's the fear that *I don't know enough*. I'm trying to move into an entirely new field. How will I ever learn enough? How will I ever practice enough? How will I ever catch up to the folks who've devoted their entire lives to this profession?

Second, there's the fear that *I will fail*. What if this doesn't work out? What if I end up in some nightmare condition with no resources and no prospects?

Finally, there's the fear that *I'm not connected enough*. Here, it's not my own faults or failings that will hold me back. I might even feel totally confident about my new profession. But nobody I know has ever done anything like this. I have no network. No role models for success. How will I ever find a job? Shouldn't I just pick a profession closer to home?

I can think of few people who might be more vulnerable to these fears than a college cornerback with two hip surgeries. But on the other side of his own career loops, Steven reflects that everybody he's encountered struggles with the same uncertainties. "I quickly learned that it's all a big experiment," he says. "Nobody knows how it's gonna turn out."

Here's what I *can* tell you about how it turned out. It's been about a decade and a half since Steven was first wheeled into surgery. Today, he creates augmented reality (AR) adventure comics about the Black experience in America for his own studio, Iltopia. In his free time, he consults as an AR developer, creating a suite of immersive experiences for local brands. He teaches at colleges and speaks at global conferences and gives interviews to national newspapers. He helps my team train emerging creators on the Unity platform. And, oh yeah, he's completing an MD-PhD in integrative neuroscience.

When we face our fears and follow our gravitational pull and devote ourselves to study and discovery, things have a way of working out.

5.3 The First Fear

I don't know enough.

According to Lyle Maxson, this fear has things all backwards. Ignorance often isn't an obstacle. It's an asset. Like Steven Christian, Lyle also works in the mixed reality space. He creates and leads tech companies at the intersection of VR, artificial intelligence, games, health, and education. He works with the United Nations to promote "gaming for purpose," and he writes about mission-driven tech for *Rolling Stone*.

Lyle's first real job—although it seems kind of crazy to call it that—was clubbing. When people in his area went out, they might hit three or four clubs a night. It was his job to make the one they were at feel too fun to leave.

When he started out, he energized clubbers simply by socializing and dancing. But it soon occurred to Lyle that, with better tools and deeper strategy, he could create much richer experiences. This line of inquiry would eventually lead him to the music festival circuit where he became a creative director, developing joyous immersive experiences for hundreds of thousands of festivalgoers.

In many ways, Lyle had found his viable "professional path." He was checking boxes for skill and passion and pay—even mission. His festivals incorporated wellness experiences, yoga stages, education hubs, and more. But his sense of mission demanded more: Lyle didn't just want to reach thousands—he wanted to reach millions. That realization launched him on a journey into games and immersive technology that's still careening around twists and turns today, evolving with every new Silicon Valley innovation. He's leading multiple companies, serving on boards of directors, and rolling out new products all the time.

My team and I first encountered Lyle when we were putting together a special initiative to make jobs in the game industry more accessible. This employer advisory board designs and promotes new hiring practices aimed at diversifying the games workforce, reducing bias, and rethinking the skills and credentials that qualify creators to work in this space.

Lyle had cofounded a global publishing company to support VR developers who make "games for good." And that experience, combined with his industry outsider background, gave him a unique perspective. He became a vocal advocate for looking past traditional markers of technical expertise and industry experience.

Later in this book we'll discuss a number of Lyle's key insights and arguments. But for right now I want to focus on one point in particular: "It's naive mindsets that allow innovative ideas to come through," Lyle says. And to make this point, he cites his own credentials for game publishing: "I played a lot of video games when I was younger, but I had never worked in gaming. I came from the music industry. And that gave me a unique approach."

Looking at his own life, at the lives of his fellow C-suiters, and at the lives of their employees, Lyle observes that too much knowledge can become dead weight. He says that when you learn too much, it biases you, constraining you to "a set of rules" about how things work and what's possible. In Lyle's experience, innovation happens when "you're carving your own path, guided by what you want to do, figuring things out as you go."

Put it another way: innovation is born when we don't know enough to doubt that something is possible.

About 80 years ago, STEM wiz George Dantzig proved this point mathematically. By the time he died in 2005, Dantzig had made huge contributions to computer science, industrial engineering, statistics, and economics, never letting the unfamiliarity of any field deter him. His work had made huge impacts across transportation, supply chains, energy, and beyond.[1] But in 1939, Dantzig wasn't yet so distinguished. Here's what he was instead: *tardy.*

Dantzig was pursuing his PhD at Berkeley, and, one day, showed up late to class. He had just enough time to copy the homework problems off the board, then was off to his next lecture.

> A few days later I apologized to [the professor] for taking so long to do the homework—the problems seemed to be a little harder than usual. I asked him if he still wanted it. He told me to throw it on his desk. I did so reluctantly because his desk was covered with such a heap of papers that I feared my homework would be lost there forever.[2]

Six weeks later, the professor showed up at Dantzig's home, banging on the front door. It was 8 a.m. on a Sunday. Dantzig hadn't figured out the answers to the homework, the professor told him. What Dantzig had figured out were the answers to two famous unsolved problems. The professor wanted to publish Dantzig's homework in an academic journal.

There's an old adage that's often paired with stories like Dantzig's. "It couldn't be done," the saying goes. "But the poor fool didn't know it couldn't be done, so he went ahead and did it anyway."

Here in Phase 1 of the Core Career Loop, we're choosing a new profession. It's natural, as we look at our opportunity horizons and see a world full of unfamiliar fields, to feel fear. How could we ever learn enough, practice enough, experience enough?

The answer is that we can learn and practice and experience plenty. And the things we don't know can often serve us just as well as the things we do.

5.4 The Second Fear

I will fail.

This fear represents a special species of failure that we most frequently encounter at the beginning of the Core Career Loop. Strangely, this is failure both at its most dangerous and at its most harmless.

We'll be talking a lot about failure in this book. The fear of it. The embrace of it. The overcoming of it. When we start learning new skills in Part II of this book, we're definitely going to fail—again and again and again. Our challenge there will be to persevere despite those failures. To get back on the horse.

We'll likely fail again in Part III, when we search for jobs. We'll send out so many applications, shake so many hands, speak to so many strangers, and hear so many people say no. This will be another special species of failure—*rejection*—and this too we will have to overcome.

But here in the first phase of the loop, we won't fail at all. We can't. It's literally impossible to fail. Because we aren't *doing* anything yet. We're asking questions. We're noticing our feelings. We're weighing our options. We're making decisions. You can't fail at any of that. The only way you can "fail" is by *not engaging*. And, ironically, the fear of failure is one of the most common reasons we might disengage.

If we give in to the fear, it'll stop us before we even begin. Instead of expanding our opportunity horizons and searching for a viable professional path—instead of pursuing our gravitational pull—we'll do nothing.

If we're already employed in an unsatisfying profession, then we'll stay put. If we aren't employed yet, then we'll seek out the path that best protects us from failure. That might mean staying out of the job market altogether or entering the market by way of its most low-effort opportunities.

If you think about Chapter 1, you'll recall that future cyber detective James Stone tried both of those strategies. A challenging childhood had taught him to fear failure. So after he dropped out of college, he stayed home, on his grandparents' couch, playing video games all day long. And when he couldn't do that anymore, he took the path of least resistance. His grandmother circled the wanted ad, got him his suit, scheduled his interview. All he had to do was take the gig, soldering at a local electrical engineering firm.

Later in life, as he cycled the Core Career Loop again and again, James would confront much deeper failure-based fears. Many of his professional choices involved financial sacrifices—some of which would leave him indebted and homeless. Others would put him in the crosshairs of danger, exposing child exploitation, turning to spearmen for protection there.

Those experiences have left James with a transformative philosophy of fear. Here's how he puts it:

> Fear controls many people. And that's a real shame, because, actually, in most cases, you're worried about a whole bunch of theoretical things happening to you. Fear makes you focus on the worst possible outcomes, but these are all fantasies. None of them have actually happened to you.
>
> In reality, sure there are things you have to be careful of, but with good planning and preparation, bad things rarely ever happen. And overcoming things when they do is what truly changes us—shows us what we are capable of.
>
> Fear just holds us back. And once you embrace fear and push through it and see what happens, it's a really powerful thing for your career, for your relationships, for your family. Because once you do something scary and realize that nothing bad happened, what's left to be afraid of?

This is the strange thing about Phase 1's fear of failure. Unlike other encounters with failure, this one is entirely unreal. In Phase 1, we cannot fail. We can only *imagine* failure. We did just that a moment ago, when we imagined ourselves too untrained and ill-informed to succeed at any of the careers on our horizon. And we'll imagine failure again in a moment, with the third fear, when we look around at our communities and worry that we aren't connected enough to succeed.

I'm certainly not encouraging anybody to pursue professions that threaten death or homelessness ("sustainability" is a central tenet of the Professional Pathfinder), but I think it's important for us all to take James Stone's insight to heart. Hopefully we can all learn the same lesson without putting our lives on the line. If not by reading what James has to say, then perhaps by reading what the sci-fi epic *Dune* has to say:

> Fear is the mind-killer. Fear is the little-death that brings total obliteration. I will face my fear. I will permit it to pass over me and through me. And when it has gone past I will turn the inner eye to see its path. Where the fear has gone there will be nothing. Only I will remain.[3]

5.5   The Third Fear

I'm not connected enough.

After his second hip surgery, when Steven Christian wrestled with his Phase 1 Loop decision, none of the options that appealed to him seemed within reach: "I don't know anybody who does this stuff," he remembers thinking. "My parents don't do this. My friends don't do this."

Fear might be the mind killer, but Steven wasn't exactly wrong to worry here. It's no secret that *whom* you know often matters more than *what* you know.

Most obviously, that's because people usually hire, recommend, and promote from within their own communities (to their detriment, as we'll see in Part V of this book). And it's also because we learn from our communities. Our friends and family and coworkers and mentors expose us to skills, to ideas, and to visions for what might be possible.

For both of these reasons, it might seem scary or foolish to choose a profession that's disconnected from our existing communities and networks. Who's going to open doors for us? Who's going to teach us and collaborate with us and dream with us?

There is an answer though: *plenty of people.* In Chapter 6, we're going to take our first of many deep dives into the Community Loop—the process by which we build networks and friendships while looping through our careers. We'll see that while things are certainly simpler when you're born with industry connections, it's never been easier to build these connections yourself from the ground up. And the rewards can be staggering.

When Steven Christian felt gravity pulling him toward illustration and animation, he began building a new community around those disciplines. Initially, he pursued this work in small-scale ways, developing connections while testing the waters. First, he became an illustrator for his college newspaper. Then, he put out his own graphic novel. And those experiences got him a job at a small, local magazine.

Simultaneously, Steven got involved with the maker scene and small business community in his area, connecting with like-minded artists, creators, and entrepreneurs. "That really informed and offset the frustrations I had with not getting hired for entry-level positions or internships," he says.

Then he went to an industry conference that changed everything for him. "The stars just aligned," as he puts it.

At the time, he was wrestling with a frustrating issue: he was trying to show off his animation skills at conferences, but poor internet connections often made it hard for people to watch his videos. He could only show them his static comic book work. "I met a product manager who was like, 'Hey, this is a prototype to show what you could do with our paper.'"

This special paper integrated with an augmented reality app, effectively animating images on the paper page. With tech like this, Steven could use hardcopy comic books to show off his animation skills.

Not only did this encounter turn AR comic books into Steven's new medium of choice, it also introduced him to Unity—the platform that powered his new favorite tool. He bought an $11 Unity web course and started studying.

Meanwhile, when the pandemic hit in 2020, Steven took his community-building efforts online. He live-streamed his learning journeys in AR and Unity, and documented his progress in Twitter threads. And with all these efforts combined, he broke through.

At the beginning of the pandemic, Steven's credit card had been denied when he tried to buy a carton of ice cream. He'd been flat broke. But exactly a year later, he was featured in the *Wall Street Journal's* "Future of Everything" conference. He was a certified Unity developer. He was teaching AR and consulting on AR development for industry.

We don't need to come from privilege to succeed. And we don't need to inherit a network.

Fear will arise every time we return to the first phase of the loop. But if we can recall that ignorance is strength, that fear is fantasy, and that community is ours for the building, then we can succeed.

For gamers of all backgrounds, this game is beatable.

Notes

1. "Obituaries of George Dantzig." The Virtual Center for Supernetworks, Eugene M. Isenberg School of Management, University of Massachusetts Amherst, 2025. https://supernet.isenberg.umass.edu/photos/gdobit.html.
2. Mikkelson, David. "The Legend of the 'Unsolvable Math Problem'." Snopes, December 3, 1996. https://www.snopes.com/fact-check/the-unsolvable-math-problem/.
3. Herbert, Frank. *Dune* (Penguin Random House, 2005), 370.

6

Community Loop: Mentors

6.1 The Community Loop

As we discussed in Chapter 4, change is a constant. The world around us is always changing, our values are always changing, and our opportunities are always changing. But here's something that probably won't change anytime soon: *It's who you know.*

Or better yet, it's who you *meet*.

The people we meet expose us to new frontiers, challenge our beliefs, broaden our skills, and support us throughout our life journeys. It's been that way since the first two humans shook hands and decided to share a cave.

Throughout the Core Career Loop, we'll meet tons of new people, and we'll ask them for help again and again. Here in Phase 1, the people we meet will help us select professional paths to pursue. In Phase 2, they'll help us level up. In Phase 3, they'll open doors to new job opportunities. And in Phase 4, they'll help us grow on the job, leading us back to the start of the Core Career Loop.

Given the important role that the people we meet will play throughout our journey, Parts I through IV of this book will each end with a special chapter dedicated to community building. Across each of these four chapters, we'll ask: *How do you build community to support your career?* Ultimately we'll discover that the community-building process is a loop in its own right.

You might recall from the Introduction that any one video game can have many loops. The core loop is the one that defines the game (choose quest > slay monster > collect reward > repeat). But there can be plenty of other loops, too.

There might be a shopping loop that you repeat every time you earn some more money. (Enter shop > sell items > buy items > leave > repeat.) Or there might be a dialogue loop that cycles every time the game delivers new story beats. (Greet character > receive information > ask follow-up questions > say goodbye > repeat.)

Building a career likewise requires navigating many loops. At the center, we have the Core Career Loop, which we've heard about plenty (see Figure 6.1). (Choose quest > level up > job hunt > job craft > repeat.) And here in Part I, we've also encountered another kind of loop—what you might call the *Quest-Selection Loop* (see Figure 6.2). (Investigate change > expand opportunity horizons > identify viable professional path > repeat.)

Figure 6.1 The Core Career Loop

Figure 6.2 The Quest-Selection Loop

In these community chapters, we're going to navigate a third loop: the Community Loop. This loop breaks down into four phases, each of which correspond to a phase of the Core Career Loop (see Figure 6.3):

1. Mentors
2. Coaches
3. Sponsors
4. Bosses

Figure 6.3 Community Loop

By the end of this book, we'll have built a complete professional community, capable of supporting us during every phase of our journey.

That work begins here, in Phase 1, with mentors. But before we dive in, I want to clarify what I'm talking about when I talk about community.

6.2   Weak Ties

Communities, of course, are made up of all sorts. Family. Friends. Bosses. Coworkers. Teachers. Students. Soulmates. Arch enemies.

What's important to note when we talk about community is that we aren't just talking about the people we know best. We're also talking about the people we know least. And, in fact, it's those people we know least who often end up helping us the most.

Nitzan Pelman is a passionate proponent of this idea. She's spent more than two decades improving education and career outcomes in underserved communities as an entrepreneur in residence at LinkedIn and as a leader at Teach for America and the New York Department of Education—not to mention at three of her own mission-driven ventures. Among those ventures is an upskilling organization called Climb Hire, which Nitzan founded and ran for the last six years, with the aim of giving job seekers the upper hand in their careers "even when life didn't give them a head start."

Climb Hire launches working adults into high-income tech jobs, unlocking social capital and economic mobility by teaching in-demand job skills alongside relationship-building skills. It's this latter bundle of skills that Nitzan's especially passionate about. Speaking about Climb Hire, she often says, "We're a community, not a class."

Across all of her experience, Nitzan's learned that community is a powerful force for creating networks where peers open doors for one another. And, surprisingly enough, our community doesn't have to be tight to open those doors.

Casual acquaintances. Distant colleagues. Friends of friends. That person you sort of met at that party that one time—or at that conference, or at that soccer game, or at that community garden. These so-called weak ties are the ones that most often connect job seekers to transformative opportunities.

"Weak ties have tentacles that are far further reaching than our strong ties," Nitzan says. "Strong ties lead to referrals and opportunities, of course. But the real innovation and opportunity is to leverage strong ties and weak ties together. That's when you are optimizing your social capital most effectively."

We'll take a close look at these weak ties later, during job hunting in Part III. For now, the important thing to note is this: for those who worry that they don't have the right networks, or weren't born into the right sort of privilege, there's good news. We don't need bone-deep, age-old, multigenerational connections to get ahead. Weak ties reach so much further, and we can make those ties ourselves.

Who you meet is no longer restricted by where you grew up or how much your parents earned. Today, it's easier than ever to find like-minded peers and mentors. It's easier than ever to knock on doors and meet experts. It's easier than ever to design careers in collaboration with community. All we need is a little know-how.

And most gamers already have a lot of know-how.

6.3 Ready Player 1—and 2 and 3 and 4

Ironically, it's violent shooting games that turned gaming into a medium of friendship and community.

In 1962, scientists at MIT had just gotten their hands on the PDP-1, the first ever "minicomputer." It was cheap (about $100,000), it was tiny (the size of a fridge, the weight of a car), and it had revolutionary new capabilities. As accidental game designer J. Martin Graetz puts it, "you could turn it on any time by flipping one switch, and when you were finished you could turn it off. We had never seen anything like that before."[1]

Graetz and his team were thrilled to start using the PDP-1, but there was just one problem: they didn't know what to do with it. Computers were new, and although people could intuit that they would eventually be useful, it wasn't yet clear how.

The team talked it over and decided to create some kind of computer program—one that would show off all of the computer's resources and tax it to the limit. They wanted this program to feel different every time it booted up. And they wanted it to actively "involve the onlooker," as they put it. The result was one of the world's first video games. *Spacewar!* pit two players against each other in an extraterrestrial dogfight to the death.[2]

One MIT generation later—and one minicomputer generation later—came *Maze War*, the first-ever first-person shooter. Three high school students developed the game during a work/study program at NASA in 1973.

Initially they'd built the game for two players, but when one of those kids brought it to MIT, the game quickly expanded. *Maze War* evolved to support eight simultaneous players. And once plugged into the ARPANET, those players could join from anywhere with a network connection.[3]

By the time the 1990s rolled around, the ARPANET had become the internet, and the federal government had tasked a little intern in a windowless room with figuring out whether it should be regulated. While she studied up, gamers turned this new network into a roaring hub of communal play.

By the early aughts, first-person shooters like *Quake* and *Counter-Strike* had transformed communal games from mere multiplayer experiences into "clan" experiences. These clans were groups of gamers who played together regularly—competing, strategizing, and skilling up as a team.

Today, community is a vital part of the online gaming experience. Players encounter and bond with strangers, seek out mentors and advocates, band together to achieve shared objectives, and rely on one another to discover possibilities and open doors. More and more, designers build games with these community experiences in mind.

And we don't only see communities growing in multiplayer contexts. Designers of contemporary single-player games likewise assume that players will turn to friends and experts for help. It's a tradition that dates back to the hardcopy walkthrough guides of the 1980s and 1990s. In the early 2000s, we had web-based wikis and forums to turn to. And now, the walkthrough has spawned an entire industry of its own, encompassing let's plays, live streams, speed runs, and commentary videos.

Although community building might be challenging for some, it's second nature to gamers. We've been doing this since the 1960s. Gamers appreciate that community is the key to surviving, thriving, and enjoying the wide world of play.

Why should our careers be any different?

6.4   Career Clans

As in games, the communal dimension of career looping begins with our peers. By now we know what the first phase of the Core Career Loop involves. We must monitor and investigate the changes happening both in the world and inside ourselves. Through this process, we expand our opportunity horizons and refine our Professional Pathfinder. Then we compare our opportunities to our values, looking for places where the two align, and we choose a profession to pursue. Along the way, we must overcome the three fears—the fears of ignorance, of failure, and of disconnection—and we must choose courageously, embracing our gravitational pull wherever it leads.

At each of these turns, our peers can support us. Much of this help will be casual, conversational, and abstract. Our peers can help us make sense of our values by reflecting what they see back to us. *What do you think my passions are?* we might ask a close friend. *What skills stand out most to you? What causes won't I shut up about?*

During Phase 1, our peers become our sounding boards, too. We tell them about the opportunities we see, the values we've identified, and, together, we evaluate which professional paths seem best aligned.

Our peers also become our cheerleaders. When we wrestle with the three fears, friends and family step in to remind us of what we're capable of. They remind us that we know more than we think we do, have the capacity to learn more than we think we do, and don't need to know nearly as much as we think we do. They meet our fears of failure with reality checks and offer to catch us if we fall.

Then, when it comes to the third fear—the fear that we don't know the right people—our peers remind us that we're more connected than we might realize. And this is where peer support moves from the abstract to the concrete.

It's also where we start moving from local, in-person networks to remote, digital ones.

6.5 Peer-to-Peer Networks

As we know from Chapter 2, the first major challenge of Phase 1 is that of expanding our opportunity horizons. If we think about the five tactics that enable this expansion, the first and most powerful was *community*. "The people around us do stuff," we said in Chapter 2. "We should ask them about it."

Our friends can tell us about what they do, why they do it, how they feel about it, and whether they think we'd like it. And, to Nitzan Pelman's point, our friends can introduce us to their friends, who can do the same.

Importantly, this process isn't just about taking advantage of our existing community. It's about *growing* that community, branching out from peer to peer, from friends to friends of friends, from close ties to weak ties. And although this branching out doesn't necessarily have to take us online, it often does—to great effect.

In Chapter 4 we encountered Andrew Connell, the virtual reality (VR) developer who launched an exciting new chapter of his career by building a YouTube community on how-to videos. We also encountered in Chapter 5 Steven Christian, the former football star whose live streams and Twitter threads helped launch his second act in animation and augmented reality.

There are a lot of things that these internet communities can contribute to our careers. But perhaps the biggest one is *diversification*.

To explain what I mean, it's helpful to get under the hood of why weak ties matter so much. When you think about close ties, these are the people we know best. They're the people we see most, speak to most often, and share the most interests with. As a consequence, we tend to run in the same circles. That means we're likely meeting the same sorts of people and hearing about the same sorts of opportunities.

By contrast, weak ties are quite different and distant from us. We know them just enough to consider them "ties," but that's the extent of our connection. The people they talk to are different, the professions they hear about are different, and, as a consequence, the opportunities they encounter are different. Which means they're uniquely well positioned to expand our opportunity horizons and, later in the

Core Career Loop, they're uniquely well positioned to connect us to future jobs (see Figure 6.4).

To put it another way, it's the diversity of weak ties that make them powerful. The more different these people are from us, and the more different they are from each other, the more helpful they can be.

The internet is a gathering place for all types of people. The people we love and the people we hate and the people we've never heard of. People from other professions, from other states, from other countries. People of different classes, genders, races, and ages.

All these different people run in different circles. Connecting to them connects us to their worlds. And connecting to their worlds expands our opportunity horizons. Meanwhile, this diversity isn't just important because it diversifies our access. It's also important because it diversifies our insight. Which is where mentors come in.

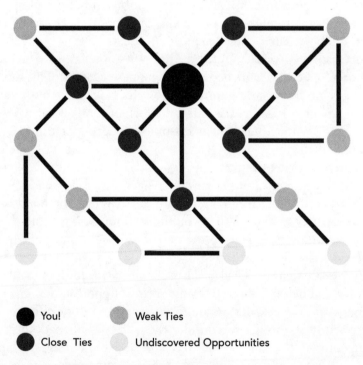

Figure 6.4 Peer Network

6.6 Meeting the Mentor

Mentors exist to diversify our insights. Each of us is limited by our own experiences and by our own perspectives. Without noticing it, we can become trapped in a single story about our lives and our world. Our visions of what's possible might be constrained, and so might our visions of who we are or who we could be. In short, no matter how old we are or how much of the world we've seen, there's a limit to our insights.

Mentors expand those insights. They motivate, inspire, and advise, guiding us through holistic personal and professional development.

When I say *holistic*, I mean that mentors focus on the whole person. A great mentor doesn't just help us get one job, they help us make sense of who we are and what we're meant to do. And when there's a change in our world or in our values, they help us make sense of these things all over again.

Sometimes mentor relationships are brief—weeks or months long. But often our mentors will stick with us for years, guiding us through many cycles of the loop. In that time, they might help us with the following:

Provide clarity. Mentors help us assess our passions and skills, missions and needs. And they help us evaluate where those values align with opportunities on the horizon.

Track changes. Our mentors often hear about external changes before we do, and they often notice changes in us before we spot them. Mentors can help us notice these changes and adapt to them.

Share experience. Mentors are often older than we are, but not always. Sometimes they've just seen more of a particular corner of the world, or spent more time working through a particular problem. Drawing on these experiences, mentors share what they've seen and heard and felt and discovered. They help us learn from their mistakes and reproduce their victories.

Make introductions. Our mentors have often collected many close and weak ties of their own. When their ties become ours, that creates exponential network growth.

Offer accountability. Regular check-ins with a mentor can help us stay on track, requiring us to make progress in the time between meetings.

Give emotional support. Our mentors often know the three fears well, having faced them many times before. Drawing on their own experience, they can bolster our certainty that necessary knowledge is within reach, that failure is survivable, and that the connections we need are all around us.

Tell the truth. A lot of people don't like talking about the dark side of their industries. Sometimes, the painful parts feel too personal to share. Other times, people just prefer to give us encouragement. But we need the truth to choose our quests well. And a good mentor will give that truth to us.

The value of mentorship is a constant, persisting throughout our first loop journey and throughout every subsequent cycle. For that reason, the best time to onboard a new mentor is right here, right now, at the very beginning.

6.7   Onboarding the Mentor

Ray Graham is a tech leader who's spent 30 years creating the games and tools that people love most, first as an engineer for EA and 2k and Ubisoft and Apple, then as a director of tech and graphics at Unity. Now he's the CTO of his own game studio—Cornerstone Interactive Studios—and he heads up engineering for an exciting new VR venture.

When he isn't managing the genius inventors of today, Ray's usually mentoring the genius inventors of tomorrow. For six years, he's served as a board member of Gameheads, a summer accelerator program that provides teaching and mentorship to high schoolers with engineering and game-designing ambitions. And Ray mentors plenty of people outside of Gameheads, too.

One year, during an industry conference, a young guy started chatting him up in the elevator. As an aspiring developer, this guy was looking for evidence that he might have a chance, and Ray was that evidence. "He was just like, 'You're the first Black person I've seen here so I want to talk to you,'" Ray recalls.

Ray hears this refrain often, and it's a big part of why he started mentoring in the first place. At Gameheads, Ray says, "We focus on kids [who] are underrepresented. We warn them that working in this industry, you'll feel out of place. And we teach them how to deal with that."

Initially, Ray was thrown by how forward that guy in the elevator had been. But the passion came through, and Ray was hooked: "We started talking, and then I started mentoring him, and now he works at Unity."

Every now and then, a mentor might fall into our lap. But most of the time, it's on us to go out and find them.

Admittedly, these relationships can't be mechanically predicted or engineered. They can only be seeded, grown, and tended to. Rich, deep mentorship is especially out of our control. It often comes from unexpected places and takes years to reveal itself. But, as with the pursuit of gravitational pull, there are ways that we can exercise agency, even in the midst of surrender.

What we can do proactively is send out the bat signal. Start searching for mentors. Start building relationships. The best strategies here will sound familiar. They're not so different from the strategies we used to expand our opportunity horizons or grow our peer networks.

For instance, Ray's story reminds us once again that industry conferences can change lives. (In Chapter 2 we heard about the importance of conferences from Niantic recruiter Lianna Johnstone. And in Chapter 5 we saw an industry conference transform the career of Steven Christian, the former football player.)

Likewise, social media sites, alumni networks, and professional associations can all connect us to potential mentors. So can mission-driven organizations like the ones we've read about here in Part I: Mona's Generation, Nitzan's Climb Hire, and Ray's Gameheads. (Soon we'll encounter a fourth such organization, Urban Arts.)

Sometimes, we don't even have to go anywhere to find mentors—they're right here, all around us. Our family, friends, coworkers, and managers all have the potential to mentor. We just have to reach out.

6.8   Is the Mentor on Board?

Of course, although everyone has the potential to mentor, not everyone will want to. Ray offers a few tips for feeling out whether someone's open to mentorship.

The easiest sign to read, he says, is a broadcasted offer of availability: "I've definitely seen people posting something like, 'Hey, I'm open to do résumé reviews, and have conversations.'" Those are obvious open doors.

To be clear, Ray doesn't recommend explicitly asking strangers to be your mentor unless they've made that offer first. Most people expect mentorships to be *grown*, not given away or acquired. Still he says that when a person offers these kinds of conversations, they're signaling that they're open to becoming mentors.

And Ray adds that, although these signals are great, we don't have to wait for them. He encourages us to do cold outreach, asking folks for informational interviews. Then, he says, we should listen carefully to how they respond. "Are they interested in what you're doing? Do they have anything to offer? Are they willing to get on a call?" If yes, then there's potential for a connection.

Still, not every mentorship conversation will lead to years of relationship and guidance. For perspective on this, I found it helpful to talk to the folks at Urban Arts, a nonprofit organization that turns game design classes into college and career pathways for underrepresented students.

"You have to be very cognizant about whom you're pairing with whom," says Genevieve King, who leads philanthropy for Urban Arts. She says that one young man wanted to work on music for the games industry, and they were able to pair him with a games composer. That proved to be a very successful mentorship.

When I ask what unsuccessful mentorships look like, Urban's CEO, Philip Courtney, explains that there really are no failures. "We'd call it a failure if it was 'just nice,'" he says. "The pair met for six hours, spread out over a few months, and that's it." But he explains that even these shorter, thinner relationships often yield benefits that manifest themselves later.

For mentees, these "failed" relationships might reveal new ideas, introduce new possibilities, or help them clarify what they need— whether from their careers or even just from their future mentors. Every conversation makes an impact.

Ultimately, Ray encourages career loopers to strike up a conversation even if it seems like a long shot. "Hey, maybe I can't help you," he says. "But I bet I know somebody who can."

6.9   Making the Most of a Mentor

Once we've found someone, how do we make the most of this new relationship? The first and most important thing is to trust that your mentor cares. If you don't trust this, then you might not take full advantage of them. But your mentor *wants* you to take advantage of them.

There are all sorts of reasons that mentors do what they do. Ray says that it's often about giving back:

> For me, it's just that I want to help. I've been there. When I first got into the game industry, there was nothing. Nothing that made it look possible.
>
> People need to see somebody who's doing the thing for them to go, "Oh, wait, I could do that thing, too."
>
> Now I'm at a point in my career where I think I have something to give back. That's why I do it.

Ellen Flaherty offers another reason. Ellen's spent more than 20 years designing and leading digital learning initiatives. She earned her master's degree in learning design from Stanford and then went on to spearhead projects for teaching organizations like Adobe, PBS, and IDEO U—the learning branch of a world-leading experience design firm. These days, she works with me here at Unity.

Ellen adds that, for many mentors, "the value is in their own curiosity." Like us, our mentors crave opportunities to keep learning and growing, no matter how senior they might seem. For these guides, mentorship is a values-driven vehicle for continuing that development.

Other times, Ellen says, "it's just about kindness." Simple as that.

Whatever their reason, we have to trust that our mentor wants to work with us as much as we want to work with them. It's that trust that'll help us build structure.

6.10   Building Structure

Ultimately, it's structure that will make or break a mentorship, says Genevieve King. And Ray Graham agrees. "In every situation, always lay down the ground rules," he says.

You need to figure out how often you'll talk and for how long. That agreement will keep you both committed to this partnership, and give you a framework for understanding how it is or isn't serving you.

Once in meetings, Ray says that it's on us, the mentees, to use the time well. We're responsible for telling our mentors what we're thinking about, what we're struggling with, what questions we have. Here's Ray again:

> Don't expect the mentor to just come in and start talking to you about all sorts of stuff without any sort of direction. You should say, "Here's what's on my mind." Say, "Here's what I need help with today."
>
> You're driving that relationship. You're prepared. You're not wasting their time. And you have questions for them.

This proactive attitude will serve us well throughout the mentorship process. We should tell our mentors what we need and how they can help us, and we should help them see their own value.

You might be surprised to discover how often experts don't realize their own expertise. When first asked for advice, many will tell you that they don't have anything useful to share. That likely isn't true, but it also doesn't mean your mentor is lying to you.

They might simply not be able to see the water they're swimming in. After so many years so close to their field, they might not realize how much arcane wisdom they've picked up. So stay curious. Ask questions. Your gentle interrogations will help them see just how much they have to offer.

Finally, invest in these relationships and stick with them. Like any great heroes, our mentors become more powerful over time.

6.11   From Padawan to Master

The Core Career Loop isn't a sequence that we complete once and put aside. We'll return to Phase 1 many times, investigating change, expanding our opportunity horizons, seeking out viable professional paths.

Along the way, we'll also cycle the Community Loop again and again throughout our careers. Our peer networks will continue to broaden and diversify. We'll meet new mentors and deepen relationships with the ones we have. Our communities will grow. And we'll grow, too.

Obi-Wan Kenobi was a padawan once, before he became a mentor to Luke. Luke was a padawan once, before he became a mentor to Rey. One day, you too will be the wise mentor. Remember to pay it forward.

Notes

1. Graetz, J. M. "The Origin of Spacewar." *Creative Computing*, August 1981. https://www.wheels.org/spacewar/creative/SpacewarOrigin.html.
2. Graetz, "The Origin of Spacewar."
3. Moss, Richard. "The First First-Person Shooter." *Polygon*, May 21, 2015. https://www.polygon.com/features/2015/5/21/8627231/the-first-first-person-shooter.

Part II

Level Up

After selecting a Professional Path, previous generations skilled up only once, in their youth. Then they spent their lives putting those skills to use.

But the new economy requires a very different attitude. Our professions change frequently, so we must change with them. Today, we must continue learning and growing throughout our careers. Some of that leveling up might happen with the help of an institution, and much of it might also happen independently.

How do you build the skills you'll need for a contemporary profession?

7

How Gamers Learned to Learn

7.1 Choose Death

There are so many ways to die. You could fall off a cliff. A monk could light you on fire. A bat the size of a yacht could kick your head in. You've only just begun the game, and yet here you are, stranded on some strange mountaintop, surrounded by ruins. If you're a newcomer, you'll be dead within moments. If you're a hardcore gamer, you'll probably be dead a few moments later.

But death isn't the end. Death is the beginning. You'll respawn in a graveyard, and that graveyard will lead you to a vast chasm—a pitch-black pit of certain doom. Taking the plunge down into that pit will surely lead you to more death. If the fall doesn't kill you, it's reasonable to assume that the monsters lurking down there will.

You can bypass this chasm if you want to—the game will let you keep exploring and playing for hours and hours and hours. In fact, as far as the game's concerned, you need never take the plunge at all. And if you were a reasonable human being, you wouldn't.

But you aren't a reasonable human being. You're a gamer. You choose the plunge.

You jump down into the crevasse, and it's a good thing you do. Because in *Elden Ring*, the only way to access the built-in tutorial is by taking that leap. It's there, in that graveyard, down that pitch-black pit of certain doom, that your learning begins.

7.2   The Drop-Out

Stacey Haffner dropped out in her senior year of high school. She had enough credits to graduate, but "life just kind of pulled me away," she says. In years to come, she would return to schooling three more times, and each time, life would pull her away before she finished. She did eventually get a high school diploma, but that was it.

She never got a two-year degree. She never got a four-year degree. And she certainly never got a graduate degree.

Where did this dropout life lead her?

To Microsoft, where she worked on a Windows product serving hundreds of millions of users. To Xbox, where she launched the Xbox Live Creators program, democratizing console game development. And then to Unity, where she became the director of product working on DevOps and eventually transitioning to AI and machine learning. Her role focused on guiding large, multidisciplinary teams with the goal of launching new products within the company. "Basically, I ran a mini startup within the company," she explains. "My collaborator and I built the whole strategy and vision, from org[anization] culture to final product."

Stacey didn't get where she is today by studying like an A-plus student. She got there by studying like an A-plus gamer, leveling up the way every gamer levels up: you see something scary, you take the plunge.

That's how she learns new software ("I kind of just jump into it."). It's how she learned to overcome her fear of public speaking ("I just started putting myself on stage."). And it's how she navigated every step of her career—just following the next challenge wherever it led.

After dropping out of high school, she says, "I didn't know what I wanted to be. I really had no clue. So I just tried things that sounded interesting." With each job, she got inquisitive about what she loved and what she hated, and then she used those insights to guide her next cycle around the loop.

Eventually that process would lead her into game development, where she'd go toe-to-toe with the NBA in a virtual duel to the death. But not until she'd tried a string of dead-end jobs.

First she answered phones at a staffing agency. She found that work unbearably mundane, but loved learning new skills every time she got to fill in for recruiters who played hooky. So she switched to human resources (HR) and recruiting.

Working in HR and recruiting, Stacey realized that her role was pretty adversarial. She was tasked with protecting her company rather than its people. And its people feared her. That wasn't going to fly for Stacey, but she did love playing analyst every now and then—crunching the data on employee performance, turnover rates, recruitment metrics, and so on. So she became an analyst next.

It turned out that analyst work was only fun in short bursts, not as a full-time job. When Stacey told her staffing agency that she wanted something new, they offered her a project management role at Microsoft. And it turned out that project management was the perfect fit.

About a decade later, she manages the managers.

Stacey's cycled the Core Career Game Loop many, many times, and each time, she's had to level up. She's used all kinds of strategies along the way, always evaluating what skill she needs to learn, what learning opportunities are available to her, and which methods will support her best.

She's used booths at conferences, classes at a local college, company-provided training, coaching from bosses and peers, and the most reliable tactic of all: taking the plunge and figuring things out on the fly.

"I'll watch tutorials, or read a book, or do whatever," she says. "And then at some point, I'll get bored of the tutorial, and I'll just go try, and play around, and do a thing."

That's how she's learned everything she's learned. It's how she's achieved everything that she's achieved. And it's how she eventually beat the NBA at its own game.

7.3 Nothin' But Net

When Stacey isn't handling AI for Unity, she creates games for her studio, What Up Games. She's the CEO, and her husband, Ben, is the CTO.

About 10 years ago, she went to a conference where she tried virtual reality (VR) for the first time. For Stacey, it was love at first sight, and she raced home to tell Ben about it.

Ben hadn't experienced VR yet, but what he had experienced was sticker shock: the developer equipment was outlandishly expensive.

Stacey insisted he give it a try anyway, and Ben was willing. So they got some goggles and, as Stacey puts it, "Two hours later, Ben finally took off the headset, and he was like 'Let's go make a game.'"

Before doing anything else, Ben wanted to get his head around the virtual physics of VR experiences. So the two of them got to work on a basketball simulation.

Basketball seemed like a fun way to figure out the mechanics of VR gravity, but the duo didn't actually know anything about sports. They didn't care much either. And, again, they were entirely new to VR technology.

I'm reiterating this because I really want to emphasize: these two could not possibly have been worse prepared to go up against a multi billion-dollar pro-ball brand. But did that stop them? Of course not. We already covered this. Gamers are not reasonable human beings.

Once they'd nailed the basic physics, Stacey and Ben figured they might as well introduce some competition. So they built their first game mode: a VR version of H.O.R.S.E—the schoolyard basketball game where players compete to out-aim each other. Then came multiplayer mode, and before they knew it, What Up Games had a fully operational basketball experience on its hands. They called it *Nothin' But Net*.

The next time a major games conference hit their calendars, Stacey and Ben brought the game with them. And it absolutely killed. The pair had to lay down duct tape to accommodate the unexpected queue of enthusiastic players, which grew and grew as the day went on.

Then came the official release date. And then came the weeping. "We were devastated," Stacey says. "I cried so hard!"

Completely unbeknownst to Stacey and Ben, a major studio with official NBA licensing had also been developing their own VR basketball game all this time. By some cruel twist of fate, that blockbuster game dropped on precisely the same day as *Nothin' But Net*.

In an instant, years of development were made completely moot. Everything Stacey and Ben had worked for. Every innovation they'd pursued. "When we saw that game release, we thought that no one would even look at ours," Stacey says. They were about to be blown out of the water by a gaming goliath.

Except, when Stacey stopped crying and checked the industry news a few days later, it turned out that this goliath couldn't reach the net. The official NBA game had tanked. "Hard pass. Avoid it," read one review.[1]

Meanwhile, reviewers said, *Nothin' But Net* was a slam dunk. It had "immediately overshadowed" and "outshined" its blockbuster competition, "with an experience obviously better built for virtual space."[2]

With no college diploma, no industry credentials, and no "relevant experience," Stacey had gone head-to-head with the pros and won. Her tactic had been simple. All she'd done was train like a gamer.

7.4   How Gamers Started Training

For as long as I've played video games, they've encouraged continuous skill growth. But they didn't always work that way. Released in 1978, *Space Invaders* cast players as Earth's last great hope. Players controlled a surface-to-air cannon, which they could slide right and left, shooting down enemy aliens as they entered the planet's atmosphere. If the aliens defeated your cannon or made landfall, it would mean the end of humanity forever. Game over.

But while humanity was ending, a whole new kind of game experience was beginning. *Space Invaders* revolutionized the use of high scores and music and, most important for us, "dynamic difficulty," which opened the door to a new kind of playful skill growth.[3]

Before 1978, video game difficulty had been static. A game might be easy, or it might be challenging, but whatever it was, it would stay the same. This was true even for legendary greats like Atari's *Pong* and *Breakout*. Then *Space Invaders* changed the game.

This was a classic case of necessity mothering invention. Frustrated by the limitations of early arcade hardware, creator Tomohiro Nishikado decided to build new hardware for the game all on his lonesome, combining both Japanese and American parts. His do-it-yourself arcade system became known as the Taito 8080, and went on to build a glorious legacy of its own. But the hardware had many failings. Among them: the 8080 couldn't actually handle the game it was created for. *Space Invaders* didn't work.

The game's hordes of enemy aliens taxed the 8080 to its limit. The system could render them all if it had to, but that quantity came at a price—the aliens would move at a painfully slow pace, defanging the game's central challenge: keep up and shoot 'em all.

Here's the thing though. Once players started killing off alien invaders, there were fewer aliens to render. The fewer aliens there were, the faster the 8080 could render them, the faster they'd move, and the harder the game would become.

Players loved that this game became more difficult as they played. They loved the challenge and the demand to keep growing their skills—to keep getting better. It turned out that this slow-rendering bug wasn't a bug at all. It was a feature.[4]

In Japan alone, that feature sold 300,000 units of *Space Invaders*. The game even caused a national coin shortage, forcing the Japanese mint to triple production of its 100-yen piece.[5]

Space Invaders would go on to become the highest-grossing video game yet, selling nearly half a million arcade cabinets (not including counterfeits) and raking in nearly $14 billion—all of it thanks to what game designers now call "the difficulty curve."[6]

7.5 The Difficulty Curve

To really understand how difficulty curves changed the way gamers learn, it'll be helpful to fast-forward to *Ultima*. Remember *Ultima* from Chapter 1? Released in 1981, *Ultima* was one of those early computer games that tried to give players the same expanse of possibility and freedom of choice that they'd experienced in *Dungeons & Dragons*. It was the first ever open-world role-playing game, and it was a direct inspiration for *The Legend of Zelda*.

Well, in 1997, 16 years after its initial release, *Ultima* revolutionized the industry again. It went online. *Ultima Online* was an MMORPG—a massively multiplayer online role-playing game—and it was the first such game to reach a hundred thousand players. Within six years, it would reach a quarter million players.[7]

By standards of the time, *Ultima Online's* game world was huge and unparalleled in its interactivity and possibility. Just to give you a taste, here's an excerpt from a blog post by lead game designer, Raph Koster. He's describing the unplanned in-game economy that blew up about "dye tubs," which could be used to change the colors of objects. He and his team hadn't meant for dye tubs to be valuable, but players loved them.

Players could find objects that spawned in the world with rare colors, copy them to a dye tub, and then dye clothes with that rare color, cornering the market on a specific shade of green. . . . This led to lily-white wedding dresses, guilds that color-coordinated their uniforms, a pimp named Fly Guy on the docks with a purple feathered hat, and much more. When a bug in the system created "true black" as a hue (a palette with only #000000 black in it) it instantly became a highly coveted color that led to mass murder and economic mayhem.[8]

Ultima Online was a massive world, full of these sorts of surprising player interactions. Players would craft blank books, write novels in them, then distribute them all across the game world. They'd craft in-game mics and in-game loudspeakers and emcee in-game events. They'd create in-game neighborhood watch groups to protect in-game homes from player-controlled burglars.[9]

Later in this book, we'll talk more about this special species of surprising, so-called emergent play. But for now, I want to call your attention to *Ultima Online*'s lead designer himself—the creator we just heard from, Raph Koster. He's going to help us understand difficulty curves.

Right around the time that *Ultima Online* was hitting 250,000 users, Koster published a book called *A Theory of Fun*. Today, it's required reading in pretty much every game design course out there. And that's because it explains much of what we're talking about in this chapter.

Koster wrote this book with a mission: to investigate what makes a fun thing fun. In it, he questions why certain games are more fun than others, and why some fun games eventually become boring. Ultimately, he reaches this conclusion: "Fun from games arises out of mastery. It arises out of comprehension. It is the act of solving puzzles that makes games fun. In other words, with games, learning is the drug."[10]

This is the accidental insight that made *Space Invaders* the most profitable video game that the world had ever seen. It's what kept players coming back again and again, dropping quarter after quarter—about 56 billion quarters in all. It all comes back to the difficulty curve.

If you graph the difficulty of a game over time, charting how much that difficulty increases, decreases, or stays static as you play, what you get is a *difficulty curve* (see Figure 7.1). And that difficulty curve is important because, when designed well, it's what keeps players learning. It's what keeps players *hooked*.

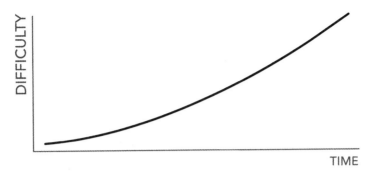

Figure 7.1 Difficulty Curve

Before *Space Invaders*, video game difficulty was static. A game was hard or it was easy, and it stayed that way. But, thanks to poor technology, the difficulty of *Space Invaders* was accidentally dynamic. It changed as you played. The better you got at shooting down aliens, the faster those aliens would move, and the harder they'd become to shoot down.

Every time you learned more about the game, you'd get better. Every time you got better, the game would get harder. And every time the game got harder, you'd have to learn more about it.

Learn, earn, advance. Learn, earn, advance.

In *A Theory of Fun*, Koster explains that fun games are fun because they challenge us. It's the challenge that leads to learning. And fun games *stay* fun when they're able to maintain a level of challenge that's difficult but not insurmountable.[11] Because—to use some of our own phrasing here—those games empower us to keep learning, earning, and advancing.

If the game gets too easy, the player doesn't need to learn anymore, so they get bored. If the game gets too difficult, the player can't earn or advance anymore, so they get bored. The game's difficulty needs to keep ratcheting up without ever straying out of that sweet spot. It needs to stay just right.

In cognitive psychology, a task that's perfectly calibrated in this way is called an *optimized challenge*. Optimized challenges boost happy neurochemicals, motivate student and worker productivity, encourage deep focus, and—as we well know—get us all hooked on great games.

It's the challenge that keeps us hooked. Learning is the drug.

7.6   The Shake-Up

The 1970s and 1980s were the age of coin op games, so the drug meta-phor is an apt one: designers had to get you hooked so that you'd keep coming back with more coins. And, once *Space Invaders* demonstrated the power of difficulty curves, dynamic difficulty became the new normal. Every game was looking to deliver the perfect optimized challenge.

So, by the late 1990s and early 2000s, when Raph Koster was writ-ing his *A Theory of Fun*, games had become all about challenge, and they'd stayed that way for decades.

It was high time for a shake-up. Someone had to push back against this games-as-challenge phenomenon, and that someone would be Fumito Ueda.

Ueda was a visual artist, drawn to abstract styles. His mission: to reframe art "in terms of ideas, rather than depictions." After completing his degree at the Osaka University of the Arts, he created performance art, bizarre installations, and visual abstractions. Then he sold his motor-bike to buy a computer, and the rest of his life began.[12]

Learning to use this computer took no small effort. Ueda had picked this model—the Commodore Amiga—because it had a graphical dis-play, and he thought it would be fun to teach himself computer graphics. But pretty much nobody else in Japan was using the Amiga, so nobody could show him the ropes. Plus, the manual was in a foreign language. Ueda tackled this challenge the same way Stacey Haffner would:

> The operating environment was all English language, so I learned with a dictionary in one hand. I wanted to get my hands dirty so I dove in and figured it out as I went along. Iterating and learning from doing, really.[13]

Ueda says that it wasn't his "original intent" to become a computer graphics professional. He was just messing around with computer art for fun, but "soon enough I felt like there was something I could discover in or express through the computer." His gravitational pull started kicking in.[14]

So Ueda went to work in the games industry. Then when, in the course of his work, Ueda finally got the chance to pitch his own game, he decided to set it apart from what he'd seen elsewhere. Rather than pitch a game powered by challenge, he pitched one powered by visual artistry.

"I was going to make my game by removing all the 'game-like' ele-ments from it that I could," he says. "I think partly it was my youth, but I wanted to do the opposite of what others were doing."[15]

The pitch worked. Ueda's game got the green light. He assembled a team and dove into design.

But the more Ueda committed to his vision, the more concerned he became that the game might fail:

> For a long time, I was very worried whether a game created in this way would be accepted by players. There were no stats, no scoring . . . would players really accept a game that only had a story and a realistic map/world?

The answer: absolutely, yes. In 2001, *Ico* was born—a game now celebrated for transforming the medium. *Ico* stunned gamers with its unprecedented visuals, welcoming players into a surrealist-inspired, expressively lit, dreamy world of abandoned castles and crumbling bridges. And once you entered that world, you discovered an entirely new kind of gameplay.

In *Ico*, the game's mechanics weren't designed to be addictive. They were designed to express characters' emotional experiences. For instance, the instinct to love and protect was articulated mechanically through moments when your character would hold hands with another, leading them through treacherous territory, tying your fates together.

The character design itself was revolutionary. So too was the sound design, and the devotion to minimalism throughout. For the first time, players were experiencing games as art. And the industry took notice. People outside the industry took notice, too. One of those people would be Hidetaka Miyazaki, who would fail his way to the ultimate expression of games-as-learning-challenges.

7.7 Celebrating Failure

When *Ico* launched in 2001, Hidetaka Miyazaki was an early-career IT specialist, working in tech to finance his sister's college tuition. Money had always been tight for the family. As a child, they hadn't even been able to afford books. But that never stopped Miyazaki. He'd go to the library and borrow English-language novels. Fantasy. SciFi. And, finding these foreign language books incomprehensible, he'd dream up his own stories to fit their illustrations.

Decades later, when Miyazaki played *Ico* for the first time, he found himself transported back to that childhood. Here he was again, at age 29, lost in mysterious imagery, dreaming up his own story to explain a visual world that defied understanding.

Ico floored Miyazaki, as it had floored so many others before him. It was gorgeous. Unprecedented. And, for Miyazaki, it held the promise of something more. Miyazaki saw a change happening in the world around him, felt a change happening inside himself, and took notice. He left his IT job and got himself a gig at the only game studio that would hire him—Tokyo's little-known FromSoftware. The pay cut was huge, but so was the possibility it promised.

At first, Miyazaki's role was confined to coding. But he spotted a failing project that nobody wanted, and offered to take it over. (In Part IV of this book, we'll learn to call this *job crafting*.) It was precisely the failed nature of this project that attracted Miyazaki. "If my ideas failed, nobody would care," he says. Because the game "was already a failure."[16]

For Miyazaki, failure spelled freedom. The freedom to experiment and mess up and experiment again. The freedom to learn and innovate. Failure was a thrill, and it opened the door to possibility.

Just a moment ago, we heard that Fumito Ueda, the creator of *Ico*, hoped to create work that would communicate "ideas, rather than depictions." And we saw how this mission influenced his design choices. *Ico's* game mechanics, for instance, became a medium through which to express ideas like love, attachment, and the instinct to protect.

Now that Miayazaki was designing his own game, he took inspiration from Ueda, articulating his own ideas through the game's core mechanics. His game became a philosophical exploration of failure. It was uniquely difficult, requiring deep practice and study to master. The result was a one-of-a-kind experience that blended the atmospheric and artistic innovations of *Ico* with the challenge of gaming classics like *Space Invaders*.

In Miyazaki's game, the difficulty curve wasn't balanced. By design, it was brutally steep. But this wasn't difficulty for its own sake. Miyazaki says that for him "difficulty is more of a means to an end." Difficulty reveals the extraordinary pleasure of taking on a challenge, failing, and then overcoming. "Those elements of hardship and that feeling of accomplishment simply have value as an experience," he says.[17]

It's good that Miyazaki was ready for some hardship, because it came for him soon. When the game that he'd poured his heart and soul into finally launched in 2009, it didn't quite bomb, but it did flop. A Japanese reviewer notorious for going soft on publishers gave the game "a disastrous 29/40."[18] And the financials disappointed everyone, too.

"Initially, sales were poor," says producer Takeshi Kajii, who helped Miyazaki codevelop the game with Sony. "We sold between 20 and 30,000 copies in Japan the first week and . . . we were really disappointed and worried that the project was going to fail."[19]

Sony decided not to bother localizing the game for markets outside of Asia. There'd be no release in the United States or Europe. *Demon's Souls* would be dead in the water.

The buck for that decision stopped with the president of Sony Worldwide Studios, Shuhei Yoshida. Three years later, in a 2012 interview, *Game Informer* magazine suggested that this was one of Yoshida's all-time biggest business failures. His response: "Absolutely! Tell me about it! 100 percent agree!" Yoshida explains a variety of factors that contributed to his decision, chief among them that he had found the game's difficulty deeply alienating: "I spent close to two hours playing it and after two hours I was still standing at the beginning [of] the game. I said, 'This is crap. This is an unbelievably bad game.' So I put it aside."[20]

Fortunately, another publisher saw the game's potential. They secured the rights to publish it in North America, and the wheel of fate turned. So did public opinion.

In some ways, nothing had changed. American reviewers likewise found the game infuriatingly difficult. One called it "a controller breaker" with another reiterating this idea more colorfully: "Warn your television to watch out for flying controllers," it read.[21]

But these reviewers also gushed about the magic of desperately struggling their way through a game, learning from their failures, and overcoming. "You will die in minutes," said one review. "You're supposed to. That's not a bad thing, mind you. . . . You're supposed to get up, dust yourself off, learn why you died there, and then come back."[22]

Here's another reviewer—this one from game journalism titan IGN:

> It's not just fogey nostalgia powering the absolute love I have for this game, I promise; it's the almost euphoric feeling that will come from *finally* besting one of the end-level bosses and raking in tons of cash. . . . There's a blissful sense of relief, of knowing you've overcome all those ridiculous odds to triumph, and to the victor goes the spoils—except in this case the knowledge of enemies and their tactics often weigh more heavily than any purse. . . .[23]

In the United States, it took just one month for the game to match a year of Japanese sales, clocking in at 150,000 units.[24] That number doubled the total lifetime sales expected for this game in the United States.[25] The game then quadrupled sales expectations by the end of Q1, and by the end of that year, it had sold half a million units worldwide.[26]

The game went on to sell 930,000 units in the US alone, and was dubbed one of Sony's "Greatest Hits" by the publisher.[27] When it was eventually remade for Sony's PS5, it sold more than 1.4 million copies in a single year.[28]

Miyazaki had built the ultimate game about failure, and it had failed. Then it had persevered, and it had come out on top. Failure, then mastery. *Demon's Souls* was a hit.

7.8   What Demons Teach Us

After *Demon's Souls* proved that gamers would take on any challenge for the joy of learning and triumphing over it, Miyazaki got the greenlight to make another game like it. *Dark Souls* became its spiritual successor and an even bigger hit.

From there, *Dark Souls* went on to birth not only a slew of best-selling sequels but also an entire genre: "Soulslikes." These games combined the atmospheric artistry of *Ico* with the extraordinary challenge of early arcade and console games like *Space Invaders*.

A decade after *Dark Souls*, Miyazaki released *Elden Ring*—a next-gen Soulslike designed to reach more players. In *Elden Ring*, there's no ambiguity about Miyazaki's philosophy of failure.

There are so many ways to die. A chandelier could fall on your head. You could accidentally teleport into a 30-mile freefall. A pair of sculptures could saw you in half. And the quickest path to the tutorial is through death—through failure.

Then, on the other side of that failure, you must signal to the game that you crave more challenge and more failure. You must wade through the graveyard and leap into the pitch-black pit of certain doom.

This eager embrace of challenge is what sets gamers apart from other professionals in the modern economy. Perhaps better than any other medium, games teach us to run toward the difficulties that scare us most. Miyazaki puts it this way:

> In other media especially, it's difficult to replicate that hardship and accomplishment. . . . In terms of that risk and reward and that sense of accomplishment you feel with the act of play, that's very unique to games and I think it's very powerful.[29]

With *Elden Ring*, he says, "I just want as many players as possible to experience the joy that comes from overcoming hardship."[30]

Miyazaki's description of games as a medium defined by effort and accomplishment rhymes uncannily with Raph Koster's insight in *A Theory of Fun*. "Fun from games arises out of mastery," Koster wrote. "With games, learning is the drug."[31]

It's clear that, like Fumito Ueda before him, Miyazaki sees games as artistic media that don't merely depict the world, but teach us something about it, and how we ought to meet it. In *A Theory of Fun*, Raph Koster zeroes in on why these game skills translate so well to reality:

> The holy grail of game system design is to make a game where the challenges are never ending, the skills required are varied, and the difficulty curve is perfect and adjusts itself to exactly our skill level. Someone did this already, though, and it's not always fun. It's called "life." Maybe you've played it.[32]

7.9 From Games to Life

Stacey Haffner says that about three years into her time at Unity, something shifted:

> It just started to get boring because it was everything I knew. I understood the business. I could have somebody show me customer insights and not give me any data about the customer, and I could tell you exactly the demographic that they were talking about just by what the customer said. And that was so boring to me. Which is why I wanted to move into AI [artificial intelligence].
>
> Even now, nobody knows anything about AI. Every week, there's something randomly new about it, and there's some tech that's progressed. And that pace of innovation is perfect for me.

I learned early on in my career—if I'm not learning, I get bored.
There's just a point where I max out and I'm just doing the same thing
I've done over and over. That's when I just tend to switch jobs and go
find something else.

Stacey isn't kidding here. Eight days after I wrote this chapter, she
announced that she was leaving Unity for her next big level-up.

For gamers, learning is the drug.

Since the birth of difficulty curves, gamers have studied the
power of continuous leveling up, and the mindsets required to thrive
through it all. Gamers have learned to fail forward, practice hard, and
maintain resilience. And they've seen the rewards on the other side of
trials and errors. They've learned that when you see a giant, menacing hole in the ground, the best thing you can do is leap. That's the
path to growth.

Here in Part II of this book, we're going to take a closer look at
the career benefits born of gamers' penchants for seeking out challenges, running toward failure, and learning by doing. Until now,
we've been focused on Phase 1. We've investigated change happening
in the world and in ourselves. We've expanded our opportunity horizons. And we've chosen professional paths to pursue with the help of
our communities.

Now that we've chosen a professional path, we need to level up. We
need to learn the skills necessary to score a job and thrive in it. These
efforts will begin in Chapter 8, where we'll lay the groundwork necessary to master Phase 2 of the loop. We'll identify which skills we need to
learn, choose platforms for learning them, and fine-tune our mindset
for success.

Then, in Chapter 9, we'll take a look at the specific tactics that gamers use to level up. And in Chapter 10, we'll broaden our training beyond
technical skills, developing the transferable, "durable" skills that contemporary careers require.

Finally, in Chapter 11, we'll return to the Community Loop, exploring how coaches can support us in our level-up journeys.

It's a steep road ahead, and to old-timers, it would be daunting. In
the modern economy, you don't level up just once. You do it again and
again, every time you circle the loop. But to gamers, this is old hat. We've
done this our whole lives—since the age of *Space Invaders*—and we've

done it well. Gamers appreciate that leveling up is the heart of the fun, and that the learning never ends.

Notes

1. Singletary, Charles. "New HTC Vive Releases for the Week of 11/20/16." UploadVR, November 25, 2016. https://www.uploadvr.com/htc-vive-new-releases-112016/?ref=uploadvr.com.
2. Singletary, Charles. "VR Basketball Sim Nothin' but Net Adds Online Multiplayer and New Mode." UploadVR, March 21, 2017, https://www.uploadvr.com/vr-basketball-sim-nothin-but-net-adds-online-multiplayer-new-mode/.
3. Freeman, Will. "Space Invaders at 40: 'I Tried Soldiers, but Shooting People Was Frowned Upon'." *The Guardian,* June 4, 2018. https://www.theguardian.com/games/2018/jun/04/space-invaders-at-40-tomohiro-nishikado-interview.
4. "Space Invaders." GiantBomb.Com. Accessed September 17, 2024. https://www.giantbomb.com/space-invaders/3030-5099/.
5. Kent, Steven L. *The Ultimate History of Video Games: From Pong to Pokemon—the Story Behind the Craze That Touched Our Lives and Changed the World.* (Three Rivers Press, 2001), 130.
6. Gallagher, Jason M. "How Space Invaders Became a Gaming Phenomenon." Den of Geek, August 12, 2018. https://www.denofgeek.com/games/how-space-invaders-became-a-gaming-phenomenon/.
7. Olivetti, Justin. "The Game Archaeologist: The Legacy of Ultima Online." Massively Overpowered, September 11, 2022. https://massivelyop.com/2022/09/11/the-game-archaeologist-the-legacy-of-ultima-online/.
8. Koster, Raph. "Ultima Online's Influence." Raph Koster's website, September 28, 2017. https://www.raphkoster.com/2017/09/28/ultima-onlines-influence/.
9. Koster, "Ultima Online's Influence."
10. Koster, Raph. *A Theory of Fun for Game Design* (O'Reilly Media, 2013), 40.
11. Koster, *A Theory of Fun for Game Design*, 98.
12. Parkin, Simon. "Fumito Ueda's Slow Route to Perfection." *The New Yorker,* December 4, 2016. https://www.newyorker.com/tech/annals-of-technology/fumito-uedas-slow-route-to-perfection.
13. Parkin, Simon. "Fumito Ueda: Colossus in the Shadow." Medium, December 13, 2016. https://medium.com/@SimonParkin/fumito-ueda-colossus-in-the-shadow-80e200a727dd#.b9flhk420.
14. Parkin, "Fumito Ueda's Slow Route to Perfection."

15. "ICO – 2002 Developer Interview," Shmuplations. Accessed September 17, 2024. https://shmuplations.com/ico/#:~:text=I%20think%20partly%20it%20was,ve%20told%20me%20that%20before.

16. Parkin, Simon. "Hidetaka Miyazaki Sees Death as a Feature, Not a Bug," *The New Yorker*, February 25, 2022, https://www.newyorker.com/culture/persons-of-interest/hidetaka-miyazaki-sees-death-as-a-feature-not-a-bug.

17. Nightingale, Ed. "Elden Ring Creator Hidetaka Miyazaki on Originating the Soulslike Genre." *Eurogamer*, February 21, 2024. https://www.eurogamer.net/elden-ring-creator-hidetaka-miyazaki-on-originating-the-soulslike-genre.

18. Reed, Kristan. "Demon's Souls Retrospective." Eurogamer, March 23, 2014. https://www.eurogamer.net/demons-souls-retrospective.

19. Edge Staff. "Interview: Demon's Souls." *Edge*, August 13, 2010. https://web.archive.org/web/20130404134819/http:/www.edge-online.com/features/interview-demons-souls/.

20. Reilly, Jim. "Sony Talks the Last Guardian, Demon's Souls, and the Vita Launch." *Game Informer*, February 10, 2012. https://web.archive.org/web/20230211194159/https://www.gameinformer.com/b/news/archive/2012/02/10/shuhei-yoshida-interview.aspx?PostPageIndex=2.

21. North, Dale. "Non-Review: Why I Couldn't Finish Demon's Souls." Destructoid, October 5, 2009. https://www.destructoid.com/non-review-why-i-couldnt-finish-demons-souls/; Kollar, Phil. "Demon's Souls Review: From Software Gives RPG Players Tough Love." *Game Informer*, October 20, 2009. https://web.archive.org/web/20230322163605/https://www.gameinformer.com/games/demons_souls/b/ps3/archive/2009/10/20/review.aspx.

22. North, "Non-Review: Why I Couldn't Finish Demon's Souls."

23. Bishop, Sam. "Demon's Souls Review." IGN, October 8, 2009. https://www.ign.com/articles/2009/10/08/demons-souls-review.

24. Remo, Chris. "Sony Regrets Not Publishing Demon's Souls in North America." Game Developer, March 15, 2010. https://www.gamedeveloper.com/game-platforms/sony-regrets-not-publishing-demon-s-souls-in-north-america.

25. Goldman, Tom. "Demon's Souls' 'Amazing Success' in UK Gives Sequel Hope." *The Escapist*, August 4, 2010. https://www.escapistmagazine.com/demons-souls-amazing-success-in-uk-gives-sequel-hope/.

26. Goldman, Tom. "Demon's Souls Price Slashed by Gigantic Halberd," *The Escapist*, September 15, 2010, https://www.escapistmagazine.com/demons-souls-price-slashed-by-gigantic-halberd/.

27. RedHuntingHat. "A Look Into the Sales Figures of the Souls Series." Reddit, 2014. https://www.reddit.com/r/bloodbornethegame/comments/2x8zrc/a_look_into_the_sales_figures_of_the_souls_series/.

28. Bailey, Kat. "Bluepoint's Demon's Souls Remake Has Sold More Than 1 Million Copies." IGN, September 30, 2021. https://www.ign.com/articles/bluepoint-games-demons-souls-remake-sales.

29. Nightingale, "Elden Ring Creator Hidetaka Miyazaki on Originating the Soulslike Genre."

30. Parkin, "Hidetaka Miyazaki Sees Death as a Feature, Not a Bug."

31. Koster, *A Theory of Fun for Game Design*, 40.

32. Koster, *A Theory of Fun for Game Design*, 130.

8

Fundamentals, Platforms, and Mindsets

8.1 Lock and Load

We're rebels in a galactic conflict, and we need your help.

Titanfall 2 casts you as a pilot for our rebel army. And as a pilot, you've got a lot to learn. Hand-to-hand combat? You'll need that. Close-quarters firefights? You should be ready for those too. Also long-range sniping. Also short-range explosives. In total, *Titanfall 2* offers more than 30 firearms for you to master.

And none of that yet touches on the core skills that set *Titanfall 2* pilots apart from other war-game heroes. These pilots are called as such because they're uniquely equipped to pilot "Titans"—giant, bipedal fighting machines, which come with a whole host of additional skills to learn.

Oh, and when you aren't piloting a Titan, you're expected to master jetpacks for fast-moving, gravity-defying battlefield parkour. Got it? Great! Let us know when you're ready to start!

8.2 Suit Up

Back in Phase 1 of the Core Career Loop, we chose a profession to pursue. Now that we've got a new professional path in our sights, we don't just head right toward it—nor do we delay, spending the next decade chasing mastery from afar.

In Phase 2 of the loop, we level up, developing the fundamental skills necessary to thrive in our new profession. And we're strategic about that process, maximizing relevant skill growth while managing our limited time and resources practically.

In the next few chapters, we're going to take a close look at that level-up process and the tactics that gamers use to make the most of it.

But before we start leveling up in earnest, there's some initial recon and prep that we need to do. And that's what this chapter will cover:

- Identify which fundamental skills we need most
- Determine our platforms for study
- Adopt the mindset necessary for leveling up

By the end of this chapter, we'll be ready to launch our training montage in earnest.

8.3 Preparing for Launch

A moment ago, when I listed all the stuff you'll have to do as a rebel pilot, I only scratched the surface of skill challenge in *Titanfall 2*. The true challenge cuts deeper. One of *Titanfall's* designers, David Shaver, puts it this way:

> When you play a game, a classic shooter like Doom . . . the top third and the bottom third of the screen aren't really that dangerous. But in Titanfall the top two thirds of the screen could be a threat from any direction, pilots are flying through the air as they wall run above you and shoot from above.[1]

This expanded battlefield creates an entirely new play paradigm. That, plus the aforementioned range of tools to master, makes for an extraordinary skill challenge. Of course, the designers know that it would be crazy to throw you into all that unprepared. And they also know that nobody wants to play a multi-hour tutorial. So *Titanfall 2* isolates individual skills for you to learn, one at a time, stacking skill on top of skill on top of skill.

Your adventure begins with a tutorial, which teaches you basic combat maneuvers. Then you continue learning new skills throughout the main campaign, as you play through it. You don't actually learn to pilot the titular Titan until well after the tutorial. And some of the most important parkour abilities aren't clarified until much later, once you're deep into the game.

In well-designed games like this, skill building isn't haphazard. It's strategic and intentional. Behind the scenes, *Titanfall 2*'s designers have mapped out all of the skills that you'll need to succeed as a pilot. They've identified which of those skills are most important and which of those skills build on other skills. Then they've frontloaded the most essential, most fundamental skills at the top of the game.

We'll want to take a similar approach as we level up in Phase 2. We're going to identify the skills needed to thrive in our new, chosen profession. And we're going to remember that we can always expand and deepen our skills later. Here in Phase 2, we're going to figure out which skills are most essential—most fundamental—and we'll focus on those.

8.4   The Fundamentals

The research we do to identify fundamental skills will look a lot like the research we've done elsewhere: searching the web, stalking forums, posting questions, reading blogs, talking to career assistance counselors, joining workforce development organizations. But, as is so often the case, the best method of research will be to find people who do the thing and then ask them about it.

Investigating skill gaps through these kinds of conversations offers two big benefits. First, it gets you grade-A intel: you know exactly who's advising you and what kind of experience they're drawing on. Second, seeking out experts for these conversations expands your career-looping community.

Later, we'll dive back into the Community Loop and get specific about which people to talk to and where to find them. For now, I just want to offer this rule of thumb: we're looking for folks who are knowledgeable about their field, and who are one or two steps ahead of us in their own professional journeys.

Once we've found the right people to talk to, we want to ask them about two big categories of fundamental skills in their profession: technical skills and durable skills. Technical skills are the sorts of skills we think of most often when entering a new field. New coding languages. New software. New tools. If we're moving into a new profession, there's a good chance that it has some of its own, specialized, arcane secrets, and we'll need to learn those secrets to excel.

By contrast, durable skills get their name from the fact that they can weather anything: different technological eras, different professions, different jobs, different companies, different teams. These aren't the specialized skills of any one guild—they're the fundamental abilities that apply in all contexts. Some durable skills include the following:

- **Adaptability:** a capacity to thrive in conditions of frequent change
- **Resilience:** the capacity to maintain effort and determination in the face of difficulty
- **Emotional intelligence:** the ability to understand and navigate the emotional dimensions of life—both with respect to one's own emotions and the emotions of others

These abilities often get mislabeled as *soft skills*, suggesting that they possess less power or import than technical skills. But the reality is that durable skills take us farther, faster, for longer.

Later, we'll talk lots more about the importance of durable skills—both for job hunting and for long-term success. For now, suffice to say that we need to identify both fundamental technical skills and fundamental durable skills in order to level up well. And we should anticipate that many of the same tactics will work to learn both.

We can use many of the same platforms, too.

8.5 Pick Your Platform

Once we've identified our chosen profession's fundamental skills, we have to identify which learning platform will serve us best. There are so many to choose from: certificates, bootcamps, community college, traditional degrees, professional coaches, web-based learning platforms. On and on the list goes.

When choosing among them, I find it helpful to consider return on investment (ROI). ROI is a business calculation that measures how much money you get back (return) versus how much money you put in (investment). If you invest $10 and get back $15, that's an ROI of +50%.

Learning is more abstract than money, so we won't be doing literal math here. But the general concept of ROI will help us all the same. And we'll expand it to encompass two different kinds of ROI—what I call *external* and *internal* ROI.

For both kinds, the investment is the same: we're spending our time, money, and energy on training. What sets the two kinds of ROI apart is that they measure two different kinds of *returns*. External ROI yields *social* currency (reputation), and internal ROI yields *growth* currency (skill).

If we earn a PhD from MIT—even if we cheat on every assignment and never learn a thing—we'll walk away with a ton of social currency. Our reputation will go up among hiring managers, recruiters, movers, and shakers. These people will assume that we're brilliant. Sometimes, this sort of social currency alone can buy us better connections, better jobs, better titles, even better salaries.

The other type of currency is what I call *growth* currency. This is the actual amount of skill or knowledge we gained from our training. If we cheated on every assignment at MIT, we probably earned very little growth currency. People might think our degree sounds great, but we didn't learn anything while getting it. In this scenario we might be able to get a super-flashy job with a great salary, but then struggle to keep it because we have no core skills.

Instead of going to MIT, we could get tutoring from our brilliant, high school drop-out next-door-neighbor. And we could learn a ton. In that scenario, we'd walk away with very little social currency (+0 reputation) but lots of added growth currency (+10 skill).

Now, we're still only comparing these options from the perspective of returns. We also need to consider initial investment. ROI doesn't just measure how much currency you *get*. It measures the ratio of how much you get versus how much you *spend*.

In business, for example, it sounds great for the sales department to bring in $1 billion. But if we earned those sales via a $10 billion marketing campaign, then we've gotten terrible ROI: −90%. We've lost more currency than we've gained.

We should do this kind of calculus for every platform we consider: certificate programs, bootcamps, masterclasses. How much time, money, and energy are they asking us to invest? How much social currency are they returning? How much growth currency are they returning? And, in the final calculus, are they a good deal?

When evaluating possible learning platforms, many of us will consider college and graduate degrees. On their surface, these seem like great investments. A college degree is one of the first indicators of credibility that employers look for. And there are many for whom the university learning environment will foster excellence, so these degrees can yield tons of social currency and growth currency.

The trouble is that not every field requires a college degree, not everyone thrives in academic settings, and we have to invest quite a lot before we see any of that return. College and grad degrees can be extraordinarily expensive, and they also take us out of the job market for multiple years. For some people, those will be good trade-offs. For others, it'll feel like giving away $10 billion and getting back $1 billion.

Think about Stacey Haffner, the game developer who went head-to-head with the NBA before taking over Unity's AI work. She enrolled in degree programs a few times, but each time, opportunities out in the world pulled her away. "I almost finished my associates degree," she says, "and then I got offered a full-time employee role at Microsoft. So I stopped going to school, and I never finished it."

Stacey says that she was only pursuing her associates degree for the external ROI—for the line on her résumé. And, in her final calculus, it wasn't worth turning down full-time Microsoft employment for a little extra social currency.

This isn't to say that degree programs are always a bad choice. For many, they will be the unequivocal right choice. The important thing is to enter eyes open. And that's true for any other level-up platform—certificate programs, bootcamps, you name it.

This eyes-open approach requires us to make an accurate estimate of our potential return. We need to clearly define what we're looking to get from this learning platform and whether the platform is equipped to deliver.

This is another key place where we often misstep in college and university decisions. Many of us enroll in these programs because *that's what's done*—not because these programs are the right choice for *us*. And when we do pursue schooling with purpose, these purposes often aren't aligned to what degree programs actually have to offer.

To sum all this up, I find that it can be helpful to ask these questions when selecting a learning platform:

- Do I have the money to pay for this platform?
- Do I have the time/energy to give to this platform?
- Do I have a clear purpose driving me to this platform?
- Is my purpose well aligned with what this platform has to offer?

Once we've found the platform that best suits us—accounting for both internal and external ROI—there's just one thing left to do before we start leveling up in earnest: we have to adopt the right mindset.

8.6   Mind Games

The biggest setback to successfully leveling up isn't getting the wrong teacher or the wrong textbook—although those things aren't great. The biggest setback is entering Phase 2 with the wrong mindset.

Great achievers throughout history have reinforced this mindset-first mentality through their own anecdotal insights. Take Einstein for example. You won't find any quotes from him telling you which college you should go to, but you will find plenty of quotes about mindset.

One of my favorite Einstein-isms goes like this: "I have no special talent. I am only passionately curious." Curiosity is where I'd like to start. Because, in the best level-up journeys, curiosity is what gets us started.

8.7   Starting with Curiosity

About 1973, at about the same time that *Dungeons & Dragons* first hit tabletops and about 30 years before Raph Koster published his *A Theory of Fun*, Stanford researchers were getting curious about why kids enjoy some school activities and dread others. So they launched a study.

First, they observed children in classrooms during free-play time, noting how much time these kids spent drawing. Then, a few weeks later, they handpicked the most dedicated of these little illustrators, split the kids into three groups, and observed them again. This time, one group was promised a reward if they spent time drawing.

The two groups that weren't promised rewards drew about as much as they had before. Which is to say *a lot*. They had a great time. The only group that changed was the group that had been promised a reward. They drew way, way less—which the researchers considered a red flag: these kids weren't enjoying drawing anymore.[2] Somehow, the reward had diminished the fun.

This study launched a whole new field of research—research that investigates how and why rewards regularly undermine joy. At the center of that research is a battle between what psychologists call *extrinsic* and *intrinsic* motivation. Extrinsic motivators are external rewards: money, trophies, job titles, good grades, a smile from your parent. These are the rewards that we think people want. And indeed, they'll motivate folks to do undesirable tasks.

But research shows, again and again, that extrinsic motivation is short-lived and unsustainable. Plus, whatever natural interest a person had will be mysteriously quashed by these extrinsic motivators. When motivated by external factors, drawing just won't be fun anymore.

By contrast, intrinsic motivators come from within. A sense of mission. Of personal satisfaction. A desire to learn. And, as Einstein says, *curiosity*. When motivated by intrinsic forces like curiosity, people experience sustained engagement, enhanced creativity, and a stronger sense of pleasure and satisfaction.[3]

During our career-looping journeys, it's natural for income to become a key motivator. But we shouldn't just follow the money. The research is quite adamant: we'll achieve more and have a better time doing it if we follow our curiosity.

8.8   Curiosity Killed the Bug

Curiosity isn't just key to leveling up because of the way it motivates us. It also naturally generates the strongest process I know for designing our own skill-building tutorials. That process is all about asking questions and pursuing answers. And it's entirely driven by our own internal impulses to investigate.

You'll recall that it's precisely this sort of self-generated curiosity that propelled Stacey Haffner and her husband Ben into the virtual reality (VR) space, where they ultimately beat the NBA at its own game. They just really wanted to figure out the physics of digital gravity. And the result was a terrific first foray into VR.

In the tech world, many call this the *hacker's mindset*.

Ferhan Ozkan is the cofounder of XR Bootcamp, a global training program to level students up in fields surrounding virtual and augmented reality (collectively called *XR*). Alumni of his program have gone on to successful careers at places like Boeing, Microsoft, Meta, and Riot Games.

Ferhan says that the hacker's mindset is what sets these outperforming alumni apart. It's natural that every time new hardware, new software, and new updates drop, they'll be under-documented and unfriendly to developers. Ferhan says that outperformers get curious about these challenges as they arise. They don't wait for help. Instead, Ferhan says that these folks ask, "How can I hack my way through to find a solution?"

Ferhan calls these solutions *hacks* because they often don't play nicely with a product as designed. "Sometimes the solution is a shortcut," Ferhan says, "and sometimes it's just a patch."

But you can't patch together a solution if you're not first deeply interested in the problem. Curiosity opens the door to hacking, and, as we'll see in much more depth soon, hacking opens the door to leveling up.

There's a downside to all this curiosity though: if we're curious enough, we'll try new things. If we try new things, we'll often fail. And if we fail, that failure might hurt. Embracing these failures is the most challenging, most important mindset move we can make in Phase 2. It's also the most important one for our careers as a whole. And, fortunately, it's one that gamers come to naturally. Gamers are masters of just *getting over it*.

8.9   Getting Over It

You are the burly torso of a human man stuck inside a bouncy black cauldron. Your only tool: a sledgehammer. Your goal: to climb this perilous mountain of rock and refuse and then, once you reach the top, fling yourself into outer space.

You've been at this for two or three hours now, and you've managed to climb a long way up the mountain. But just as you reach for the next rung of a precarious ladder, you slip and topple. And topple. And topple. And when you stop toppling, you find that you've landed back at the very beginning of the trail.

You're playing a game of course, but one that doesn't play nicely. It doesn't give you a way to undo mistakes. You can't reload to your last save point. The game's creator made this clear in his voice-over at the very beginning of your journey: "Don't worry," he said. "I'll save your progress. Always. Even your mistakes."

This is *Getting Over It*, a little indie game that's drawn millions of players into its maw, and which, at its peak, attracted about a hundred thousand simultaneous Twitch streams.[4] *Getting Over It* is designed to be difficult—impossibly difficult. It's designed to *provoke* in every sense. To beguile. To enrage. To inspire.

The game's creator, Bennett Foddy, is yet another of the self-taught, just-wing-it game designers we'll meet in this book. Not only was game design not his intended career, it wasn't even the first accidental career he had, or the most successful. Every time Foddy actually tried to control the outcome of his career, he chose academic philosophy. But we already know what happens to people who try to control the outcomes of their careers.

Foddy was in the middle of pursuing his philosophy doctorate when a friend asked him for a favor. The friend needed a bassist for his synth-pop band. Could Foddy help out?

Sure.

You know that feeling when you agree to drive your friend to the airport, and then, halfway through the drive, they ask you to make a pitstop? Something kind of like that happened next. Foddy's band blew up, and they were invited to tour with the hit-making, best-selling, Grammy-nominated, indie rock breakout Franz Ferdinand.[5]

To this day, Foddy expresses no doubt about the path he chose. He promptly retired from the band and recommitted himself to philosophy—at Melbourne, at Princeton, and at Oxford.

But Foddy is a compulsive procrastinator. So instead of doing the work that he'd chosen over rock-n-roll stardom, he got to fiddling around on his computer. His curiosity led him to a game development tutorial. And that led him to his next accidental smash-hit career—one he wouldn't be able to resist. Today, Foddy teaches game design at

New York University while releasing new games every few years. *Getting Over It* has been one of his greatest hits.[6]

Many see *Getting Over It* as a landmark entry in the "rage game" genre, a niche corner of the world where games are designed to frustrate rather than delight. Usually the intent of these games isn't to entertain players; it's to entertain their audiences. Streamers capture themselves exploding or melting down, and audiences have a great time watching them do it.

But *Getting Over It* is a different kind of rage game, designed to deliver insight, not just to troll—designed to affect the player, not just their audience. And we know this for a fact because, in a mellow voice-over accompanied by jazz piano, the game's creator tells us so. He and his piano drop in periodically throughout the game to wax poetic about this game and other games and life itself. "Your failure here is a metaphor," Foddy's voice says when you fall over and lose a bunch of progress. "To learn for what, please resume climbing."

It doesn't take much work to decipher how this metaphor works. Foddy spills the beans right at the beginning of the game, in his opening monologue:

> There's no feeling more intense than starting over. If you deleted your homework the day before it was due, as I have, or if you left your wallet at home and you have to go back after spending an hour in the commute. If you won some money at the casino, and then put all your winnings on red, but it came up black. If you got your best shirt dry-cleaned before a wedding, but then immediately dropped food on it. If you won an argument with a friend and then later discovered that they just returned to their original view. Starting over is harder than starting up.

Getting Over It is a game about failure and resilience. It's a game that celebrates players' willingness to fail and get back up and fail again. This is a skill that gamers have been cultivating since *Space Invaders*, and it's one that will serve us well here in Phase 2 of the loop.

"There's no way left to go but up," Foddy says.

8.10   One Way Up

Most of us default to seeing failure as a bad thing. It's an attitude that usually dates back to childhood—the lessons we learned from school, from parents, from peers, from pop culture.

And we shouldn't blame childhood alone. Throughout our careers, we will inevitably encounter colleagues, bosses, and clients who reinforce this fear of failure, sometimes even weaponizing it. Think of the manager who gets results by threatening to fire underperformers. (Yikes.)

In Chapter 2 we met Joy Horvath, a VR game developer and program manager here at Unity. Joy was the creator who intended to work in fashion before her friends pulled her into gaming. Now she and our Unity team are working with games leadership nationwide to change hiring practices and make the industry more accessible.

Joy points out that one of the key reasons why all of us—aspiring game developers, aspiring fashion designers, aspiring cauldron-bound mountaineers—fear failure is because failure feels like the end: "We're taught as children that, if you fail, it's game over, and you stop pursuing something. It's the endpoint. You failed, and that's it. You're done." She notes that it's also common for us to identify with failure at a personal level: "If I fail, then I *am* a failure."

Our curiosity might inspire fantasies about trying new things, but these attitudes about failure hold us back from following through. And if we do brave the danger—if we do try new things—a single failure can stop us in our tracks.

Fortunately, gamers have spent their whole lives failing forward—which is to say, failing, trying again, and failing again—learning, earning, and advancing with each failure. Gamers know that, without failure, there's no fun, and there's no achievement. "Game over" is never really a game over. You just respawn and try again.

This failure-friendly attitude bleeds into the larger, real lives of gamers. "If I pick something up, and I'm immediately an expert on it," Stacey Haffner says, "I'll put it down and move on to something else. Cause that's boring. It's only fun if I can fail."

Meanwhile, it's not just game players who embrace failure. Game *creators* do, too. "This is key in game design," Joy says. "I cannot actually imagine becoming successful without failing first."

Eric Zimmerman is the celebrated CEO of Gamelab and a giant of game design academia. Here's how he explains the role of failure for creators:

> You produce a playable prototype of a game as quickly as possible, then playtest the prototype, and you decide how to evolve the game based on the experience of the playtest. . . .

No game designer I know has ever released a game without play-testing it. . . .

The behavior of complex, interactive systems—like games—is incredibly difficult to predict. You generally cannot know exactly what players are going to do once they start playing your game. The only way to find out is to actually build some primitive version of your game, have people play it, and see what happens. Each time you play-test, you find out what does and doesn't work, make some adjustments, and then play again. That's why it is called the iterative process—you create successive versions, or *iterations*, of your game as you go. . . .

One of the hardest things about iteration is seeing your ideas fail. But it's really important to experience failure—most ideas will not work the way you expected them to play out. That's why it is important to iterate like mad, trying out ideas, seeing what works and doesn't work, evolving your design forward as you learn from your mistakes. Failure is like spicy food—it hurts at first . . . but then you acquire a taste for it—and soon you just can't get enough. You never completely lose the hurt, but you also learn to enjoy the pain.[7]

Joy explains that game developers enjoy this pain because it signals the start of something new. Each failure demands inquiry. That inquiry yields insights. And those insights lead to new creations.

Thomas Edison wasn't a game designer, but he is another one of those great achievers with a classic line about mindset. "I haven't failed," he supposedly said, "I've just found a thousand ways *not* to make a light-bulb." Each misfire gave him data, and that data eventually helped him light up the world.

This was a recurring theme with many game creators I interviewed for this book. Folks like James Stone, Stacey Haffner, and Joy. Not only did the creation processes for each individual game require failure, but, looking back, many of these creators see their early games as failed experiments from tip to toe. James called one of his earliest games "utterly terrible." Stacey called one of hers "crap."

Yet, funnily enough, it's these "failed" games that they talked about most in our interviews. And, looking back at our interviews, it's clear why: because I was asking them about the moments when they learned life-changing lessons. For all of them, those moments were connected to glorious failures.

For great achievers in games and in life, failure isn't something to fear. Failure isn't an endpoint, and it isn't a reflection of who they are.

Failure is inevitable.
Failure is data.
Failure is the beginning.

Notes

1. Purslow, Matt. "How Titanfall 2 Made Movement the Star of the Show— Art of the Level." IGN, September 30, 2022. https://www.ign.com/articles/ how-titanfall-2-made-movement-the-star-of-the-show-art-of-the-level.
2. Lepper, M. R., D. Greene, and R. E. Nisbett. "Undermining Children's Intrinsic Interest with Extrinsic Reward: A Test of the 'Overjustification' Hypothesis." *Journal of Personality and Social Psychology* 28, no. 1: 129–37. https://psycnet.apa.org/record/1974-10497-001.
3. Morris, Laurel S., Mora M. Grehl, Sarah B. Rutter, Marishka Mehta, and Margaret L. Westwater. "On What Motivates Us: A Detailed Review of Intrinsic V. Extrinsic Motivation." *Psychology of Medicine* 52, no. 10 (2022): 1801–16. https://www.ncbi.nlm.nih.gov/pmc/articles/PMC9340849/.
4. "Getting Over It with Bennett Foddy." SteamDB, August 28, 2024. https:// steamdb.info/app/240720/charts/.
5. Dornbush, Jonathon. "The Appropriately Strange Journey of QWOP's Creator From Philosopher to Game Professor." Polygon, October 7, 2013. https://www.polygon.com/2013/10/7/4786622/the-appropriately-strange-journey-of-qwops-creator-from-philosopher.
6. Purdom, Clayton. "QWOP Turned Failure into Comedy and Found Viral Immortality." AV Club, May 30, 2018. https://www.avclub.com/qwop-turned-failure-into-comedy-and-found-viral-immorta-1826394272.
7. Zimmerman, Eric. "How I Teach Game Design: Lesson 1: The Game Design Process." Being Playful, October 19, 2013. https://ericzimmerman.word press.com/2013/10/19/how-i-teach-game-design-lesson-1-the-game-design-process/.

9

Build Your Own Tutorial

9.1 Do-It-Yourself Tutorials

So far in Part II, we've talked quite a bit about tutorials and the tactics that designers use to incrementally teach us core game skills. We discussed *Titanfall 2*, for example, and the way it breaks complex skill sets down into smaller pieces, introducing one skill at a time.

Tutorials like these are great when they're available. But in Phase 2 of the loop, if we want to learn new skills through independent study, much of the tutorial design work will fall on us. Fortunately, having established the right mindset, this design work will be easy.

In Chapter 8 I said that curiosity doesn't just motivate us. It also naturally generates the process by which we design our own tutorials. And, in many ways, we've already seen this play out. We've seen how *Ico* creator Fumito Ueda followed his curiosity to teach himself computer graphics. We've seen how Stacey and Ben Haffner followed their curiosity to teach themselves virtual reality development. And we've seen how Ferhan Ozkan and virtual and augmented reality creators of all stripes follow their curiosity to invent hacks for technological bugs.

In this chapter, we're going to take a closer look at that process, exploring how we can lean into our own natural inquisitiveness to develop home-brewed professional development tutorials.

At the heart of this chapter will be a principle that I call the *law of little quests*. The law is simple. It says that the best way to learn is by breaking up study into small projects. And anytime we get stuck on a project, the best thing we can do is break that project into even smaller pieces.

This can mean intentionally pursuing small initiatives. Instead of making a 24-hour open-world role-playing game, we make a single-level run-and-gun game. Instead of building a fully functional e-commerce site, we build a simple landing page. Instead of creating a full-scale speculative ad campaign for our portfolio, we design a single product label.

But we can also go big if we must. Rather than pursue small initiatives, we can pursue large ones, breaking them up into smaller component pieces, which we tackle either one at a time or concurrently. So if we take on a big project like building a full-scale game, we can break that project into many component pieces. Narrative design. Mechanical design. Level design. Character design. Animation. Underscoring. Marketing. Sales. And we can break any one of those pieces into many more component pieces.

Narrative design includes plotting and world building and script writing. Character design includes concept drawing, modeling, and texturing. Marketing includes crafting the game's visual identity, establishing its web presence, and building its community. Then we could break each of those tasks down even further.

Each of these mini-tasks could be tackled one at a time. Or we could alternate between them—for instance, spending an hour on character costuming, then an hour on logo design.

Joy Horvath is the mastermind behind many of the ideas in this chapter. She sums up the law of little quests like this:

> The smaller your question, the more binary the answer, and the faster you can get to success.
>
> Like, "What does the wiring in my house do?" That's not a single answer. Whereas "What does this light switch do?" Hopefully that has a single answer.
>
> If you look into each switch and each wire individually, you get easy answers. Ask enough questions, and eventually you understand the wiring in your house.

9.2   Wired for Little Quests

Joy's just previewed one of the benefits to pursuing little quests. But there are many benefits.

9.2.1   Neutralizing Failure

It's one thing to decide, intellectually, that we're going to embrace failure. It's quite another to *actually* embrace it at an emotional level. We have to unlearn a lifetime of fear and teach ourselves a new desire. That doesn't happen overnight.

So when we're first learning to embrace failure, it can be helpful to do so gradually. We don't want to fail at a bunch of things at once, and we don't want any huge, ego-crushing failures either. We want to fail in small, manageable doses. And that's where little quests come in.

If the quest we've given ourselves is to resize our logo for our mobile website. I mean, how many times can we fail at that before we get it right? Will a few misfires seriously affect our will to go on? Will those failures seriously dent our ego?

The littler the quest, the less likely we are to fail. And the less likely we are to take failure personally.

We'll especially appreciate this fail-safe approach early on in the level-up process, when we're likely to experience the most intimidation and self-doubt. Early little-quest successes will bolster our confidence that the level-up climb is surmountable. And early triumphs over failure will inoculate us, helping us internalize the central principle that failure isn't scary enough to deserve our fear—that it's actually quite helpful.

9.2.2   Boosting Fun

Games generate constant stimulation. At every moment of play, a well-designed game gives us an optimized challenge. Then it delivers immediate feedback on our performance, validating every success.

Outside of games, life doesn't often deliver optimized challenges or instant feedback. We have to create those things for ourselves. And we can do that with the law of little quests. Pursuing little quests naturally optimizes our challenges: we break down tasks into smaller and smaller pieces until they reach a size that we can handle. And we're able to get quick feedback: we don't have to wait weeks or months or years to find out whether we've succeeded. If our tasks are little enough, we can evaluate the results within minutes, hours, or days.

As we know from *A Theory of Fun*, "Fun from games arises out of mastery. It arises out of comprehension. It is the act of solving puzzles that makes games fun."[1] Chasing curiosity, tackling optimized challenges, and experiencing well-earned triumph—these experiences make Phase 2 of the loop more than just a necessary step. They make it a joy.

9.2.3 Ending Boredom

A Theory of Fun again:

> Boredom is the opposite of learning. When a game stops teaching us, we feel bored. Boredom is the brain casting about for new information. It is the feeling you get when there are no new visible patterns to absorb.[2]

When we get bored during level-up projects, it's because the task we're chipping away at has become too familiar. We're too deeply entrenched in its patterns. The best way to shake off the boredom is to chase a novel problem—a new learning experience.

Later, when we come back to the task that bored us, we often feel refreshed and reengaged. That's because distance has helped us step back and see new patterns. We return ready for new discoveries and new learning. (A successful vacation from work operates the same way.)

What's great about the law of little quests is that *there are so many little quests*. If we're too close to one—too entrenched in its patterns—we can always step away and work on some other quest. And we can keep working on other little quests for as long as it takes to get the distance we need, returning to that original task only once we're ready to see new patterns and rediscover the fun.

With the law of little quests, we can always keep boredom at bay.

9.2.4 Solving Complex Problems

Whether we have a big project or a big question, tackling it all at once can feel daunting. Even impossible. There's so much we don't know!

Little quests give us smaller, more manageable questions to answer and tasks to perform. We've already seen how this works—how we can segment our way down from "I'm building a full-length video game" to "I'm resizing my game's logo for the mobile website." From "What does the wiring in my house do?" to "What does this light switch do?"

And we can also think about this benefit in reverse. Rather than conceptualizing the law of little quests as a system for breaking down complex problems into simple ones, we can conceptualize it as a method for growing simple discoveries into complex ones.

"It's much easier to answer five binary yes-or-no questions," Joy Horvath says, "than it is to answer one philosophical question about the universe." But if we answer enough yes-or-no questions, we can eventually form a fairly complex philosophy of the universe.

As we complete little quests or answer little questions, we'll discover that each discovery yields more quests. Every answer creates more questions. We develop advanced skills and expansive knowledge by tackling each of these new little quests as they arise. Build a bunch of little answers on top of each other, and you get expertise.

Joy puts it like this:

> The more you know, the more you want to ask. You learn how to make your character jump, and it makes you wonder—how does that character double-jump? Or how does the character hover? And then you figure that out, and that prompts more questions.
>
> It's kind of like Lego bricks, right? If you want to build a Lego castle, you have to stack a series of bricks. Each brick on its own seems like it's just one brick. But if you start stacking those up, it starts becoming really significant. So honor the brick.

9.3 Feedback

When we talked about boosting fun a moment ago, I touched on the importance of feedback. I said that feedback was a key ingredient in making both games and little quests fun. Here's what I meant.

In design disciplines, feedback tells users how they're affecting the system. When you push an elevator button, the button lights up to let you know that a lift is coming. That's feedback. When you fire off a text message, your phone goes "Whoosh!" to let you know that the message sent. That's feedback.

One of the things that makes gaming so fun is the constant, real-time supply of feedback. You swing your sword at the dragon, and you see its health bar go down. You fail to dodge its fire breath, and *your* health bar goes down.

This instant feedback makes it immediately apparent to us whether we're failing or succeeding. Which means that we can immediately assess what our weaknesses are, how we can get better, and whether we are indeed learning. When we eventually succeed at slaying the dragon, the game lets us know immediately, and we feel a sense of triumph.

As we know from *A Theory of Fun*, it's these aha moments of successful learning that make games fun. And we wouldn't be able to get those quick, vivid, gratifying aha moments without clear, instant feedback.

To some degree, the pursuit of little quests yields similar benefits. Because we've given ourselves such straightforward tasks, and because those tasks take such a short time to complete, we'll often find out pretty quickly whether we've succeeded or failed. And when we do succeed, we'll get that sweet hit of learning pleasure. But not every little quest will yield instant, crystal-clear feedback.

We're especially likely to miss out on instant feedback in cases where we don't have the expertise to evaluate success or failure. Or in cases where success is subjective, so our individual assessment doesn't give us enough data. Other times, we might know that we've failed, but struggle to identify where we went wrong.

In all of these cases, we need to look elsewhere for feedback. We need to look to our community. In the games industry, this solicitation of community feedback is called *play-testing*, and everyone does it as often as they possibly can. Solo developers. Top-tier studios. Everyone. In fact, the best-financed studios hire people to do this full time.

Eric Zimmerman, game design academic extraordinaire, told us about play-testing just a short while ago. "No game designer I know has ever released a game without play-testing it," he said. "It is important to iterate like mad, trying out ideas, seeing what works and doesn't work, evolving your design forward as you learn from your mistakes."

In our own level-up journey, whether we're creating a game, or building a website, or compiling an investment portfolio, it's vital that we play-test with our community. As often as possible, we want to put our work in front of other people and get their feedback. And we want to solicit that feedback the same way game designers do, by asking precise questions. Here's more from Eric Zimmerman:

> Preparing . . . for the play-test is very, very important as well. You always want to know . . . what is the question that you're hoping your play-test will answer . . . "Why are we making this prototype? What is the question that we're hoping that this prototype begins to address?"[3]

Most obviously, zeroing in on precise questions will help ensure that your play-testers are giving you helpful feedback, rather than answering questions you don't need answered. Joy also points out that these precise questions help ensure that play-testers actually respond to you:

> People come to me for feedback all the time. And if they're very vague, I don't really know how to approach it. And I'm really busy. So the odds of me just kind of forgetting to deal with that are pretty high.
>
> But if somebody comes up to me and says, "I have problem X. Why? What is going on?" That I actually tend to prioritize, because there's a problem to solve, and I have that capability. I really want to give that feedback because I know this. I can fix it.

In a way, by asking precise questions, we're helping our play-testers implement the law of little quests themselves, breaking down the larger, more intimidating process of "giving feedback" into a few discrete answerable questions.

Who should our play-testers be? Our peers, our mentors, our managers, experts we hunt down on social media sites. In games, pretty much anyone can be a good play-tester, because pretty much everyone can play a game and report back on whether they're having fun. But in professional level-up journeys, we specifically want to solicit feedback from folks who really know their way around our topic, and who are open to offering guidance.

In the world of workforce development, we call these folks *coaches*, and they'll be the heroes of Chapter 11. But before we talk about them, I want to take one little detour. I want to talk about durable skills.

Notes

1. Koster, Raph. *A Theory of Fun for Game Design* (O'Reilly Media, 2013), 40.
2. Koster, *A Theory of Fun for Game Design*, 41.
3. "Eric Zimmerman: Sharpen Your Sword as a Game Designer." Game Thinking, accessed September 17, 2024. https://gamethinking.io/podcast/108-eric-zimmerman/.

10

Mastering Durable Skills

10.1 Speaking of Skills . . .

The lights were hot. Stacey wasn't getting as much air as she needed, and the room had begun to spin. She was delivering a live-streamed talk for a major conference, and she was going to pass out. With the little presence of mind she still had, she called for her colleague to join her on camera.

> I said, "My colleague's got some questions for me," and he comes out, and he's like, "No, I don't," and I'm whispering, "I don't feel good," and he's like, "What?" and I said, "I don't feel good," and he claps his hands, and he looks at the camera and he goes, "That's all we have for today!"

For years, Stacey Haffner feared public speaking. For her, that meant addressing any group larger than four, which accounted for pretty much every meeting she was ever in.

She knew that she couldn't dodge five-person meetings forever, and she also knew that speaking to crowds would open up new opportunities for career growth. So she bit the bullet, got some coaching, and embarked on a journey of exposure therapy.

"I decided that I wanted to get over my fear of public speaking," she says. "So I started putting myself on stage."

In the very first of these experiments, she failed. Hard. She very nearly passed out, and had to call her colleague on stage for an on-tape rescue. But every attempt, failed or successful, gave her more exposure. "And then, eventually, the fear went away," she says. "I could start talking in meetings. I wasn't scared to talk in groups. Now I'm at the point where I really, really enjoy presenting." And she's done so often, at places like the annual Xbox Showcase and GDC, the world's largest games industry summit.

Much of Stacey's level-up journey has involved speaking, speaking, and speaking again—in the car, at home, and on stage. But she's also pursued lots of technical study—both through an employer-provided workshop and through her own independent study of other speakers' techniques. She worked on pacing, on tone, on structure, on sounding natural even when she's prepped. Now strangers stop her at conventions to thank her for speeches that she gave months or years earlier.

Over the years, Stacey's taught herself many technical skills—game development, web development, 3D modeling, and many more—but no single skill level-up has had as profound an impact as this one, which isn't technical at all.

10.2 Leveling Up Durably

Durable skills are capabilities that apply across many fields and contexts. They're durable both in the sense that they transfer with you as you move between domains, and in the sense that they make you more durable—prepared for any career.

When leveling up, it's common to focus on building technical skills, and that is certainly important. But ultimately it's durable skills that elevate outperformers. And more and more, employers are looking for these skills specifically.

Meg Garlinghouse, vice president for social impact at LinkedIn, explains that durable skills—sometimes called *soft skills*—matter more than ever in the new economy: "In this environment, where the world of work is rapidly changing," she says, "employers are turning their focus to soft skills." And the data bears that out.

America Succeeds is a nonprofit that engages business leaders in the work of modernizing education, boosting equity, and increasing opportunity. A few years ago, they were trying to figure out how schools can improve long-term economic outcomes, so they launched a study of skill demand in the workplace.

They looked at 80 million job postings across 22 sectors, and found that 77% of them—about 62 million postings—requested at least one durable skill. Of the most frequently requested skills, 70% were durable, rather than technical, skills. And the top five most-requested durable skills were requested five times more often than the top five technical skills.[1]

All signs suggest that durable skills will only continue gaining momentum. Presenting research on this topic, LinkedIn VP Aneesh Raman says, "People skills are going to come more to the center of individual career growth. And people-to-people collaboration is going to come into the center more for company growth."[2]

Later in this book, we'll talk more about how and why employer attitudes are shifting, but all we need to know for now is that they are. Nine out of ten global executives agree: in the new economy, durable skills matter more than ever before.[3]

The beauty of this is that durable skills travel with us, from job to job, company to company, profession to profession. If we level up durable skills for any one industry, those skills will drive success throughout our careers, no matter where those careers take us. And, contrary to popular impression, durable skills can be learned, taught, and even self-taught.

10.3   Building Durable Skills

Stacey Haffner's already shown us much of what it takes to level up durable skills. When improving her public speaking, Stacey found platforms for learning, then broke her level-up journey into a series of smaller projects. Initially, she challenged herself to sign up for five speaking engagements. She took a workshop on tone. She watched videos about pacing. When necessary, she failed, failed hard, and failed forward.

The importance of failure, the virtues of little quests, even the selection of learning platforms for maximal return on investment (ROI)—in nearly every way, the level-up process for durable skills matches the process for technical skills. If we were to build any durable skill, we'd see the same principles play out.

In fact, let's demonstrate that real quick. This time, instead of looking at public speaking, let's look at one-on-one interpersonal communication.

10.3.1 Failing Forward

Even masters of communication fail at communication sometimes. And if communication is a weak spot for us, then we're bound to fail more. We'll fail in conversations with our coworkers, our managers, our collaborators, and those failures will hurt. But each failure will also give us data to learn from—starting points for becoming better communicators. The important thing is to notice these failures when they happen. Pause. Interrogate yourself about what went wrong. Then take that lesson into our next one-on-one encounter.

10.3.2 Little Quests

We probably won't get far if our plan is just to "become a better communicator." We're going to make the most headway if we break that project down into a series of little quests. Examples could include (1) asking three friends about our communication style, (2) making a list of key communication skills to build, (3) picking one communication skill to focus on per week, (4) finding a communication "coach"—a friend or mentor who can act as an outside eye and a sounding board throughout our journey.

10.3.3 Picking Platforms

We can pick from many platforms when studying communication. Each will have to be evaluated for external and internal ROI. For instance, there are workshops and retreats specifically designed to boost communication skills, many of which focus on things like "compassionate communication" or "leadership communication." These might carry hefty price tags and demand serious investments of time, but also yield lots of social currency and growth currency.

Or we could watch a random smattering of short online videos about communication. This approach requires virtually zero investment and yields no social currency. Whether it yields meaningful growth currency will depend on the individual learner's style and preferences.

There are also books on communication, podcasts, articles, lectures—you name it. We ought to evaluate all of these for ROI and find the ones that match our needs best. In this way, much of the learning process for durable skills will feel familiar. We're picking platforms, giving ourselves little quests, and failing forward.

There's also another key tactic—one which applies for all level-up efforts, but which we haven't addressed yet: turning to our communities for support. But before we get there, I want to highlight a few of the most powerful durable skills and why they matter.

10.4   Emotional Intelligence

Arguably the foundation of all other durable skills, emotional intelligence is the ability to understand and navigate the emotional dimension of life—both with respect to one's own emotions and the emotions of others.

The internal mastery over our own emotional lives will give us a huge head start in the pursuit of so many other durable skills. We've already seen that all skill growth hinges on our embrace of failure—an embrace that requires us to notice the *fear* of failure as it arises, understand where that fear comes from, and operationalize practices to keep it at bay. All of these are exercises in emotional intelligence.

Likewise, many other durable skills—communication, collaboration, leadership, self-starting—require us to identify how our emotions are influencing our behaviors. We must learn how and when to cultivate, interrupt, or redirect those emotions. And that's all to say nothing of the power to be found in comprehending, predicting, and responding well to the emotional lives of others.

As individual contributors, how do we navigate boredom, apathy, frustration, anxiety, or stress? As communicators, how do we correct for our own instincts to hog the spotlight or to hide from it, to push too hard or back down too soon? As collaborators, what do we do when our team members drive us up the wall or when they mistreat us or when they signal that they're in distress? As leaders, how do we manage difficult personalities or direct reports who've hit their own emotional walls? How do we correct our own senses of superiority or inferiority, our tendencies toward micro-management or detachment?

Leveling up in every one of these areas requires robust emotional intelligence. Fortunately, emotional intelligence can indeed be taught and learned. And gamers have an advantage over everyone else.

Many contemporary game designers specifically create work to encourage emotional intelligence around a particular issue. *What Remains of Edith Finch* requires us to confront a variety of perspectives on family, grief, and mortality. *Depression Quest* teaches compassion for those experiencing mental illness. *Florence* captures the sensation of first love, turning its highs and lows into playable mechanics. *That Dragon, Cancer* explores grief and faith and loss and hope.

And it's not just the indies that do this, plenty of blockbusters do it, too. In fact, it's right there, in the name of one of the industry's best-selling genres. RPGs are role-playing games: games in which we inhabit the bodies and minds of others, taking on their perspectives and their problems, their dreams and their circumstances.

Detroit: Become Human takes this about as far as it can go, with expansive opportunities for choice making. We're given extraordinary agency to decide how we'll confront the challenges of marginalization, how we'll respond to calls for civil disobedience, how we'll react to and embody violence, loyalty, and betrayal. *The Last of Us, Mass Effect, Red Dead Redemption 2*—even as these games thrill and captivate and sell sell sell, they challenge us to expand our own emotional lives and our compassion for the lives of others.

10.5 Adaptability

Previously we said that durable skills are durable for two reasons: first because the skills remain valuable across many contexts, and second because the skills make *us* durable—ready for anything. There are two skills that especially support our personal durability. One is *resilience*, which we'll address in just a moment. And the other is *adaptability*.

Adaptability is the capacity to thrive in conditions of frequent change. Life has always been inconstant, so adaptability has always mattered. But, every year, it keeps on mattering more.

We met Mona Mourshed in Part I. She's the founding CEO of Generation, a global nonprofit devoted to expanding opportunities for folks of all ages. Mona often talks about four gaps that separate people from the work that will serve them best. When we met her last, she was talking about the gap between known and unknown professional opportunities, helping us expand our "opportunity horizons."

Another of the gaps that Mona addresses is the gap between technical skills and "behavioral" (aka durable) skills. "Technical skills may be what get you the job," she says. "But your behavioral skills are what keep you in the job." Mona goes on to explain why, as among all the durable skills, adaptability has become particularly important, and why its importance just keeps on growing:

> Your ability to adapt to new technologies, to new processes, to learn new tools, has probably never been at a higher premium than it is today because the pace of change is so high. Every six months, there is something new that you need to master to be able to do your job well. And that pace is picking up rapidly.

We discussed this rapidly increasing pace of change in Part I when we encountered Moore's law and the law of accelerating returns, which, together, described the exponential quickening of technological innovation. With every lap around the innovation circuit, we gain momentum, moving faster and faster. We used to measure the duration between innovative laps in thousands, or even millions, of years. Now you blink and you miss 'em.

This means that our technical skills aren't going to have a whole lot of longevity. Every time new tools show up, they're going to render our existing skills obsolete. Apple's probably going to keep changing its coding language of choice, and I'm sorry to be the bearer of bad news, but humanity will never just pick one damn project management app and stick with it.

All this tech talk is to say nothing of the other winds of change that blow through the ecosystems of our personal lives and the global marketplace. Health and family. Politics and economics. Change will remain constant, and that's just about the only thing that won't change.

Much of what empowers us to weather those winds and remain durable is our adaptability. It's our ability to drop old tools and pick up new ones, to switch industries without flinching, to let go of old stories and expectations and respond to what's right in front of us—like a gamer pivoting seamlessly from platformer to shooter to sandbox to whatever the heck *Untitled Goose Game* is.

You might say that the key subskills in adaptability are the abilities to *relax* and *adopt*. When a new software tool emerges or a new market paradigm takes hold, we need to *relax* our grip on what came before and *adopt* the tools and strategies necessary for what lies ahead. In part, this requires that we continuously monitor for change—and it requires that we try out new tools and strategies every now and then, just for the heck of it.

Together, these behaviors will shore up our adaptability, creating space for us to focus on resilience.

10.6 Resilience

Previously I said that our personal durability especially hinges on two behavioral skills: adaptability and resilience. Whereas adaptability requires keeping our heads in the face of change, resilience requires keeping our heads in the face of *challenge*. Can we stick with a project, a relationship, a job hunt even when things get tough?

This is a particularly gnarly extension of embracing failure. The embrace of failure that we've spoken about till now has mostly been about *reframing* failures. ("I've found a hundred ways not to make a lightbulb!") But resilience is about remaining strong even in the face of failures that defy reframing—the ones that just hurt. Think of serious career setbacks. Serious financial setbacks. Familial splits and personal tragedies.

In Chapter 5, we met Lyle Maxson, the erstwhile professional club goer who later found mission in his work on health-oriented technology and games for good. As a member of our employer advisory board, which advocates for better hiring practices across the industry, Lyle's been a vocal advocate for spotlighting resilience in hiring searches.

In the same breath, Lyle addresses job seekers, recommending that they devote special energy to enhancing resilience during Phase 2 of the loop. He recommends doing this through therapy, mindfulness meditation, and physical wellness practices that give us the bodily health to weather psychological setbacks.

There's also one more avenue that Lyle recommends. It's the one that matters most to him:

> When community is missing, we don't know that we're missing it until we actually receive it. And then we're like, *Holy shit, I needed this.*
>
> Building community is, I think, literally the most important thing of all. It's what actually creates accountability and creates inspiration. It stabilizes our mental health and our other practices.
>
> When your community supports you, even if you try over and over again and seemingly fail, you can continue moving forward.

10.7   Moving Forward

America Succeeds has identified 82 durable skills.[4] We've only scratched the surface here. But, if you'll recall, our objective in Phase 2 of the loop isn't to level up every relevant skill. It's to identify the most *fundamental* skills and level up those.

It's been my aim to highlight some of the most foundational durable skills—the ones that form bedrock for virtually all other level-up efforts. For each of these, our previously discussed level-up tactics will support us. And, as Lyle points out, there's one more tactic that will support us too. It's the most powerful of them all: community-building.

Notes

1. "About the Durable Skills Advantage." Durable Skills Advantage, accessed September 18, 2024. https://www.durableskillsadvantage.org/about/.

2. Brodnitz, Dan. "The Most In-Demand Skills of 2024." LinkedIn, February 8, 2024. https://www.linkedin.com/business/talent/blog/talent-strategy/linkedin-most-in-demand-hard-and-soft-skills.

3. Brodnitz, "The Most In-Demand Skills of 2024."

4. "Unlocking Career Success with the Durable Skills Advantage Framework." Durable Skills Advantage, accessed September 18, 2024. https://www.dura bleskillsadvantage.org/.

11

Community Loop: Coaches

11.1 No Dead Mentors

"Always start with the money," she remembers him saying.

Stacey Haffner had a great boss. He was helping her build better pitch decks—and better pitches. Years later, when Stacey moved into her first management role, another peer-turned-boss guided her through leading her first team. Meanwhile, much of her public speaking growth came thanks to a professional trainer at Microsoft.

As Lyle Maxson reminded us in Chapter 10, the most powerful resource we have—at any stage of our careers—is our community. And when we're leveling up, the most influential of these community members will be the sorts of people who trained Stacey: our coaches. They're the focal point of Community Loop Phase 2.

As we discussed in Chapter 6, the Community Loop is a subordinate loop that moves in parallel with the Core Career Loop. In Phase 1 of the Core Career Loop, we were choosing our quest, and the Community Loop responded in parallel: it had us seek mentors to advise us on that decision. Now we're in Phase 2 of the Core Career Loop, leveling up, and the Community Loop will respond in parallel once again—this time introducing us to coaches who can help us train (see Figure 11.1).

Figure 11.1 The Community Loop

Now, these coaches won't *replace* our mentors. In epic tales of heroic derring-do, there's an idea that the mentor must die. Only then, without the mentor's guidance, can the hero truly test their mettle and become a master. Mufasa dies so that Simba can prove himself against Scar and retake Pride Rock. Dumbledore dies so that Harry can meet his destiny and face Voldemort alone. Qui-Gon dies, Obi-Wan dies, Luke dies— each for the narrative sake of the galaxy's next hero.

But in life, and in our careers, nobody has to die for us to grow. People *will* die, sure. But we're not looking to rush anyone along. Not literally, and not metaphorically either.

The fact that we've moved on to a new phase of the Community Loop doesn't necessarily mean that we've outgrown our mentors. And when we move past Phase 2, we won't necessarily outgrow our coaches either. Ideally, our mentors will follow us not only through the loop but also through many, many *cycles* of the loop. And ideally, our coaches will stick with us for as long as we can learn from them.

Although it's natural for some folks to come and go with time, the population size of our community should generally trend upward. Relationships should both deepen and accumulate. And it won't just be the wise guides who stick with us. We want our peers to stick with us too. In fact, now that we're in Phase 2, let's start with them.

11.2   Our Peers

It's natural to look upward for guidance—to those whose superior abilities or job titles or graying hairs seem to afford them elevated status. And indeed, it's terrific to look upward for guidance. I highly recommend it. But before we do, we ought to also look side-to-side.

Our peers are like us. They're at similar stages of their careers. Their skill levels might be similar. And although they often can't offer the benefit of advanced experience, there are other vital ways that they can contribute to our level-up journeys.

Lyle named two of these ways in Chapter 10. Our peers contribute accountability and inspiration. It should be clear by now that leveling up will be hard. It'll also be great fun! But it'll be hard. We will hit failures. We will hit walls. And there'll be moments when we struggle to stick with it. Sometimes we'll want to give up because of an especially difficult setback. Sometimes it'll be because life is busy and distracting and full of meaningful priorities that demand our attention.

Finding peers to join us on our level-up journey will create a sense of accountability. It'll create the sense that someone is watching and caring, and that, as a consequence, we have a responsibility to keep at it. We can shore up this accountability by doing the following:

- **Setting goals:** We need to tell our peers what skills we want to learn or little quests we want to complete, with clear timelines.
- **Sharing progress:** We also need to check in regularly with peers to motivate us to make headway between conversations.
- **Asking for feedback:** Even if peers don't have the expertise that we'll find in true coaches, their questions and feedback can help us reflect on our progress and bring more focus to our efforts.

And then there's Lyle's other insight about peers during level-up—that they offer us inspiration. Sometimes our peers are on the same journey: we're both becoming better animators, or better cooks, or better mathematicians. Other times, we'll level up different skills in parallel: I'm becoming a better animator while you become a better cook.

If we're sharing our progress with each other, it's natural that we'll inspire each other. When I see how much better your crème brûlée has become—you who, until a month ago, couldn't toast bread—it will reinforce the belief that I can get better, too. And that's doubly true if I see you getting better in the same discipline that I'm pursuing.

Which brings us to a third way that our peers can contribute to our level-up journeys. Maybe our friend isn't just studying animation at the same time we are—maybe they actually already know quite a bit about animation.

We must never underestimate the skills of our peers. Everyone knows a lot about *something*. When we're leveling up, there's a decent chance that the people who know a lot about our target skill are already in our community. They're not just our bosses and our parents' golfing buddies and our big sisters. They're also our peers and our friends. A person can be younger and earn less and have no credentials to speak of, but happen to know a lot about our target skill. We should ask them for help.

But I'm getting ahead of myself. We're starting to veer into true coaching, which I do want to talk about, but not quite yet. First, I want to return to Lyle's insights. Much of the sharing that fosters inspiration and accountability will take place in one-on-one encounters. But there's a much bigger world of inspiration and accountability out there. It brings many people into the fold simultaneously—both friends and strangers. That world is online.

11.3 Sharing Online

Austin Kleon is an expert on creative practices. His work has been translated into dozens of languages, reaching well over a million creators, artists, and hobbyists worldwide. In particular, he's an evangelist for the power of showing your work—a topic he covered vividly in his book, *Show Your Work!*:

> Almost all of the people I look up to and try to steal [inspiration] from today, regardless of their profession, have built sharing into their routine. . . . They're open about what they're working on, and they're consistently posting bits and pieces of their work, their ideas, and what they're learning online. . . . By generously sharing their ideas and their knowledge, they often gain an audience that they can then leverage when they need it—for fellowship, feedback, or patronage.

There are lots of places where we can share our work online: social media, Reddit, WhatsApp, Discord, and so on. As Kleon says, these virtual communities will help us attract more fellowship (accountability) and feedback (inspiration and peer-to-peer learning).

He also points out that these efforts can connect us to "patronage," by which he means *income*. Joy Horvath echoes this idea: "There are countless stories about people who got a job because somebody at a company saw a piece of art they posted online."

We'll save this discussion about attracting job opportunities for the next phase. For now, I want to emphasize that, whether they're our closest friends or strangers from Discord, our peers form a vital force in the effort to level up. And, as we're about to see, our coaches do, too.

11.4 Coaches

Whereas Phase 1's mentors gave holistic counsel on life and career decisions, Phase 2's coaches shoot for a smaller bulls-eye: they help us achieve specific goals and overcome specific challenges.

How do I get my animated hero's arm to stop moving like spaghetti? Should I prove this theorem by induction or by contradiction? Why does my crème brûlée keep catching fire? Coaches have the answers.

And whereas mentorship often involves many long, freewheeling conversations, the best coaches are likely to take a more structured approach, giving us incremental benchmarks to hit and tasks to perform. (Show me three different lighting schemes. Derive these three formulas. Go buy a fire extinguisher, then try again.)

Before we can find the right coach, we have to define clear goals. Fortunately, we've done that throughout Phase 2, identifying fundamental technical and durable skills to build and breaking those objectives into little quests. Once we know what we want to achieve, the next step is to look around and find someone who can help us.

As we've already established, this isn't just about looking up. It's about looking side-to-side too. Even downward. Your kid brother might know Photoshop better than you do, even if he did just spent last night TPing the post office.

We might discover coaches in our peers, or our friends, or our families, or our virtual communities. And then there are the most traditional sorts of coaches: professional experts. These can be our managers, pros we meet at conferences, or role models we cold email. There are even coaches-for-hire—tutors and trainers and consultants.

When it comes to leveling up, there's a lot of responsibility that falls to us. It's on us to figure out which fundamentals we want to study. It's on us to overcome our fears of failure and to cultivate our own curiosity. But that doesn't mean we have to go it alone. And, in fact, we shouldn't.

Our peers and our coaches will accelerate our growth and open up new possibilities for learning. Plus, there's another benefit. Building and deepening these relationships now will set us up well for the most community-driven phase of all: Phase 3.

As Austin Kleon said, it'll help us find patronage.

Part III

Job Hunt

Once we've chosen a professional path and leveled up toward it, it's time to put all of our setup to work, connecting our skills to existing work opportunities. It's time to job hunt.

Back in the day, this was a process entirely defined by quantity. How many skills could you lay claim to? How many résumés could you mail out?

But, in the new economy, quantity alone won't cut it. More than ever before, job hunters must focus on finesse. We have to become pinpoint precise about what jobs we're after. And we have to craft application narratives that pair skills and experience with the promise of something more.

How can we excel at job hunting in the contemporary marketplace?

12

How Gamers Learned
to Hack the Grind

12.1 Groundwork for Grinding

Back in Part II, we spent a lot of time with Raph Koster, author of *A Theory of Fun* and lead designer for *Ultima Online*. And we're about to spend more time with him. But not just yet.

Before *Ultima Online*, there was *Ultima*. And before *Ultima*, there was *The Game of Dungeons*. That's where the third phase of our story begins: in 1974 with *The Game of Dungeons* in Southern Illinois University's library basement, where the early-computing "PLATO terminal" lived, and where Whisenhunt met Wood.

"There was only one PLATO terminal at SIU," says Ray Wood. "It was common for one person to run the terminal and another 5–10 people to be in the room with you watching the terminal. Gary and I would meet during these 'joint viewing sessions.'"[1]

Gary Whisenhunt studied psychology and political science. Ray Wood studied electrical engineering. And, together, they began messing with that PLATO terminal, building a "dungeon crawl" game, where players explored caves, fought monsters, and searched for loot.

Whisenhunt and Wood brought on two collaborators and joined Chapter 1's holy grail hunt for a computer game akin to *Dungeons &*

Dragons—the pen-and-paper tabletop game where you could go any-where and do anything. In fact, the team was so committed to this task that they named their game's computer file after *Dungeons & Dragons*, rendering the abbreviation *D&D* as *dnd*. (Today, most game historians refer to Whisenhunt and Wood's game by this filename.)

The Game of Dungeons incorporated a grail quest of its own. Players navigated through a maze-like, multilevel dungeon, searching for two priceless treasures—a grail and an orb—each of which were guarded by especially powerful monsters—gaming's first ever "bosses."[2] To capture the go-anywhere feel of *Dungeons & Dragons*, *The Game of Dungeons* also became one of the first nonlinear games, where players could move backwards to levels that they had bested before.

That's where things got weird. Players weren't using this nonlinear feature the way that the creators intended. In *The Game of Dungeons*, you hunted for treasure, and monsters' ferocity scaled in proportion to your treasure-hunting success. The more valuable the individual treasures in your pack, the more monsters would want to kill you for them. Whisenhunt and Wood thought this would make the game brutally dif-ficult. But players were beating the game easily. Whisenhunt wanted to know why:

> I made a trip up to the University of Illinois to watch people playing the game in the PLATO lab. Once I saw one person who would walk into the dungeon, grab the first valuable item (which at that level was not much) and then leave. Then proceed to do this for hours on end. We never thought that anyone would have the patience and would spend the time to do such a simple thing over and over again to gain large amounts of wealth.[3]

Players had figured out that monsters' strength was tied to the value of *individual* treasures in their packs. If players instead collected lots and lots of low-value treasure, the monsters wouldn't want to kill them so badly, and the game would be easier to beat.

This was a new kind of player behavior, one in which players would triumph not merely through skill or through strategy but also through their devotion to performing simple, mundane, repetitive tasks, over and over and over and over again—leveling up their characters and collect-ing valuable in-game resources. This was what gamers today call *grinding*. And it wasn't what the game's designers had intended at all.

12.2   Grinding to Meet the Boss

In the beginning, grinding was about outsmarting the designers—finding the most efficient way to beat a game's challenges. And that tradition would continue after *The Game of Dungeons*. But the roles would eventually reverse as well: designers would intentionally build repetitive grinding into their games, and players would invent workarounds. Players would find ways to accelerate the grind, elevate its output, or bypass it altogether. And ultimately, these hack-the-grind skills would transform gamers into natural job hunters for our new economy.

I can think of no better example than my colleague Sam Distaso, who began his career about as far away from games as possible: in corporate accounting. He'd always played games in his free time—in fact, he says that gaming was central to the bond he built with his younger brother. But when he got to college, he studied accounting and economics. Then he became a financial auditor for one of the world's largest accounting firms, Deloitte. But after a few years, he became dissatisfied with his chosen profession.

Something was changing about Sam's internal values. And when he tuned into that change, he found that a new mission was emerging. He wanted to make an impact on the world, and he wanted to do it by "scaling exciting technologies into mainstream adoption."

"That was going to be my life's work," Sam remembers thinking. "But I'm not gonna be able to do that at Deloitte." So he identified a new professional path: he would join a startup. Someplace where he could launch something. *Anything*.

He began this effort as any gamer would, by leveling up. He'd never launched a tech product before, so he gave himself a little quest. After work and on weekends, Sam built and produced his first mobile app.

Once that project was done, Sam got to work applying to jobs. Seventy-four of them. (Talk about grinding.)

Sam got 73 rejections. Only one startup made an offer, and Sam accepted. That startup wanted to provide housekeeping, landscaping, and maintenance services at a national scale. It was Sam's job to open new markets, winning clients in cities that the business had never reached before.

This sort of worked with Sam's sense of mission. He was scaling a business toward mainstream adoption. But he wasn't launching "exciting technology" as he'd hoped. That gravitational pull still tugged at him, and he had to move closer toward it.

"Virtual reality [VR] became the technology that I had the most passion for," Sam says. "I was like, 'I love that. I know that VR wave is coming. I don't know if it's gonna be in a year, in a decade, in two decades. But I want to be part of that. I can help scale this business up.'"

So Sam put VR in his sights.

But merely grinding through another 74 applications wouldn't be enough to get Sam into the VR space. Later, when he learned about the technology that powers VR—3D game engines—he tried for a role here at Unity. And traditional grinding didn't work here either. Unity ended up rejecting him. Twice.

To break into these spaces, Sam would need to *hack* the grind, moving past the 73 rejections model, inventing a method for accelerating his search and elevating the impact of his efforts. Fortunately, the world of gaming had already paved the way many years earlier.

12.3 Grind, Incorporated

In the years after *The Game of Dungeons*, players kept getting around game difficulty by illicitly grinding for in-game resources and experience points, which they used to level up armor, weaponry, and skills. When enough players started doing this, creators caught on.

Creators realized that intentionally incorporating grind into their games would extend the length and perceived value of those games. It would keep players engaged and devoted, fostering senses of investment, progress, and achievement. And when games went online, grind-based design would also keep subscribers paying their monthly dues.

But as grinding became pervasive, players began pushing back. Grinding had originally been a player-driven effort to optimize play for maximum efficiency. Many players weren't interested in designer-mandated grinding. Player pushback hit new heights when *Ultima* went online.

We've encountered *Ultima* a few times now. Like *The Game of Dungeons*, *Ultima* represented one of the earliest efforts to capture the magic of *Dungeons & Dragons*. *Ultima I* is commonly considered the first ever open-world role-playing game. And that game's success launched a franchise, culminating in the release of *Ultima Online (UO)*, one of history's most successful massively multiplayer online role-playing games (MMORPGs).

With *Ultima Online* (*UO*), the ambition was to create what producer Richard Garriott called "the very first ever, completely virtual world for the mass public to go live out alternate lives in."[4]

Raph Koster, future author of *A Theory of Fun*, became the game's lead designer. And, as we already know, Koster saw skill building as the be-all, end-all of gaming. So, true to form, he wanted to put skill building at the center of *UO*.

Koster didn't want to handle skill building the way other games had. He disliked "arbitrary 'experience points'. . . [that] can be applied to anything, leading to oddities like getting better at crafting because you have slain a lot of orcs. . . ." Instead, Koster wanted *UO* players to, as he puts it, "get better at crafting by, well, crafting."[5]

So *UO* implemented a "use-based" progression system. The more you used a skill, the better you got at it. You'd get better at swordsmanship by slaying monsters. You'd get better at blacksmithing by forging metal. Even musicianship: you'd get better by practicing your instrument.

This meant that players had to return to the grind, clicking away for hours at monsters and anvils and lutes. Many players did play the game as intended, reveling in the grind. But many other players looked for alternatives. They wanted to accelerate the grind. They wanted to elevate its yield—maxing out skills and resources. Some even looked to bypass the grind altogether. These players wanted optimal play.

12.4 Optimal Play

Long after the heyday of *UO*, Wyatt Cheng, a senior designer on the game *Diablo 3*, would coin a term that describes what *UO* players experienced back in the late 1990s: "the burden of optimal play."[6]

The VR game designer Edward McNeill describes the burden this way: "Players will tend to make the choices that lead most directly and surely to victory. If you set up a goal that players care about, you should expect them to try to reach it as efficiently as possible."[7]

We saw the burden of optimal play take effect back in *The Game of Dungeons*. Players had clear goals: gain wealth, kill monsters, retrieve magic artifacts. But, by design, as players collected more valuable treasures, the process of achieving their other goals became slower and more difficult. So players found a way to optimize: by grinding for low-value treasure, they could maximize wealth and still achieve their other goals with relative ease.

Cheng and McNeill call this inclination to optimize a "burden" because it seems to operate more like a compulsion than a decision. It often leads players away from the designed experience of the game toward a less wondrous, more tactical approach. But I prefer to think of it as a *drive* toward optimal play—because this drive often yields wonderful benefits, as we'll soon see. Although I'm not sure that Raph Koster was such a fan.

12.5   Ultima Optimized

The problem with *UO*'s use-based skill system was that the game gave you reason to swing your sword much more often than it gave you reason to play an instrument. If skill growth was merely based on frequency of use, then *UO* would become a game world full of sword masters with no other skills.

The design team tried to balance this out with the use of probabilities. Every time you used a skill, virtual dice would roll on the back end, determining whether you gained experience. The design team lowered the probability that you'd gain experience from frequently performed actions while increasing the probability that you'd gain experience from infrequently performed actions. You'd have to swing a sword many times to gain swordsmanship, but play your instrument only a few times to gain musicianship.

This worked just fine for folks who enjoyed grinding. But many players felt the drive toward optimal play tugging away at them. The process of mastering swordsmanship had just become much slower, and these players needed to optimize.

For this, they turned to macros, scripts, and bots—a suite of virtual tools for automating in-game activities. Tools like these had been around for decades. Players had even used them in *The Game of Dungeons*. But *UO* gathered more players together in one virtual space than any game ever had. With so many players competing for the same trophies and participating in the same virtual economy, automation-based optimization entered into a kind of renaissance.

Players started hacking skills like swordsmanship, automating keystrokes so that they could instantly swing their swords many times. If each swing was like a roll of the dice, then these automated keystrokes enabled players to roll the dice faster and more often, raking in a higher quantity of successful rolls than they would playing by the rules.

Koster explains why this was a problem for developers:

> It meant, fundamentally, that players were more efficient, and the game had been tuned to a given player efficiency rate. A higher efficiency meant that the game ran out of content faster on several different axes—not only did players finish the levelling process faster, but at any given moment, there were fewer monsters left alive, and therefore less for everyone else.[8]

UO's development team raced to respond to these automation efforts. And players raced to respond to those responses. What began as a game of cat and mouse eventually spun out into a full-scale arms race. *UO's* successors—online games like *Everquest* and *World of Warcraft*—would face similar challenges. Where *UO* peaked at about 250,000 players, *World of Warcraft* (*WoW*) would eventually reach 12 million. That's 48 times more players, giving developers 48 times more headaches.[9]

WoW would implement all kinds of anti-bot systems while also working to disincentivize optimization, increasing the playfulness of grind through narrative design and in-game events. Today, the optimizer-versus-designer arms race continues. Players continue looking for ways to accelerate the grind, get more out of it, or bypass it altogether. They look for ways to save time and beat the randomness.

It should be mentioned that this often violates the terms and conditions of contemporary games—not something I endorse doing. But what I do endorse and celebrate and admire is gamer ingenuity, and the relentless drive toward optimal play. Plus, not all grinding hacks require violating terms and conditions.

Perhaps the most powerful optimization tools of all are player communities. Gamers post in online forums, they share strategies and insights—tips and tricks for grinding faster and more effectively. *Go there,* they say. *Try this.*

And many of them gather together in-game, where their avatars grind as a team, recognizing that many hands make light work. They distribute labor, protect each other from hazards, and combine abilities to accelerate, elevate, and bypass the grind.

That's precisely the sort of hack-the-grind mentality that makes gamers killer job hunters—and it's just the kind of thinking that Sam Distaso needed.

12.6   Hack the Grind

Sam felt ready to leave his housekeeping/landscaping startup. He wanted to launch exciting new technologies. Most especially, he wanted to help boost virtual reality into mainstream adoption. But VR studios weren't biting.

Merely grinding his way through applications wasn't working. The drive toward optimized play began kicking in. Sam knew: it was time to hack the grind.

This didn't mean that the grind was over. Sam wouldn't take the "bypass" approach. Instead, he'd focus on accelerating the grind and elevating the impact of every effort.

As he tells it, he began by putting himself in recruiters' shoes: "I figured that if I was an HR recruiter, my job would be to serve the other employees at my company. That's who my customer is." So if he could get the other employees at a company—say 10 or 15 of them—to bother HR about his application, recruiters would have to listen.

"Once I realized that, it kind of became a game within a game," he says. "Can you network with [about] 25–30 people at the company, knowing that only maybe half will follow up with HR on your behalf?"

Sam reached out to current employees asking for chats. He prepped like crazy for those conversations. And then, after every one, he made his ask: *will you email HR about me?*

That's how he broke into VR, eventually becoming a vice president for Linden Lab, the developer behind *Second Life*. Later, he'd put Unity in his crosshairs, and he'd receive two rejections. But then he implemented this approach, and turned things around. Today he manages our partnerships with creative collaborators like Riot Games, Apple, and Meta. True to his mission, he spends every day scaling exciting technology into mainstream adoption.

He got here by grinding, yes, but also by *hacking* the grind, drawing on ingenuity and community relationships to accelerate and elevate his efforts.

12.7   Ingenuity and Community

There's an idea out there that jobs are distributed based on merit. If we've shown how deeply we care, how well we've leveled up, and how great we'd be in the role, then we'll get the job.

I don't know if that was ever true, but it certainly isn't true today. Without a doubt, each of those things is vitally important. But, ultimately, today's jobs are won through grind. With so many applicants competing for the same vacancies, success often has a quality of randomness: every application feels like a roll of the dice. And it takes many, many die rolls to break through.

But gamers have a leg up. In part, because they're so comfortable with the grind—they've been performing repetitive tasks for long-term gains since the 1970s. But also because of their drive toward optimal play. Gamers find ways to accelerate the grind, elevate its yield, or bypass it altogether—often by building community and collaborating with other players.

This is the essence of the Core Career Loop's Phase 3. In Phase 1, we chose a professional path. In Phase 2, we leveled up. And now, in Phase 3, we hunt for the job where we'll finally get to put our decisions and skills into practice. This won't be the only job we ever get—every time we cycle the loop, we'll job hunt again. And, every time, we'll come back better prepared. We'll be more comfortable with the application grind, better trained to automate and optimize, and we'll bring more community with us.

We'll see how both grinding and hacking the grind play out across Part III. In Chapter 13 we'll address the grind-friendly mindset required to score great offers. In Chapter 14, we'll look at the hacks that accelerate and elevate the job-hunting process. In Chapter 15, we'll evaluate our offers and negotiate great contracts. Then, finally, in Chapter 16 we'll address the importance of community—the hack that arguably plays a bigger role in job hunting than in any other phase of the Loop.

But before we turn outward to our communities, we must begin by turning inward.

Notes

1. RPG Fanatic Carey. "Interview with the Creators of Dnd (PLATO)." RPG Fanatic, April 26, 2012. https://web.archive.org/web/20131027034539/http://www.rpgfanatic.net/advanced_game_wiki_database.html?p=news&nrid=5049&game=dnd.
2. "DND: A.k.a the Game of Dungeons." Universal Videogame List, January 6, 2007. https://www.uvlist.net/game-160118-dnd.

3. RPG Fanatic Carey, "Interview with the Creators of Dnd (PLATO)."

4. "Is Richard Garriott Really Building a Better World?" *Next Generation*, March 1996, p. 9. https://archive.org/details/NextGeneration27Mar1997/page/n4/mode/1up.

5. Koster, Raph. "Use-Based Systems." Raph Koster's website, July 18, 2006. https://www.raphkoster.com/2006/07/18/use-based-systems/.

6. Rush. "Wyatt Cheng's GDC 2013 Panel: Illustrated Transcript, Part Two." Pure Diablo, July 11, 2013. https://www.purediablo.com/wyatt-chengs-gdc-2013-panel-illustrated-transcript-part-two.

7. McNeill, Edward. "Grinding and the Burden of Optimal Play." Game Developer, July 20, 2014. https://www.gamedeveloper.com/design/grinding-and-the-burden-of-optimal-play#.

8. Koster, Raph. "A Brief History of Botting." Raph Koster's website, March 25, 2008. https://www.raphkoster.com/2008/03/25/a-brief-history-of-botting/.

9. Williams, Mike. "How World of Warcraft Was Made: The Definitive Inside Story of Nearly 20 Years of Development." VG247, September 26, 2022. https://www.vg247.com/how-world-of-warcraft-was-made-the-definitive-inside-story-of-nearly-20-years-of-development.

13

Free Your Mindset

13.1 Opportunity and Despair

Job hunting can brew up brutal storms of self-decimating anguish and despair. But not for everyone. For many, Phase 3 of the Core Career Loop is the most fun phase of all. It's a thrilling time when theory turns into practice, when ambition turns into opportunity, when our chickens finally come home to roost. We build community, open doors, and create possibilities where none existed before.

The difference between despairing job hunters and delighting job hunters is merely *mindset*. Mindset determines what we feel, which determines how we behave, which determines what we can achieve. We saw this in Phase 2, and we'll find it equally true here in Phase 3.

There are two key mindsets we'll need if we're to enjoy Phase 3 and triumph in our job hunts. The first is attitudinal: we must brace for rejection. The second is belief-based: the individualists among us must internalize that it's our communities, not our brilliant lonesome selves, that create job opportunities.

For the most part, we'll save that community talk for Chapter 16 at the end of Part III. For now, let's look more closely at rejection.

13.2 Embracing Rejection

Tomb Raider's Laura Croft. *Uncharted's* Nathan Drake. *Indiana Jones's* Indiana Jones. Treasure hunters never find their quarry in the first place they look. They chase wild geese, drive headfirst into dead ends, pull up red herring after red herring, and—I hate to quote *National Treasure*, but as Nick Cage's dad says—treasure hunters discover that many clues lead nowhere: "That will lead to another clue, and that will lead to another clue!"

If you've seen *National Treasure*, then you know that Nick Cage's dad is the brutal-storm-of-self-decimating-anguish-and-despair type. He refuses to believe that Nick's treasure hunting efforts will pay off. But, of course, Nick Cage doesn't listen to his dad. He turns to his friends for help, and together they find eons' worth of priceless artifacts.

I don't often say this, but we should all aspire to be more like Nick Cage.

Job hunting involves all the same dead ends as treasure hunting. We'll encounter huge flocks of wild geese. Huge schools of red herrings. We really can find treasure on the other side of all those creatures—just as long as we don't let them throw us off.

In Phase 3, there's a tendency to anticipate overnight success. And if we don't get that overnight success, many of us tend to crumble. But overnight success is a myth. It's virtually unattainable.

Lyle Maxson is the games-for-good tech leader that we met first in Chapter 5. He rubs elbows with many of Silicon Valley's most successful movers and shakers. And he says, "All my friends who've had 'overnight successes' took—you know—*14 years* to make it happen."

Outperformers do years of hard work in obscurity. Their successes only seem to happen overnight because that's when people start paying attention.

Lianna Johnstone—recruiter for *Pokemon Go* developer Niantic—adds that many of her studio's most successful employees get rejected the first time they apply. "A lot of times, if somebody isn't a fit for a certain role, recruiters and hiring managers will reach back out for a different role," she says. "We've had that happen a few times already this year."

This all boils down to a variation on the same mindset requirement that we discussed in Phase 2: the embrace of failure. In Phase 3, we're dealing with a special subtype of failure: rejection. We're hearing no. We're being told that we aren't a fit. We're feeling like we aren't enough. And we need to remember that these rejections don't necessarily mean anything at all. They're just part of the treasure hunting process.

Often, it's a numbers game. We're competing with so many other job hunters for any given vacancy. The question of whether our résumé gets considered by the right person on the right day at the right time comes down to a roll of the dice.

This isn't to say that every rejection is without cause. Often, there's a reason for the rejection—even if it feels unfair. Our résumés or our interview answers aren't quite working. And, in these cases, we must respond to job-hunting failure the same way we responded to level up failure: treat it like data for future iteration.

Joy Horvath is the Unity program manager and game developer who masterminded our Phase 2 guidance. She puts it this way:"

> The major failure when you're trying to find a job is getting a rejection. When that happens, ask yourself: what's something that you could do differently? And then just trying doing it differently."

As in Phase 2, rejection is inevitable.
Rejection is data.
Rejection is the beginning.

13.3   From Qualified to Connected

So far we've talked about the mindset necessary to navigate disappointments during job hunting. But there's another important mindset that we'll need in order to thrive: we'll need to shift from a skills focus to a community focus. We'll need to stop asking whether we're qualified and start asking whether we're connected.

Until now, in our Core Career Loop, we've focused on developing our *selves*. We've focused on clarifying our values, identifying our professional paths, and building our personal skills. But what we know and what we're capable of won't make the final determination about what jobs we can access.

In reality, the number one contributor to job-hunting success will be our community. Our peers, mentors, coaches, and sponsors (whom we'll meet soon) alert us to opportunities, connect us to hiring managers, and make referrals. The vast majority of the time, it's these community members who determine what we can achieve.

In fact, not only are we ourselves not the most important contributors to our job-hunting journeys—our closest connections aren't either. Ironically, it's our weakest connections who are most likely to create opportunities. The strangers we meet at conferences. The experts we chat up online. They're the ones most likely to open doors.

13.4 From Grind to Gig

So much of what Phase 3 will ask of us boils down to two things: grinding for opportunities and hacking that grind. We'll need to face rejection. Lots of it. Remember that Unity rejected Sam Distaso twice, and when he wanted to join a startup, he faced 73 rejections before landing his first gig.

We need to keep grinding through all that rejection. Keep sending out apps. Keep starting conversations. Roll enough dice, and we'll beat the random number generator. Better than anyone else, gamers know how to put in those hours and enjoy themselves in the process.

Simultaneously, we'll also need to bring gamer ingenuity to the job hunt, working strategically to accelerate, elevate, and bypass the grind. Largely, that will involve moving past individualism, turning to our communities for help. Just as we might form in-game clans to farm resources together, we'll form career-looping communities to hunt down jobs.

And there's one other way we can hack the grind, too. We can accelerate and elevate our efforts if we learn to tell our stories well—in ways that speak to modern hiring managers. We'll still need to draft lots of documents and speak to lots of insiders—we'll still need to grind—but we'll boost the probability of success for every roll of the dice.

14

Tell Your Story

14.1 Story Games

Space Invaders. Pac-Man. Pong. Back in the stone age of video games, skill was all there was. Games gave us challenges and double-dog-dared us to take them on.

Skill up. Win. If you aren't too chicken to try.

But as the medium matured, difficulty became just one tool in the designer's box, and skill became just one component of play. Other elements rose in prominence—among them, *story*. Today, and in recent years, studios like Rockstar, Telltale, and Quantic Dream have dialed narrative up to 11, while dialing skill challenges down so far that it sometimes seems like they're barely there at all. Other studios like BioWare and Naughty Dog have made similar moves, if perhaps less extremely.

This all amounts to half a century of great luck for gamers. Our medium has always been perfectly calibrated to the job-hunting demands of the moment. Back in the stone age of video games, the job hunt was also a skills-first-skills-only endeavor. Employers wanted to know your qualifications and abilities, nothing more. Because employers valued stability and straightforward ladder climbing, the ideal job applicant wouldn't have much story to tell anyway. *You've only ever worked at one other place, and nothing ever happened there? Perfect! You're hired!*

Today's landscape is entirely different. Employers aren't looking for people to solve problems 10 years down the road. They need people who can solve problems 10 weeks or 10 days down the road. They expect applicants to have lived busy lives before coming aboard—lives that have taught them how to meet challenges and win.

So today's job hunters need to do what so many of today's games do: tell stories. As job hunters, we need to demonstrate that we can solve employers' problems, and that, in some way or another, we've solved those problems before. Each of us needs to explain that we're on a heroic journey, and it's led us straight to *this job*.

This principle applies in all industries, not just creative ones. Yes, marketers and game writers should be able to tell compelling career stories. But so should engineers, financial analysts, and chemists. No matter what professional paths we're on, any employer we encounter will need a problem solved. And we'll need to explain why we're the perfect heroes to solve that problem.

Yes, there certainly are people who get jobs with the old-school résumé dump method. In fact, at the time of writing, the average candidate seems to be sending out about 51 résumés before landing a job.[1] Some outliers dispatch 500+ résumés before locking down a gig.[2] But modern gamers know better: they hack the grind. They put in time and effort, they rinse and repeat, but they do it with a drive toward optimal play, using storytelling to accelerate the grind and elevate returns.

14.2 Story 101

Theme. Circumstances. Conflict. Resolution. These are the story elements that we're going to highlight during our job hunt.

14.2.1 Theme

The Last of Us is a game about the zombie apocalypse, but isn't really about the zombie apocalypse. It's about love and loss and helping where we can while putting family first—even found family.

Every company we apply to is going through some kind of zombie apocalypse. Sales are down. Costs are up. Their product's delayed. They misjudged the market, made an honest mistake, and now everyone hates them. In our stories, we, as job hunters, will explain how we can help employers navigate those zombie apocalypses.

But before we launch into the heart of that story, we need to step back and ask what this is really about. What is this company's long-term mission? What does this company value? Innovation? Play? Stability? Found family? Whatever the answer, we'll want to keep those themes front and center when we tell our stories.

14.2.2 Circumstances

Back in 1897, a guy called Konstantin Stanislavski started a new acting troupe called the Moscow Art Theater, which did what nobody had done before; they made acting feel real. Natural. Today, this is the norm in movies and TV precisely because every actor studies Stanislavski on day one.

Stanislavski used a bunch of different tactics to achieve his natural effect. But before any other tactic, he began with what he called the *given circumstances*.

He didn't want his characters to feel like they just popped into existence when the curtain went up. He wanted their lives and their worlds to feel real and lived in. This required actors to get specific about the "circumstances" of the play. Before the show began, who loved whom? Who hated whom? What did each character want from life, and what had they done to get it?

As job hunters, we also need to think through these given circumstances. The teams we're joining don't just pop into existence the day we're hired. We need to understand what they've been up to all this time. What stage of life is the company at? Is it a startup? Is it maturing into profitability? Is it an incumbent, trying to maintain market share?

And what about the specific team we're applying to join? How many people are on it? How long have they worked together? What does their collaboration look like? What kinds of transitions have they been through? What are they up to now?

These given circumstances will lead us to conflict.

14.2.3 *Conflict*

The juicy center of story. *This* is the zombie apocalypse. Why does this team need a new hire? What's gone wrong? What opportunities are emerging? Is the team headed in a new direction? Are they struggling to hit sales targets? Launching a new product without enough support? This is the problem that we're going to solve by taking the job.

14.2.4 *Resolution*

Now—only now—the spotlight turns to us. How will we solve this team's central conflict? How will we end the zombie apocalypse?

14.3 Prewriting

Piecing together this story for our job hunt requires some serious research. We begin with the company website, then expand outward. We should be looking at the company's press releases and social media, as well as looking up employee reviews, financial reports, and news articles.

Then, as Sam Distaso's journey suggests, we should be reaching out to current and former employees for conversations, piecing the story together from multiple perspectives. (When we get to the Community Loop, we'll talk more about setting up these conversations and nailing them.)

This prewriting process culminates in the creation of a "job story outline"—a single document that collects our key learnings about theme, circumstances, and conflict, as well as our plan to deliver a resolution.

How have our past experiences, technical skills, and durable skills prepared us to solve the conflict at hand? We can answer by citing our work experiences, side hustles, volunteer activities, school leadership roles—anything we've ever done—just so long as our answer promises a resolution.

14.4 Make Stanislavski Proud

Now that we've got our story locked down, it's time to draw up the curtain and put on a show. Our résumé, cover letter, interviews, emails, references—every deliverable that we send and every interaction that we have with this employer should articulate the same story.

This storytelling effort *must* include a portfolio of work no matter what industry we're applying to. (Chemists and analysts, this includes you!) Portfolios highlight our best work and prove that we have what it takes to handle this employer's zombie apocalypse. We can include projects, reports, testimonials, anything that will help tell our story. (Anything but not everything. Quality beats quantity here.)

And then, of course, there are the interviews. Sam Distaso says that these are "90% preparation, 10% execution":

> I put together like an 11-page doc, and it just lists out all the questions that I can foresee them asking, including "gotcha" questions asking the hardest things. For each one, I type out my response. Then I record myself reading through the doc.
>
> I take walks in the evening, playing that recording back so I can hear myself. How do I sound? How direct is my answer? How's my delivery?

14.5   Rehearse, Rehearse, Rehearse

Job hunting is a skill in its own right, and gamers level up that skill the same way they level up any other. Every application becomes a little quest. Gamers playtest their application materials and their interview responses, seek feedback, and iterate. They learn from rejections. When necessary, they seek out learning platforms with maximum return on investment: books, articles, workshops, and webinars that level up their storytelling skills.

Gamers revise and evolve, and they remember that this time around the loop won't be their last. The actions taken here in Phase 3 build long-term durable skills that will return to relevance every time we cycle the loop.

With that hack-the-grind, learn-earn-advance approach, gamers guarantee themselves job offers on the other side of every hunt.

Notes

1. Fennell, Andrew. "Resume Statistics." StandOut CV, January 2023. https://standout-cv.com/usa/resume-statistics.
2. Wells, Charlie. "Job Seeker's 500 Applications Reveal Frustration in Labor Market." Bloomberg, October 27, 2023. https://www.bloomberg.com/news/articles/2023-10-27/how-many-jobs-should-i-apply-to-candidates-aim-for-500-in-cooling-labor-market?

15

Ask, Then Negotiate

15.1 How Gamers Choose (Again)

Somehow, against all odds, you find yourself in a brick-and-mortar game shop. You're 10 years old, and you've got just enough money in your pocket to bring home one game—the game you're going to play for the next 6 to 20 months.

Your back's to the lady behind the counter. She's got pink hair and a T-shirt that says *I'm Commander Shepard, and this is my favorite store on the Citadel*. She's talking to a flannelled guy with big glasses and a Harley-Davidson beard, debating whether, in truth, it's *Mario* who's the real villain of Mushroom Kingdom. He *is* terrorizing all those poor innocent Goombas after all.

While they hash out the ethics, you look up at this huge wall of games, towering over you, and your little heart races. The pressure's on. You haven't heard of half these titles, and you need to make this decision quickly, before dad's done getting the groceries.

Single-player or multiplayer? Role-playing game, shooter, or plat-former? Will those people at the counter judge you if you buy a Mario game? Which fantasy game is better: the "best-seller," or the "game of the year"? At 10 years old, it doesn't even occur to you to wonder whether you should prioritize mechanics, or graphics, or story. It does, however, occur to you that if you pick a game that *doesn't* have a weapon on the cover, your parents might let you play it more often.

The best thing to do in this moment?

Don't make a choice.

Instead, turn around, clear your throat, and interrupt the conversation going on behind you. Pink-hair lady and big-beard guy—they're going to help you pick a way better game than you ever could've picked on your own.

15.2   Asking for Help

By now, we've finished hacking the grind. We've gotten our story straight, sent out a bunch of résumés, been through a bunch of interviews, and, in an ideal world, we've got more than one job offer to choose from.

This won't always happen of course. Sometimes we cycle the loop, and we're grateful that one offer finally came through. We take that offer because we have to. But at other times throughout our careers, we'll reach the end of Phase 3 and find ourselves with a number of options—or with the financial flexibility to turn down an offer and keep searching.

When we have this freedom to choose, the best thing we can do is stop, about face, clear our throats, and ask around. Is this the right workplace for us?

In Chapter 2, we met Mona Mourshed, the founding CEO of a global workforce development nonprofit called Generation. In her work, Mona discusses four gaps that separate people from the work that will serve them best.

In Part I, we encountered the first gap, between known and unknown professions, which inspired us to expand our opportunity horizons. Then, in Part II, we encountered the gap between technical and durable skills. Here, in Part III, we've already addressed gap number three—it's the gap between job *interest* and job *placement*. Which just leaves gap number four.

For Mona, the fourth gap is between opportunities and *quality* opportunities. It's the gap between a place you *can* work and a place you *want* to work. Mona says that we can identify quality opportunities by asking three groups of questions.

15.2.1   Retention and Attrition

How long do people stay on this team? How often do people leave? In part, this helps us gauge what our own longevity there might look like.

It's also a quantifiable metric for determining, as Mona puts it, "whether the conditions are such that people want to stay."

15.2.2   Shared Background

Are people like us thriving on this team? We're looking for people with similar social identities, work histories, educations, or life experiences. Do people like us exist on this team, and, Mona asks, "have they progressed in the organization?"

15.2.3   Growth Opportunities

Third, Mona asks, "What types of professional development opportunities do they provide?" She clarifies that this doesn't necessarily refer to funds for continuing education. "How will they expose you to different skills?" Mona asks. "And how will that enable you to grow within the company?"

We get answers to these questions by doing the following:

• Searching for employee testimonials online
• Asking current/former employees
• Asking the hiring team once we've received an offer

We want to ask the pink-haired ladies and the big-bearded guys and all the other insider folks. Then, once we get their answers and identify the best offers, we want to do one more thing before we accept.

15.3   Negotiate

Fewer than half of all job seekers say they always negotiate on salary. Only 37% do so occasionally. Nearly one in five people never try negotiating at all. And the numbers get worse when we sort for gender or youth.[1] Only 7% of women try negotiating when accepting their very first job offer. A full 93% don't even try.[2]

This is a huge deal because salaries snowball as we work. Neglecting to negotiate that very first salary can lose us $1–1.5 million over a lifetime.[3] So even if we've been offered what Mona called a "quality opportunity," we still must, must, *must* negotiate.

And it's important to note that salary isn't the only domain where we can bargain. We can negotiate for better quality-of-life: more remote days, more vacation time. And we can also pursue monetary compensation beyond base salary: equity and bonuses that pay out once we've proven our value to the team.

When preparing to negotiate, we should first try to figure out the employer's opportunity cost. What will the employer lose if they don't get a yes from us? Do they have a strong incentive to fill the role quickly? Do they have other equally capable candidates ready to fill the role if we say no? This tells us how much leverage we have.

Next, we want to research industry standards. The internet can usually clue us into average pay among people with this job title in this geographical region. That'll help us gauge what's reasonable to request.

Then, when making our ask, we want to plan that approach carefully, ensuring that we come across as respectful, enthusiastic, and grateful for the opportunity to work with this team. We're not trying to *beat* the employer at the negotiating table, we just want fair compensation. It's good to work with both HR and the hiring manager in these negotiations. And we must always, *always*, get the final details in writing before moving forward.

Note that this game has a lot of replayability. We can revisit terms with our employer later—often annually. And, of course, we'll field new offers many more times in our careers, every time we cycle the loop. Hopefully, we can set a new high score every time.

Notes

1. "Most People Don't Negotiate Due to Fear & Lack of Skills." Salary.com, January 18, 2012. https://www.salary.com/chronicles/most-people-don-t-negotiate-due-to-fear-lack-of-skills/.
2. Castrillon, Caroline. "How to Negotiate a Raise in an Uncertain Economy." Corporate Escape Artist. Accessed September 18, 2024. https://corporate escapeartist.com/how-to-negotiate-a-raise-in-an-uncertain-economy/.
3. Ludden, Jennifer. "Ask for a Raise? Most Women Hesitate." NPR, February 8, 2011. https://www.npr.org/2011/02/14/133599768/ask-for-a-raise-most-women-hesitate.

16

Community Loop: Sponsors

16.1 The Referral Button

I've intimated many times throughout Part III that our community will play a crucial role in job hunting. Which is to say that the most powerful way to hack the grind—accelerating, elevating, and occasionally even bypassing the work of job hunting—will be to connect with other players.

This is an idea that brings us back to the Community Loop—the relationship building cycle that spins in parallel with the Core Career Loop. Phase 1 of the Community Loop brought us mentors, Phase 2 brought us coaches, and now Phase 3 brings us sponsors (see Figure 16.1).

Sponsors are people who advocate for us, using their own communities and influence to open doors. They might make introductions, recommend us for promotions, or sing our praises to decision-makers. And, although I don't want to detract from the incredible contributions that other community members make, these sponsors are very possibly the most important contributors to our career-looping journeys.

Back in 2018, Nitzan Pelman was LinkedIn's "Social Capital Entrepreneur in Residence." She worked with the team that added one very small, very important feature to the platform: a referral button. "It turned out that the vast majority of job seekers get their jobs through referrals," she says.

Figure 16.1 Core Career Loop

We met Nitzan in Chapter 6. She's the CEO and founder of Climb Hire, an organization devoted to giving job seekers the upper hand in their careers. Community building is central to her organization's approach, and she says that this focus sometimes throws people off:

> Sometimes, my people just like the skills part. That's the part that they feel comfortable with. Like, "Okay, I'll just keep doing certifications. I'll just keep learning more." But it's also about finding the person who can link you to that job. If you don't put yourself out there, it won't matter how many certifications you got. It's not a meritocracy out there.

Here in Phase 3 of the loop, the big question isn't whether we're qualified; it's whether we're connected. Skills might be vital for on-the-job success, but they're not the most powerful determinant of job-hunting success. Relationships are.

Fortunately, these don't have to be *close* relationships.

16.2   Weak Ties (Again)

Your kickball buddy's roommate. The cheese guy you sometimes see at that one farmers market. That sniper lady who occasionally drops into your server to play a match or two. In the lingo of career looping, we call these vague acquaintances *weak ties*, and they're our best bets for scoring great job offers.

This might seem counterintuitive: we'd expect our closest friends and family to be the people who help us most. But our closest connections know pretty much all the same people we know. The weaker the connection, the more likely it is that they run in other circles, where they can connect us to surprising opportunities.

"If you have a lot of weak ties," Nitzan says, "then you can unlock a lot more economic opportunity and mobility."

LinkedIn confirmed this through a five-year study of more than 20 million users. LinkedIn tracked users as they made 2 billion new connections, submitted more than 70 million applications, and landed 600,000 new jobs. Studying all that data, researchers found a clear pattern: weaker ties got people more jobs. And, conversely, "the stronger the . . . ties were, the less likely they were to lead to a job."[1]

We meet these weak ties in many of the same places we've already explored throughout this book: industry conferences, social media sites, and online forums. Community gathering places are weak-tie hotspots, too: recreational sports leagues, religious groups, volunteer groups, that sort of thing. And these weak ties don't have to be more senior than us in order to help. Peers and elders alike can help by doing the following:

- Notice a job opportunity that we'd be a fit for.
- Sponsor us by recommending us for jobs.
- Make introductions to other peers and sponsors.

But, more than anything else, I recommend that we look for weak-tie sponsors in informational interviews.

16.3   Informational Interviews

Informational interviews are conversations that we have with experts so that we can learn more about what they do. And I'm using *expert* here lightly: we wouldn't usually consider college interns experts, but if we want to hear about the dark side of working on a particular team, then that team's intern might have the most insight.

Of course, we're also interested in more traditional experts—people who've been doing the thing for many years. These higher status, more experienced folks can help us better understand a profession, company, or job—both so that we can evaluate the fit and so that we can piece together our application story. These experts are also more likely to be able to sponsor us in meaningful ways.

This is the open secret about informational interviews. They are fast tracks to job opportunities. How many résumés win a job offer? One out of every 200. How many informational interviews win a job offer? One in 12.[2]

In Chapter 14, we saw how much Sam Distaso relied on informational interviews to land jobs at major VR studios and, later, at Unity. Once Sam set his sights on a company, he set up 25–30 informationals with current and former employees, asking each of them to email HR about him. (Sam's actual goal was to get 10–15 referrals. He figures that "maybe half the people you talk to will actually follow up.")

Where does he find all these people? Social media sites, friends of friends, company directories, and conferences, he says. "Then I would just offer to meet people anywhere. Coffee meetings, zoom calls, anywhere."

Through that process, Sam transformed himself from an accountant into a tech leader. That's a pretty big pivot. Which goes to show that these informationals really do make a difference.

16.4   Getting Informational

Prep is key for nailing these informational interviews. Prep improves the likelihood that we'll get useful information; it makes the person we're talking to feel that their time is being used well; it makes us look like we're on top of things; and, bottom line, it increases the likelihood that we'll convert this stranger into a sponsor.

If we ask good questions and give good answers, we dramatically improve the likelihood that our new weak tie will go out on a limb for us, recommending us for a job, talking us up to important decision-makers, or introducing us to valuable new connections.

The kinds of questions we ask will depend on context. If we're aiming to land a job at this person's company, then we'll want to use our conversation to research the "Job Story Outline" from Chapter 14:

Theme. What are this company's mission and values?

Circumstances. What are the latest happenings inside the company? Are changes in the market sending the company in new directions?

Characters. Who are the key players on this team? Who are the
key clients?

Conflict. What's this team's biggest challenge right now?

Resolution. What information and skills would a new hire need to
solve that challenge? What should they watch out for?

Alternatively, if we're still figuring out where to apply or what sorts
of jobs to go for, then this is an opportunity to ask for help.

Note that informationals aren't just about getting sponsorship. They
can also get us Phase 1 mentorship and Phase 2 coaching, which often
turn into sponsorship down the road. We can also put aside self-
promotion for a moment and sincerely ask ourselves, What feels confus-
ing or uncertain in our job hunt right now? What do we wish we knew
more about? Examples of questions we might ask include these:

- What jobs exist in this field?
- What's the difference between two jobs with similar titles?
- What companies should we be looking at?
- What blogs should we be reading?

16.5   Getting Personal

Regardless of where we are in our search, it's always a good idea to show
interest in the person we're talking to. Most obviously, because we can
always learn something from asking about the lives and minds of others.
But showing an interest in the interview subject also happens to be
good strategy.

Sam Distaso tells us why:

> It's rare for somebody to truly take an interest in your background, and
> your experiences, and your life. Every interview is such an awesome
> opportunity to really stand out from others by showing that you really,
> really care about that individual, and about their advice. I always put
> together a lot of well-thought-out questions so they'll feel, "Okay,
> you've actually done the work."

Sam's making two points here. First, that asking people about themselves is kind, and makes people feel good, and makes them feel good

about us. Second, that asking questions—especially thoughtful, well-researched questions—shows that we're serious and devoted enough to give this conversation time and energy in advance.

But however nice these tailor-made questions might be, Niantic recruiter Lianna Johnstone assures us that there are some sure-thing questions, which will work every time:

- "What's been your experience at this company?"
- "How did you get here? What was your career trajectory?"
- "I saw you made this transition that I'm looking to make. What were some of the first steps that you took?"

16.6   Giving Good Vibes

As much as these interviews are meant to be about information, they're also often about *feel*. Toward the end of this book, we'll warn decision-makers against hiring based on how much they like a person or mesh with them, but there's no denying that this happens plenty—both in hiring decisions and in an expert's individual decision to sponsor us.

When it comes to developing rapport with strangers, Sam says it's best to start by knowing the culture we're walking into and trying to match it: "If you're gonna come into a gaming industry interview super buttoned-up, like you're sharper than Wall Street, you're gonna be out the door before you know it."

The games industry is hyper-casual. People wear graphic t-shirts to work and carry themselves accordingly. If that's the industry we're targeting, we should dress and behave to match. By contrast, if we show up to a finance interview in a t-shirt that says *It's dangerous to go alone!*, then that's not going to go well either.

So dress and act the part.

From there, Nitzan Pelman adds that we want the chat to feel conversational. In part, that involves active listening. "If I can see that you're taking notes, you're nodding your head, you're following my eyes, those are all things that make me feel good and make me want to continue talking to you," she says. She adds that good conversation also involves asking open-ended questions rather than closed-ended questions where there are only a few possible answers.

Finally, there's the true definition of a conversation: information goes both ways. We should prepare to answer questions, not just ask them. We need to be ready to talk about our own stories, just as we would in job interviews.

With all that work done, there's just one thing left to do.

16.7   Make the Ask

We met Ray Graham in Phase 1 of the Community Loop. He's a former EA, 2k, Ubisoft, and Apple engineer who directed tech for Unity, and now is the chief technology officer for his own game studio while leading engineering at a virtual reality (VR) startup. Outside of work, Ray's spent years mentoring tech-oriented high schoolers, as well as plenty of adult career loopers.

When asked how we should put the big question to a potential sponsor—*will you refer me, will you recommend me, will you connect me?*—Ray says, "Just ask." Even if it turns out they can't help you, they probably know someone who can:

> When I'm like, "Yeah, you know, I can't really help you," then they're like, "Well, do you know somebody who can? Or do you know somebody in that area that I can reach out to?" They're just being upfront and asking. That's the best way always."

Nitzan adds that we want to make as clear an ask as we can, then make it as easy as possible for them to say yes:

> If you come to me and you're like, "You seem great. What can I do? How can I be helpful?" and then I'm like, "I don't know. I need to eat. I need a job." Then you're not going to do all of the work to help me figure out what I need next. It's just too much.
>
> But if I came to you and was like, "I went on your LinkedIn, and I saw that you know these three people, and these three people might be able to refer me to the company I want to work at—can you make an intro? Here's a blurb about me to share." That's just two seconds of work for you to do. You're gonna say "No problem."
>
> We call this *the Goldilocks ask*—an ask that takes less than five minutes, where the job seeker does all the homework and the professional simply has to pass along a blurb or an intro that is already crafted by

the job seeker. That's the optimal way to leverage social capital and specifically weak ties.

It's by making requests like this that we get the most from our communities during Phase 3 of the loop. Whether we're interviewing peers or senior experts, these are the tactics that get us referrals and connections. And it's those referrals and connections that are going to get us jobs.

It'll be hardest the first time of course. And it'll get easier each time afterward. That goes both for making the ask and landing a job. Fortunately, we'll have many opportunities to practice job hunting and community building as we cycle the loop over and over and over again throughout our careers, learning, earning, and advancing each time.

Ironically, the moment we finally land a job is the beginning of the end for our first cycle. All that's left is Phase 4, which will propel us directly into our next cycle of the loop.

Notes

1. Dizikes, Peter. "The Power of Weak Ties in Gaining New Employment." *MIT News*, September 15, 2022. https://news.mit.edu/2022/weak-ties-linkedin-employment-0915.
2. Hiring Our Heroes. "How to Use an Informational Interview to Gain Valuable Information." Accessed September 19, 2024. https://www.hiringourheroes.org/stories/informational-interview-tips/.

Part IV

Job Craft

Back in the day, if you were privileged enough to have a profession, you usually got just one. You'd pick a place to work and work there till retirement. Then they'd hand you a gold watch and say "See ya at the funeral."

Today's paradigm is entirely different. We move through many professions over the course of a career, constantly respawning through the cycle of learning, earning, and advancing.

How do we keep learning skills and evolving our career after we've been hired?

17

How Gamers Learned to Reinvent

17.1 Death by Turret

A masked swordsman, a faerie dragon, an ice witch, a leviathan with murderous purpose, and you. Each of us controls a legendary hero. Our mission: to kill our enemies and destroy their base. It won't be easy, of course. Our enemies control legendary heroes, too—each with their own special abilities. And their base is defended by powerful, automated turrets. Stray past one of these turrets alone, and you'll die in seconds.

We're playing *Dota 2*, and we'd be lucky to survive. The Valve Corporation launched this game back in 2011 with a historic, blowout eSporting event. Valve invited 16 teams to play the brand-new game, competing for a $1.6 million prize pool—a sum unheard of at the time, and one that would forever change the landscape of professional gaming.

The final matchup of the competition pitted the teams Na'Vi and EHOME against one another. By the end of the first round, team Na'Vi's prospects looked bleak. "We were maybe a little bit demoralized," says one player. "We were missing something."[1]

In a desperate effort to shake things up, the Na'Vi squad tapped one of their teammates, Dendi, to play a hero he'd never tried before—one whose moves he didn't know. Scrawny, with a shaggy, overgrown bowl cut, Dendi looked like he'd just stepped out of the original *Tron*, and he played like it, too. Which is to say, he played like a natural.

The gambit worked, and, in a shocking upset, Na'Vi took the title, 3-1.

But that wasn't the end of their story. Two years later, Dendi and his team came back to the international competition. This time, when the team fell behind, they knew what to do: throw a curve ball.

After a long match, on the verge of defeat, instead of going back to basics, team Na'Vi decided to experiment. Hardcore players had known for some time that *Dota 2* had a quirk in its design. Arguably a *bug*. Team Na'Vi decided to toy with that bug in real time.[2]

Here's how it worked. One hero had the ability to hook an enemy and reel that enemy toward them. Another hero could teleport team-mates back to their home base, where that teammate would be defended by automated turrets. Combining those moves with pinpoint accuracy, Dendi and his teammates could hook opponents and teleport them across the entire battlefield. The opponent would land in Na'Vi's home base, where an automated turret would kill that opponent instantly.

Exploiting this bug, team Na'Vi picked off their enemies one-by-one and turned the match around. Their victory didn't come cleanly. In fact, it's still controversial to this day. But team Na'Vi had done what many contemporary players do. They creatively repurposed their heroes' abilities—discovering a ploy that the game's developers never meant to make possible.

Game theorists call this *emergent play*.

Career loopers call it *job crafting*.

17.2   The Job Crafter

Veronica Brown doesn't really do her job. Which makes this conversation awkward. Because I'm Veronica's boss's boss, and I've just asked Veronica what she does here at Unity.

In Veronica's defense, she's been getting into this kind of trouble since the late 1980s.

Back at the beginning of her career, Veronica worked at a bookstore, and she noticed a problem. "Before the internet, we'd send out these catalogs of books we were looking for," she explains. "We'd send them to other bookstores, and then bookstores would snail-mail back little notes, saying, *I've got this in fine condition for $2.*"

Compiling and mailing these catalogs took ages, so Veronica got to work on eliminating that part of her job: "I programmed a computer to make the list of books we wanted and get that out in the mail for us."

Later, during the early 2000s, Veronica worked for a software marketing department that was under fire. "The sales team was fed up with us, and we really needed to show our value," she remembers.

This was a bad situation, not just for Veronica, but for her whole team. When a marketing team can't prove that they're earning money for their company, something usually has to change. Knowing this, Veronica put her actual job aside and got to work proving that her department had value.

> We had this huge collection of marketing materials. The sales team didn't know it existed, and they didn't know how to find it on the hard drive. So I made a web page to organize that database. Suddenly sales had this web page that listed like 150 different resources that they could use, and their attitude turned around.

Both at the bookstore and on the marketing team, Veronica stepped away from her official job responsibilities to do something entirely different, driven simply by her own sense of curiosity and an intuition about the team's needs. In time, we'll learn to call this *job crafting*.

When she was 50 years old, Veronica abandoned her profession altogether. She went back to school. She had bumped her head on her profession's salary ceiling, and her interests had shifted. She wanted a bigger challenge, more earning potential, and the power to make a bigger impact. She became an instructional designer.

When she reentered the workforce after school, she took a contract to design one-off trainings for Unity clients. But, once again, at every turn, Veronica broke the rules. She abandoned her job for other tasks. Thanks to this strategy, she's now a full-time senior instructional designer here at Unity. And these days, she's doing things that aren't her job yet again, becoming a de facto information architect for our team.

Despite the fact that Veronica's been defying authority like this for decades, it still makes her a bit uncomfortable. And it's especially uncomfortable to admit that she's breaking the rules right *now* because I'm recording this interview with her, and I'm a Unity VP. Ostensibly, it's my rules she's breaking.

"It's a little weird talking to you about this, given the level you're at in the company," she tells me. "Because when we pursue skills that aren't in our job descriptions, it's kind of subversive."

Veronica points out that anytime you try building a new skill at work or try doing something that isn't really your job—any time you job craft—you're taking time away from other things you could be doing. Things that *are* your job. "I could work on these essential tutorials this afternoon," she says, referring to her official responsibilities. "Or I can figure out how to build an information architecture. Which am I gonna do?"

The trick, I think, is to break out of this binary. The way I see it, Veronica's job is to identify business problems and solve them. As long as the problems she's working on are both important and timely, then whatever those problems are and however she's solving them, she's doing her job—even if she is working outside the confines of her job description.

But maybe I've been spending too much time around gamers.

See, Veronica missed the opportunity to pick up games as a kid. "When I was younger," she says, "there was no such thing as a gamer." And I think that partially explains her discomfort with all this. As Team Na'Vi demonstrated, gamers don't mind being subversive. Gamers love to be subversive. They break the rules and rewrite the rules all the time. They've been doing it since the birth of video games.

17.3   The Birth of Video Games

We encountered one of history's first video games in Chapter 6. Released in 1962 and played on cathode-ray tube monitors, *Spacewar!* was built by researchers in a lab at MIT. They'd just gotten their hands on the first-ever minicomputer and wanted to show what it could do. So they built a game about fighter jets in space.

This was a dark, naive, primordial era when it hadn't yet occurred to people that they could sue each other over video games. So when the researchers who worked in that lab left MIT, they made copies of the game and brought it with them. No problem. At new labs, they shared the game and messed with its source code.

Researchers at other labs got to work reinventing the game. They added gravity. They added a chaotic new feature called *hyperspace*, which teleported your ship to a random part of the map at a moment's notice. One variant called *Minnesota hyperspace* made your ship invisible and gave you explosive space mines to plant. Another variant gave you a first-person pilot's perspective of the action.[3]

This was the dawn of game modification—what gamers now call *modding*. Two decades later, in 1981, the game *Castle Wolfenstein* acciden-tally took modding to the next level. In *Wolfenstein*, you played as an allied prisoner of war, escaping captivity, gunning down Nazis, and steal-ing their secret plans. The game's original purpose had been to introduce a new breed of gaming thrills: stealth mechanics. And *Wolfenstein* suc-ceeded there, laying the groundwork for future sneak-and-kill games like *Splinter Cell*, *Metal Gear Solid*, *Hitman*, *Assassin's Creed*, and *Deus Ex*.

But *Wolfenstein* inadvertently laid the groundwork for something else too: the popularization of modding. After the game took off, a pair of computer wizzes cracked open the game, went under its hood, and came out with their own mod. It looked just like that WWII stealth game that we'd come to know and love, but all the Nazis had been trans-formed into little blue Smurfs. The mod was called *Castle Smurfenstein*, and it set a flurry of change into motion.

17.4   Emergence

At the heart of this flurry was an alternative type of play called *emergence*. Before emergence took off, everyone focused on just one type of play: *designed play*. This is the most obvious mode of gaming, where players do what the game's creators tell them to do. They move pawns the way that pawns move. They move checkers the way that checkers move. And, in a game about shooting Nazis, they shoot Nazis who look like Nazis—not Nazis who look like little blue Smurfs.

Those little blue Smurfs opened the door to *emergent play*, a subver-sive mode of gaming where players use the game's designed trappings to do new stuff—stuff that surprises even the game's creators. Understanding this emergence will help us understand how gamers became such natural job crafters, so I want to take a moment to drill down into the specifics.

17.5   Three Kind of Emergence

At the most essential level, there's *emergent systemic interaction*. That's a fancy way of saying that players take the built-in tools of the game and smash them together in unintended ways.

We might, for example, bypass a sword fight with our enemies by burning them to death in a forest fire of our own making. (Aren't *Zelda* games sweet?) If we do this, we're still playing toward the game's intended objective—we're still trying to kill our enemies—but we've found a surprising solution that the game's creators might not have intentionally designed for.

Then there's what the games philosopher Bernard Suits calls *trifling*.[4] Here players take the tools of the game and use them to play toward a new objective. We'll call this *metagaming* because players are building an alternative game on top of the original game (and because *trifling* sounds a little too *come-butler-hold-my-cognac*).

To understand metagaming, imagine that you're playing *Halo 2*, a first-person shooter. Every location in the game has a bunch of space-age military vehicles lying around, just begging to be driven. If you wanted to, you and your friend could drop all your weapons, hop in these vehicles, and race them for hours. Turning *Halo 2* into a racing game expressly rejects the game's original objective—and, in case you're wondering, it's really great fun.

Finally, there's *modding*. This is where we get under the hood and fundamentally transform the game's content at the level of its source code. Like when we turn Nazis into Smurfs.

17.6   A Post-Smurf World

The moment it showed up on the scene, emergence thrilled players and developers alike. It took gaming's signature trait—interactivity—and pushed it as far as it could go.

The developer id Software bought the rights to *Wolfenstein* and started making mod-friendly games of their own. In 1993, id Software released *Doom* with a new file structure, designed to encourage easy modding. Then, for their 1996 game *Quake*, id laid bare the game's entire source code and introduced a unique coding language, QuakeC, to simplify player modding. In fact, they went even further than that: they built a whole new game engine—the Quake Engine—giving *Quake* a uniquely mod-friendly software framework.

By the time 2002 rolled around, many developers had picked up id's scent and begun shipping games with other kinds of modding tools on board. One of these games was related to an old friend of ours: *World of*

Warcraft, the massively multiplayer online role-playing game that took inspiration from *Ultima Online* and pulled out all the stops to keep macros, scripts, and bots at bay.

Its predecessor, *Warcraft III*, shipped with an onboard map editor, which empowered players to create their own battle scenarios. One modder took that feature further than anyone ever anticipated.

He went by the handle "Eul" and he used the *Warcraft III* map editor to create not just a new battle scenario, but an entirely new *kind* of battle. This battle took inspiration from a previous mod where, rather than control a whole army, each player would control a single hero. Now, in Eul's version, 10 of these heroes would duel each other, drawing on a wide variety of extraordinary abilities, with the ultimate objective of destroying each other's "ancients"—the mystic structures at the center of their home bases.

This was a whole new game created using the tools of an existing game. A *metagame* and a *mod* rolled into one. Eul called it *Defense of the Ancients*, *DotA* for short.

17.7   Dota 2

Actually, wait. Let's rewind for a sec back to 1996. id Software had secured the rights to *Castle Wolfenstein* and begun making their own moddable games. Their latest game was *Quake*, which they built using the especially moddable Quake Engine.

About this same time, two ex-Microsoft guys started a game studio of their own. They called it *Valve*. The duo paid id Software a licensing fee so that they could use the Quake Engine to create their first game, which they'd develop with modders in mind. They called this game *Half-Life*, and it reinvented the first-person shooter genre. As one game reviewer puts it, "When you look at the history of first-person shooters, it all breaks down pretty cleanly into pre-Half-Life and post-Half-Life eras."[5]

Like *Castle Wolfenstein* before it, we might bisect *Half-Life's* impact into two categories: designed impact and emergent impact. On the designed front, *Half-Life* brought new depths of narrative design to the shooter genre, revealing the potential of story-driven action games. But, arguably, the game's emergent impact was greater. *Half-Life* birthed a mod that would ultimately grow to outpace its predecessor by leaps and bounds.

In 1999, two *Half-Life* players created a little mod called *Counter-Strike*. Valve hired those modders to turn *Counter-Strike* into a standalone game, and, by the time *Warcraft III* landed in 2002, *Counter-Strike* had become the most popular online game in the world.[6] Today, it's worth billions of dollars.[7]

With a runaway hit on their hands, Valve went shopping for more mods. The natural place to start: *Warcraft III*. By this time, *DotA* had spawned a bunch of lookalike mods, each of which iterated on the original in some new way. One mod was more popular than all the others, and, in 2009, Valve hired its lead developer to create their next hit game. Two years later, Valve debuted *Dota 2* at an eSports event with a $1.6 million prize pool.

17.8   Lifelong Metagamers

Team Na'Vi exploited a flaw in *Dota 2* to upend Valve's own tournament. Capitalizing on a design loophole, the team combined multiple heroes' abilities in order to pull their enemies across the map and knock them out with a single blow.

With some of the world's most talented gamers gathered and huge bundles of cash on the line, this was emergent play at the highest level. Seventy years after *Spacewar!*, we watched an emergent systemic interaction happening inside a mod of a mod of a metagame. And to top it all off, Na'Vi pulled this stunt right under the developer's nose—and on their dime, too.

Veronica Brown would call this *subversive*.

Gamers? They just call it *Tuesday*.

Gamers don't beat a game and sit still. They make games their own, creating new challenges for themselves, while inventing new ways to level up and win. They create games within games, racing to beat the game in record time, to beat it with a single life, to beat it with their hands tied behind their backs. If they can't keep leveling up or metagaming, they look for mods. And if they can't find a path to fun through mods, they quit and find a new game altogether.

In previous generations, the bosses made all the rules. They determined your job description and your path to promotion. And when you'd gotten as far as you could go, you stayed put. It was called the *Peter*

Principle: people climbed the corporate ladder until they reached a rung they couldn't master. Then they stayed there.

But in the contemporary economy, every job is an exercise in emergent play. To grow a successful, rewarding, meaningful career, we make our jobs our own. We find our own ways to win. We mod our own job descriptions. And when we find systems resistant to change, we quit and move onto the next workplace.

This is job crafting, and it's the essence of Phase 4.

By now, we've chosen a professional path, we've leveled up, and we've accepted a job offer. It's through job crafting that the cycle of learning, earning, and advancing begins again.

In Phase 4, we notice changes happening in the world, in our company, and in ourselves. We respond by choosing new professional paths, leveling up new skills, and growing on the job. Ultimately, our efforts in job crafting propel us forward into the next cycle of our career.

In the chapters ahead, we'll explore precisely how this process works. Chapter 18 will unpack what Phase 4 is all about and why it's so important. Then, Chapter 19 will roll out more detailed guidance for how we go about job crafting. And, finally, Chapter 20 will return us to the Community Loop, revealing the role of great bosses in our job crafting efforts.

Although the details might feel fresh, the underlying principles of job crafting will feel intimately familiar to gamers. They've been behaving subversively since the 1960s. And as new games foster new forms of emergent play, and as tools like the Unity Engine expand opportunities for modding, gamers are only going to keep getting better at this.

Notes

1. Dota, Wraith. "Navi – The First Champion of the International Dota 2 Championship," November 28, 2017. https://www.youtube.com/watch?v=LcHmIF1Hm2E.
2. techies_goes_boom. "Dota 2 Fountain Hook – Bug or Feature?" Reddit, 2022. https://www.reddit.com/r/HobbyDrama/comments/uav4hw/video_games_esports_dota_2_fountain_hook_bug_or/.
3. Brand, Stewart. "SPACEWAR: Fanatic Life and Symbolic Death Among the Computer Bums." *Rolling Stone*, December 7, 1972. https://www.wheels.org/spacewar/stone/rolling_stone.html.

4. Suits, Bernard. *The Grasshopper: Games, Life and Utopia* (Broadview Press, 2005), 58.

5. "Top 100 First-Person Shooters: #1 Half-Life," IGN, accessed September 19, 2024. https://web.archive.org/web/20140228203738/http://www.ign .com/top/shooters/1.

6. Yuen, Ryan. "The Rise of Steam: A Case Study on the Most Dominant Force in Gaming," November 11, 2021. https://www.linkedin.com/pulse/ rise-steam-case-study-most-dominant-force-gaming-ryan-yuen/.

7. "Valve's Revenue from CS:GO Reached $6.7 Billion — A Steam Record." Bo3, accessed September 19, 2024. https://bo3.gg/articles/valves-revenue- from-csgo-reached-67billion-a-steam-record.

18

Why Gamers Job Craft

18.1 Growing on the Job

In previous generations, the most important question we could ask ourselves at work was "Am I doing my job?" Namely, am I hitting my targets? Is my boss happy? Have I done what I'm supposed to do?

Those things still matter of course, but, in the new economy, growth matters, too. What are we learning? How are we growing? These are the questions we should ask today, and we should ask them *at work*.

That *at work* bit is new, too. In previous generations, learning happened first, then earning happened. Each activity was restricted to its own domain and to its own era. You learned in school while you were young, then you earned in the office as an adult.

But like emergence-oriented gamers who transform the game while they play it, today's career loopers learn on the job, transforming what they do while they do it. They level up from within their current roles. Sometimes, they even mod those roles, giving themselves new job descriptions on the fly. And if they get too much systemic pushback, today's career loopers move on to new organizations and new roles that allow for more growth.

This is the essence of what we do in Phase 4 of the Core Career Loop: we job craft.

18.2   What Is Job Crafting?

The researchers who first coined the term *job crafting* used it to describe a type of on-the-job evolution, in which people found ways to make their work feel more meaningful—first by changing their mindsets and then by changing their job descriptions to match.

Take hospital cleaners for example. Interviewing these folks, the original job crafting researchers found that a significant portion of them saw their work as difficult and thankless. But the researchers also met many cleaners who felt differently. This second group didn't view themselves as cleaning staff at all. Instead, they saw themselves as vital members of patients' care teams.

That care team mindset motivated some hospital cleaners to behave differently from others. They'd give themselves additional responsibilities, which, in turn, would boost the meaningfulness of their work. For example, one cleaner took on the responsibility to regularly rearrange the artwork on comatose patients' walls, seeking to infuse these patients' lives with more variety. These job crafters altered their own job descriptions in order to bring more meaning into their work.[1]

When I talk about job crafting, I'm talking about that shift toward deeper meaningfulness, too, but I'm also broadening the definition.

In Part I we talked about two types of change that affect our careers: external and internal change. External change happens out in the world, as technologies evolve, markets shift, professions transform, and our employers face new challenges. Internal change happens within us, as our values shift. What we love, what we can be good at, the impact we want to make, the income we aspire to earn—these things evolve over time.

To me, job crafting is the process by which we respond to all that change from within our current roles. That can include transforming our jobs to suit our changing senses of mission and meaning—as in the original sense of job crafting—but it can also mean transforming our jobs in response to new technologies or new economic realities.

As job crafters, we're always scanning for internal and external changes. We're always interrogating those changes, and reevaluating our professional paths in response. Then, when we discover new gravitational pull, we level up toward it, and we pursue whatever opportunities it draws us toward.

This should all sound familiar. Phase 4 will echo all of the loop phases that came before. That's because, although job crafting is a Core

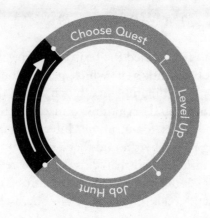

Figure 18.1 Core Loop with Arrow

Career Loop phase of its own, it's also a kind of arrow, pointing us back toward the beginning of the loop.

I've said again and again throughout this book that the Core Career Loop is a cycle, and that we'll circle it many times throughout our careers (see Figure 18.1). Job crafting is the means by which we begin new cycles. And it's usually motivated by one of three things.

18.3   Motivation 1: Thriving Through Chaos

Anuja Dharkar is Unity's global head of education. She and I work closely together to train future Unity creators, preparing them both for jobs already out there and for jobs that have yet to emerge.

"The world around us is always shifting," she says. "If we stay in a mindset that a job's just a job, then that world is going to shift, and we're not going to be in that job anymore." She explains that this is why contemporary career loopers need to care deeply about their work, moving past the bare bones of their role descriptions to craft new skills and new responsibilities on the job.

She says that we must always be asking, "How do you change or re-represent what you're doing so that you stay in the world?" Her aim is to keep us evolving as the world evolves around us.

Veronica Brown, the subversive job crafter whom we met in Chapter 17, articulates the same idea from another perspective. Even though her career has propelled her from technical writer to instructional designer to information architect—all apparently niche professions—she doesn't think of herself as a specialist. The way she sees it, she's always job crafted to become an even broader generalist. And she's done it for precisely the same reason that Anuja's describing. She elaborates:

> You have to be a generalist.
>
> You know, when I was in college in the eighties, none of the jobs that I've had really existed. Just the idea that we would have computers in our dorm rooms, in our homes, was just like, *Oh please, you really think that's gonna happen?*
>
> There was no way for me to prepare for my career, except to be a generalist.
>
> Don't think that you're going to follow a course of study, and then do that thing forever. That hasn't existed since the seventies.
>
> I think it's fair to say that there will still be companies making video games in 5 and 10 years. But what those jobs look like and how they're performed and who performs them, and whether it's even humans, that's all up for grabs.
>
> There is no way to prepare for your entire career. You've got to develop a variety of skills and then look for ways to add value along the way as things change.

The contemporary economy breeds constant innovation, disruption, and fluctuation. Thriving in this context requires that we not merely *check the boxes* at work, but that we evolve on the job, always moving intentionally toward growth and expansion.

18.4   Motivation 2: Getting Past the Gatekeepers

In Part I, we talked about the importance of following our gravitational pull. We inquired about the world around us and the world within us. Then we used our Professional Pathfinder to search for professions where values and opportunities align. We studied how our gravitational pull shifts throughout our lives, leading us through dynamic, surprising careers.

One of the things that makes this gravity-based system tricky—and that makes the Professional Pathfinder system tricky—is that neither quite accounts for the question of *what's within reach*. We stay true to our ambitions. We pursue the alignment of passions, skills, mission, and sustainability. And through our job hunt, we discover which opportunities are truly accessible to us.

But what happens when we feel gravity pulling us toward a role that gatekeepers won't open up to us? We aspire to become chief technology officers, executive producers, creative directors, vice presidents of human resources—or we simply want to pivot toward a new field—and employers don't think we're up to those jobs. In some cases, it's bias that drives their decisions. In others, it's the sincere belief that we won't thrive in those roles.

This isn't always fair—in fact, it very often isn't. But if we want to do something about it, job crafting becomes one of our most powerful tools for pushing back. It propels us back through the Core Career Loop—first to Phase 2, where we level up toward our target role, and then to Phase 3, where we evolve our job stories.

Job crafting becomes the process by which we (1) build new skills and (2) build the case that we've already done the job we're targeting. Instead of taking time off from work to achieve these things, we learn and advance on the job.

"Come up with the job that you want to be doing, and figure out what you need in order to get there," Anuja says. "It could be as light as recasting what you do, or as heavy as identifying that you actually don't have skills *A*, *B*, and *C*, and so you need to develop those in order to move into this other field."

Ultimately, job crafting in this way has the power to open previously locked doors.

18.5   Motivation 3: Searching Our Hearts

Everything we just said assumes that we already know what we want to do. We feel the gravitational pull and see where it's leading us. But often gravitational pull can be hard to find—especially when we've been emotionally disconnected from our work for a long time, or when we're only just launching our careers.

This was the case for Stacey Haffner, whom we met in Chapter 7. She'd dropped out of high school and bypassed college to enter the workforce directly. "I didn't know what I wanted to be," she says. "I really had no clue. So I just tried things that sounded interesting." She went from receptionist to human resources (HR) rep to analyst to project manager, and each time she learned more about what she hated and what she loved.

Notably, Stacey didn't just apply to a new job every time she got sick of one. Instead, she job crafted—modding her role while she worked. As a receptionist, she helped do HR work for team members who called in sick. That wasn't her job, but it did point her to her next career move.

Then, when she moved into HR, she devoted extra time to analytics. As an analyst, she took on project management duties. Each of those maneuvers moved her closer to her gravitational pull, until, eventually, she found it.

Because job crafting is the subversive process by which we do stuff that isn't really our job, it opens the door to doing lots of other jobs instead—jobs we need to explore in order to find our gravitational pull.

18.6   The Four Types of Job Crafting

So job crafting helps us thrive in an ever-changing world, it helps us kick down locked doors that block our professional paths, and it helps us chase down gravitational pull. Those are our three *whys*.

In Chapter 19, we'll talk through the *how*, working out the process by which we put all this theory into practice. But before we move on, I want to clarify the *what* a bit more. What exactly is job crafting?

We've already defined it broadly as the process by which we respond to internal and external changes from within our current roles. But there's a bit more to it than that: I think of job crafting in terms of four subtypes. And once we understand those four subtypes, I think it'll help clarify what we're after here. I'll frame these in terms of four emergent play styles.

18.6.1   Subtype 1: Emergent Systemic Interactions

In Chapter 17, we talked about *Castle Wolfenstein*, the shooter game that later got modded into *Castle Smurfenstein*. We observed that *Wolfenstein* was largely responsible for introducing stealth mechanics to the world, laying the groundwork for generations of covert mission games to come.

Among the most popular such games would be the dystopian shooter, *Deus Ex*. *Deus Ex* transports players to a cyberpunk future where they advance the cause of peace through fighting, hacking, and stealthy breaking-and-entering.

When discussing the role of emergent play in *Deus Ex*, creator Harvey Smith explains:

> Some guy in *Deus Ex* figured out that you could take a proximity mine and put it on the wall and hop up on it. It had a little lip of physics. Then you could place another one and hop up on it, then turn around, crouch, grab the first mine, and put it up higher. . . . [Using this method,] he'd climb the side of tall buildings that we never intended anyone to be on top of. It must've taken hours. But then he would take screenshots from places he wasn't supposed to be.[2]

Reflecting back on this ingenious mine climber, Smith says, "We were delighted at the flexibility of the system, of the ingenuity of the players and of the way that the game could, in some ways, be played according to the player's desires, not the designers'."[3]

This was an emergent systemic interaction at work. This mine climber, and the other players who later followed his lead, smashed together different game systems (in this case, the *climbing* system and the *proximity mine* system) to pursue the game's central objective in unexpected ways. They could still play the game of fighting, hacking, and breaking-and-entering, but they would play that game by their own rules.

Systemic interactions like these happen at work, too, and they're our first subtype of job crafting. In this mode of job crafting, we're still doing the job we were hired to do, but we're inventing new ways of doing it. This is what Veronica Brown did when she stopped creating bookstore catalogs herself and programmed a computer to create them for her instead.

If we want to level up within our existing role, or advance to a more senior position, then this might be the best type of job crafting for us. It'll prepare us to thrive in the chaos and get past the gatekeepers.

18.6.2   Subtype 2: Metagames

When Harvey Smith tells that mine climbing story, he adds that the first guy who did it "would just climb out of the world that way. . . ." This guy would stack mine on top of mine for hours and hours until, eventually, he broke past the in-game stratosphere. "It [became] a metagame, at some level," Smith says.[4]

What he means is that the player created a new game for himself using the trappings of *Deus Ex's* design. This guy was still using *Deus Ex* elements: mines, climbing, and its 3D simulated world. But instead of using those elements to play the creators' *Can-You-Beat-the-Villains* game, this guy used those elements to play a game of his own—the *How-High-Can-You-Climb* game.

Job crafters do this too when they continue operating within the boundaries of their existing jobs while pursuing objectives that nobody assigned to them. Like when Veronica continued serving her marketing team but paused her regular duties, building a collection of web-based assets instead.

She still operated within the designed boundaries of her marketing department, but instead of playing the game *Attract-New-Users-to-Our-Platform*, she decided to play the game *Organize-Our-Assets-and-Persuade-the-CEO-Not-to-Fire-Us*.

This too can be a great way to build new skills for weathering a changing world, while also growing on the job and demonstrating our potential to gatekeepers.

18.6.3   Subtype 3: Mods

The so-called nameless mod is among history's greatest mods. It completely repurposes *Deus Ex*, retaining the original game's core systems while redirecting them toward a new setting and a new story with enough new mechanics to require a whole new tutorial. In other words, it's almost an entirely new game. And it points to our third mode of job crafting: modding.

When we mod our jobs, we don't work within the established system to optimize our work or expand our purview. Instead, we take on new jobs altogether. Think of Stacey Haffner, doing HR work even though she was a receptionist. Or Veronica, who entered Unity as an instructional designer, but then started working on information architecture without anybody asking her to.

When we mod, we don't just tweak our job descriptions. We fundamentally alter them at the source code level. We effectively create entirely new jobs for ourselves. This sort of job crafting can help us achieve all three of Phase 4's whys, preparing us to thrive in the chaos of change, giving us access to previously inaccessible jobs, and helping us test-drive new professional paths as we feel around for gravitational pull.

18.6.4   Subtype 4: New Games

Finally, there's the nuclear option. If gamers can't carve out new paths toward fun through emergent interactions, metagames, or mods, they quit the game they're playing and start a new one. There's some serious wisdom there. Sometimes the best way to move forward is to move out. Quit this job and pursue a new one.

The difference between this mode of job crafting and simply "quitting a job" is that, when we quit as job crafters, our resignation doesn't pause our progress. Instead, as job crafters, quitting becomes a propulsive act, launching us toward new growth and forward advancement.

If a job crafter quits, they quit to evolve.

18.7   When to Job Craft

So how do we know whether it's time to start job crafting? For an answer, I looked to Ellen Flaherty, the director of learning at Unity. Ellen's own job crafting journey has led her on a wild ride from daycare centers to domestic violence counseling centers to law offices to her own instructional design consultancy practice, and even to a national broadcasting station.

As much as job crafting means to her, Ellen emphasizes that career looping isn't always going to be the top priority in every person's life. When her kids were young, it made sense for her to do less at work, getting her official job done and nothing more. But before those days, job crafting mattered a great deal to her. And now that her kids are older, she's back at it.

"You've got to always be gut-checking yourself," she explains. "Am I or aren't I coasting? If I am, *why*? Is it conscious? Is it not conscious?" If coasting's a conscious choice—and the right one for this moment in our lives—great. But if the coasting's unconscious, or if there's not a good reason for it, that's a cue to pause and ask ourselves what we want from our lives and from our careers.

If professional growth matters to us, then it might be time to start crafting. Because innovation, disruption, and fluctuation occur so quickly, anyone who's looking for career growth and security ought to job craft most of the time. But here are a few particular signals to look out for:

- If we see our industry evolving and don't feel prepared to meet it, it's time to craft.

- If we feel drawn toward a particular role but can't access it yet, it's time to craft.

- If we're stagnating at work, it's time to craft.

Then, once we decide to start job crafting, we'll have to figure out how.

Notes

1. My Say. "'Job Crafting': The Great Opportunity in the Job You Already Have." *Forbes*, October 25, 2013. https://www.forbes.com/sites/groupthink/2013/06/20/job-crafting-the-great-opportunity-in-the-job-you-already-have/?sh=7e995d4a25df; Wrzesniewski, Amy, and Jane E. Dutton. "Crafting a Job: Revisioning Employees as Active Crafters of Their Own Work." *Academy of Management Review* 26, no. 2 (2001): 190. https://positiveorgs.bus.umich.edu/wp-content/uploads/Crafting-a-Job_Revisioning-Employees.pdf.

2. Sheffield, Brandon. "The Subversion Game: An Interview with Harvey Smith." Game Developer, October 4, 2007. https://www.gamedeveloper.com/game-platforms/the-subversion-game-an-interview-with-harvey-smith.

3. Smith, Harvey. "The Future of Game Design: Moving Beyond Deus Ex and Other Dated Paradigms." witchboy.net. Accessed September 19, 2024. https://www.witchboy.net/articles/the-future-of-game-design-moving-beyond-deus-ex-and-other-dated-paradigms/.

4. Sheffield, "The Subversion Game: An Interview With Harvey Smith."

5. Wolens, Joshua. "14 Years Later, the Deus Ex Mod That's a Better Sequel Than Invisible War Gets a Massive Overhaul." PC Gamer, September 13, 2023. https://www.pcgamer.com/14-years-later-the-deus-ex-mod-thats-a-better-sequel-than-invisible-war-gets-a-massive-overhaul/.

19

How Gamers Job Craft

19.1 Don't Bring Rum to Work

Edward Kenway was a privateer—a naval soldier for hire. It was a good job. It served him well. But eventually he hit the max salary for his field, and he felt it was time for a change. So he did what any career looper would do. He reevaluated his Professional Pathfinder. He asked where he could earn a sustainable income (on the high seas), what he felt most passionately about (adventure and violence), what skills he could master (adventure and violence), and what mission drove him through life (adventure and violence). Then he followed that gravitational pull toward a new profession. He became a pirate.

Eventually, a chance encounter would throw his career for another loop. He'd end up skewering a professional assassin on the end of a rapier. He'd steal that assassin's robes and join his secret order. Next thing he knew, Edward Kenway would find himself in yet another new profession.

That's how job crafting works in *Assassin's Creed: Black Flag*. You loot the uniform off a dead serial killer and steal his identity. This was probably a great grow-on-the-job strategy back in the 1700s, when the game is set, but it won't work quite as well today. Today, job crafting requires more intention, more strategy, and an ounce or two less murder.

Broadly speaking, modern job crafting follows a three-step process:

1. We choose professional paths to pursue.
2. We choose methods for leveling up.
3. We tell new job stories.

Each of these steps corresponds, respectively, to a phase of the Core Career Loop. As we've already established, job crafting is its own loop phase, but it also behaves like an arrow, propelling us through our next cycle of the loop. So throughout our job crafting journey, we'll iterate on processes that were first established during Phases 1–3. But we'll do things differently now, because we're cycling the loop from within an existing job.

19.2   Step 1: Choosing a Professional Path

We'll launch our next cycle of the loop with Phase 1 activities, clarifying which professional path we want to pursue and what skills we'll need to get there. Everything we discussed in Part I of this book will help us here, but I want to highlight five new tactics we can use as job crafters.

19.2.1   *Tactic 1: Notice Predilections*

In Chapter 18, we met Ellen Flaherty, the director of learning at Unity. She recommends that we begin job crafting with an exercise: "Chart out how much time you spend on aspects of the job you like, versus what you don't like. What do you want to be doing, and how much time are you currently spending on that?"

What do you like about your job? What don't you like? And where is your time really going? This self-reflection brings us back to Phase 1's Professional Pathfinder—the profession selection tool that listed four values and helped us identify professions where they overlap (see Figure 19.1). When we enjoy tasks at work, it's usually because they play into one or more of three of those Professional Pathfinder values: passion, skill, and mission.

Meanwhile, the tasks we don't enjoy probably only play into value number four: sustainability. To put it plainly, we do unfun work tasks because we have to if we want to get paid.

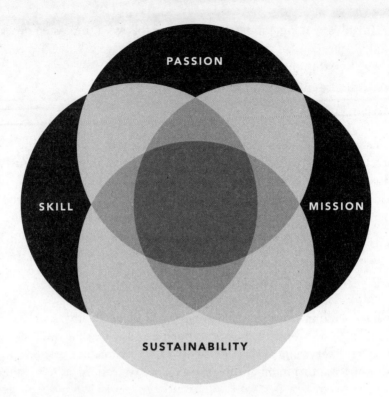

Figure 19.1 Professional Pathfinder with Highlights

Once we do as Ellen advised and chart the balance of fun-versus-unfun tasks, we might reflect on these unfun tasks and find that they come as no surprise. Perhaps they were just the bitter red pills we had to swallow in order to get the job we wanted. But there are also times when this process will reveal that formerly fun tasks have stopped appealing to us. We might find this surprising, but it's perfectly normal.

In Chapter 4, Jonathan Stull—president of the college-to-career organization (org) Handshake—told us that "what you want and value really changes throughout your lifetime and your career."

Often these changes happen because life happens. Aging, economics, politics, evolving technologies, evolving families, an evolving world—all these things can inspire shifts in our values. Think of James Stone who photographed human rights issues for charities and UN agencies until his responsibilities to family required that he pursue a safer line of work. Taking care of his family became his primary mission, so his profession had to change.

Other times, our values don't change, but our knowledge does. Think of Stacey Haffner, who was disappointed to discover that human resources (HR) reps often have to defend the company from its people rather than the other way around. Stacey's values didn't change, but her information about HR did.

Working in a role often reveals new information about our passions, skills, and mission—as well as how they do or don't align with that particular profession. The bottom line is that we can begin our job crafting journey with an evaluation: where does and doesn't our current job align with our Professional Pathfinder values. As we job craft, we'll want to move away from the misalignments and move toward the alignments, building new skills and taking on new responsibilities in the areas that we find most rewarding.

19.2.2 *Tactic 2: Source from Job Postings*

Sometimes, when we implement Tactic 1, we discover that our job doesn't actually offer many tasks that we enjoy. Other times, we might enjoy our job, but want to move toward some other role that's an even better fit. In these cases, we won't want to job craft by doubling down on existing areas of alignment. Instead, we'll want to mod our role more dramatically, taking on tasks from other kinds of jobs.

Kevin Truong is a senior program manager on Unity's social impact team. His job crafting story is a fascinating one, and I'll share it shortly. But first, I want to highlight one particular tactic Kevin uses to clarify his professional path whenever he returns to Phase 4: "I just look at job postings, doing a landscape analysis of all the professions I'm interested in," he says. "Then I study the patterns. What are the skills? What are the requirements?"

Ellen does this, too. And she explains how we can turn these job posting insights into an actionable job crafting vision. "Go look at a whole bunch of job postings, and start taking lines from jobs that you want to be doing," she says. "Then use those to create your own job posting."

Creating this fantasy job posting can help us clarify what skills we need to build and what portfolio of work we need to develop. That vision will help guide our later job crafting efforts.

19.2.3   Tactic 3: Explore the Org Chart

Ellen points out that we can also discover new professional paths by looking more closely at our own teams and companies:

> Look in your org chart. I'm in my org chart all the time. *Who's that? What are they doing? What's going on?* Reach out to folks in other departments and say, "Hey, I want to know what's going on in your department," or "Hey, I want to learn more about this. Can we talk?"

This approach can be helpful for two reasons. First, like Tactic 2, this tactic exposes us to new jobs, tasks, responsibilities, and work products. Maybe we realize that, *gosh*, this information architecture stuff sounds really fascinating and we'd love to learn more about it. Or maybe we hear about a company project that we want to help with, or a new piece of software that we want to try. Our opportunity horizons expand, and new professional paths open up.

Beyond that, meeting other folks from across the team and across the company will help deepen our understanding of the business. What are our employer's current objectives? What are their current challenges? How are people in the company responding?

Later, when we start job crafting in earnest, we'll use this intel to ensure that we're directing our job crafting efforts toward causes that matter to the company. That, in turn, will help us in two ways. It'll help us persuade managers and other leaders to support our job crafting efforts. And it'll help us use those job crafting efforts to win promotions and salary increases down the road.

19.2.4   Tactic 4: Flipping Perspectives

Back to Kevin Truong. When he began his undergrad education, Kevin intended to train for health care or engineering. To make ends meet, he took a job with a college-readiness program, where he mentored and taught hundreds of high schoolers about the college applications process.

Kevin fell in love with this work. It ended up fundamentally changing his values. He discovered new passions, new skills, and a new sense of mission. After graduating, Kevin didn't go into health care or engineering. Instead, he started his own college-readiness program for high schoolers.

When the time came for Kevin to start job crafting, it occurred to him that he could continue working on the same central project—improving learning outcomes for high schoolers—but develop that project from an entirely new perspective.

Until this time, Kevin had only ever worked for the nonprofits that implemented education programs. He'd never worked for the philanthropic funders who finance these programs. Rather than double down on what he already did, Kevin figured that he could learn tons more by exploring education from the funder's perspective.

Kevin got to work modding his role, and, today, he manages Unity's philanthropic funding programs, distributing resources to nonprofit education initiatives like the ones he used to run.

Kevin's story goes to show that not all job crafting is about vertical advancement. There can be great value in building skill on top of skill on top of skill, like so many *Deus Ex* proximity mines. But we can also use job crafting to expand horizontally, becoming—as Veronica said—"generalists" about our central project. We can explore issues, technologies, or industries from new perspectives.

If Kevin had wanted to advance vertically, he could've focused on becoming an even better nonprofit leader. He could've pursued an MBA, or taken leadership workshops, or read books on the topic. But that's not what Kevin wanted to do. Instead, he grew horizontally, studying how other professions and other organizations pursue his central mission.

We can do the same thing in any line of work. As we identify what professional path we want to pursue during Phase 4, we can think horizontally rather than vertically.

Instead of learning new design tools (vertical growth), a graphic artist could work with their company's strategy team to learn more about the business insights behind design briefs (horizontal growth). Instead of learning a new coding language (vertical growth), a software engineer could work with their company's marketing team to learn more about the users they serve (horizontal growth).

Ultimately, any horizontal growth will likely result in long-term vertical advancement. Directors, department heads, vice presidents, chief executives—in the best case scenarios, these folks become leaders because they can offer more than just depth of skill. They offer breadth of perspective, too.

19.2.5   Tactic 5: Ask About Your Gaps

Finally, Ellen points out that the best job crafting insights often come from the minds of others. Our bosses and peers work with us every day. Often, they'll have clocked qualities in us that they consider strengths, and qualities that they consider weaknesses. They might have noticed technical or durable skills that we're missing. And if we have close, trusting relationships with them, they might be willing to tell us what they've observed.

So Ellen recommends that we just ask, "What am I missing? What should I be doing? What do you need from me?" Then use that data to direct our job crafting efforts.

19.2.6   What We're After

All told, these five tactics will help us answer two questions that drive job crafting:

1. What jobs are out there?
2. What skills and credentials do we need to get those jobs?

We're expanding our opportunity horizons, choosing our professional paths, and beginning to zero in on the level-up efforts that will serve us best.

19.3   Step 2: Leveling Up

Everything up till now has been prep. Now it's time to job craft in earnest—a process reminiscent of Phase 2's leveling up journey. We can do this in four ways.

19.3.1   Raising Hands

On any team, in any department, at any company, there will be constant pop-ups—surprising projects that don't fall neatly into anybody's existing job description. As a leader, I'm often turning to my team with requests like this. *This needs to get done, but it's nobody's job. Who's going to do this?*

Ellen says that these are golden opportunities for aspiring job crafters. Before she came to work at Unity, Ellen consulted independently. Often, her clients would come to her with similar asks—requests that clearly weren't in her wheelhouse. They just needed someone to handle this stuff, and they didn't know who else to ask. Whenever she got these requests, Ellen says, "I'd be like 'Yeah, sure, another skill!' So I job crafted organically just from saying yes."

This is, by far and away, the easiest way to job craft. The opportunities come right to us. We don't have to do a thing. And it's one of the methods most likely to win us employer gratitude, which we can lean on later if we decide to pursue promotions or salary raises.

So Ellen recommends that we just get used to raising our hands and saying yes.

19.3.2 Asking Managers

If job crafting opportunities don't come to us, then we have to go get them. Ellen recommends that we start with our managers, telling them, "I'm really interested in stretching and doing this thing. Are there projects that I can take on right now to start moving toward that?"

Like raising our hands, this approach does more than just create job crafting opportunities. It also broadcasts how engaged and growth-oriented we are—factors that often contribute to future promotions and raises. And, more immediately, it turns our manager into a collaborator, giving them a stake in our growth.

Think about Chapter 17, when Veronica Brown worried that job crafting often feels "subversive." One of the great things about explicitly seeking help from our manager is that it neutralizes that subversion. Not only do we let them in on our secret—that our time is going toward tasks that aren't in our job description—but we actually turn them into active accomplices. Partners in crime.

Of course, ideally, our new job crafting tasks won't feel like digressions from the core business. And that's another place where asking our manager can help. They can help us find the overlap between our own job crafting objectives and the company's business needs.

If, for some reason, our manager can't help us find that overlap, then we've got to do some digging ourselves. Which brings us to . . .

19.3.3   Growing the Business

Every story that Veronica Brown has about job crafting begins and ends with a business need. When she worked at a bookstore, she automated their catalog ordering system for efficiency. When she worked in marketing, she made their materials more accessible, improving sales outcomes and helping to secure the department's future budget. At Unity, every turn of her job crafting wheel has helped advance our education efforts further.

The best job crafting efforts work just like this. We grow, and our team and our company grow with us. If we can find that intersection of personal growth and business growth, we can do the following:

• Secure management support for our personal growth efforts.
• Grow our value to the company (leading to promotions and raises).
• Ensure that the skills we build will indeed grow our careers.

If we can't find these intersections by raising our hand or by talking to our manager, then we'll have to widen the net by talking to other people in our org.

"Investigate your company," Ellen recommends. "Does your company have plans to go in the same direction your job crafting's going?" Even if those plans aren't in action now, leaders will likely approve us for professional development time if we're helping them prepare to execute those plans later. And in these cases, our employer will often finance our studies, too.

Veronica says this approach brings her a special kind of pleasure: "It's so satisfying. Especially when I'm on a team that says, 'If only we could dot-dot-dot. . . .' I love to be the one who says, 'Hmm! Let me think about that. There might be a way!' That's very gratifying."

19.3.4   Using Free Time

Finally, when all else fails, Ellen recommends asking ourselves, "Do you have to job craft through work? Can you do it on your own?"

Ideally, we do want to job craft *on the job*. And places where we can't job craft probably aren't good places to stay in the long term. Companies like that aren't just harming us. If they're preventing employee growth, then they're preventing their own growth, too. And frankly, I'd be pretty skeptical about the long-term sustainability of any company whose employees aren't allowed to learn.

Having said all that, every one of us will encounter resistance to job crafting at some point in our careers, and we can't let that stop us. When that happens, we've got to turn back to Part II of this book and pursue our next round of upskilling independently, with little quests and the help of our communities.

19.4   Step 3: Telling Our Stories

So far, we've seen how job crafting propels us through new iterations of Phases 1 and 2. In Step 1, we reevaluated our professional paths. In Step 2, we leveled up in new directions. But job crafting isn't just about choosing new paths and building new skills. It's also about telling our stories in new ways and pursuing new opportunities—whether those opportunities arise at our current companies or elsewhere.

In this way, job crafting echoes Phase 3 of the Core Career Loop. As we transform on the job, we rethink the stories we tell about our work and how those stories could prepare us for the next chapters of our careers.

This doesn't necessarily have to be about artificially "rebranding" ourselves. For many of us, the ways we narrativize our lives do truly evolve over time. That's because, when we're looking ahead toward future growth, we tend to look for linear paths. *I'll build this skill, then that skill, and eventually I'll become such-and-such.* And that's a good way to operate. That's what this whole darn book is about! But when we look at our lives through the rearview mirror, the paths we took tend to look much more circuitous. In retrospect, we see the strange twists and turns, which seem to lead mysteriously, and yet *inevitably* to where we are now.

In my own life, I never would have guessed that interning for the FCC would lead me to Unity. But, in the rearview mirror, the whole journey makes a crazy kind of sense.

As we job craft, we look for these evolutions in our narratives, and we externalize them. We tell our stories in new ways as we apply for new opportunities—whether inside our current companies or beyond.

When Kevin wanted to shift from running a nonprofit to working for funders, he needed to tell the story of how that shift became inevitable. If someday Veronica wants to quit instructional design and go full-time as an information architect, she'll need to tell the story of how her work here at Unity—and at all the places that came before—made that shift inevitable.

We're not playing tricks on our audience here. We're telling the true story of how past experiences have taken on new meaning for us. We're revealing how our passions and skills and mission evolved not despite our work but *because* of it, and how each of the experiences we've had prepared us in some way for this new season of our career.

In a bizarre twist of fate, I had to do exactly that just a few weeks before writing this chapter of the book. I've spent the last month collaborating with Unity's CEO to reshape my role here, and that's required me to get really practical about how I tell my new career story.

At a practical level, we can rewrite our career stories by thinking about past work through a new lens. Instead of describing our journey in terms of job titles, we can describe it in terms of *modular activities* (stuff we did) and *particular skills* (capabilities we developed). For example, in my old job . . .

- Building new teams was a modular activity that I performed. Skills used: clarifying team missions, appointing leaders, enlisting team members, helping to set goals.
- Securing Unity resources for my department was a modular activity that I performed. Skills used: understanding unmet customer needs, collaborating across the company, making the most of limited resources, creating pitch decks, pitching to decision-makers, negotiating with the CEO.
- Promoting Unity's thought leadership work was a modular activity that I performed. Skills used: public speaking, article writing, relationship building.

In my new role at Unity, I might not need to build new teams or secure department resources or promote my team's work to the world—a lot of that's being taken care of by other folks now. But I bet I'll need many of the same skills. I'll need to clarify team missions, set team goals, uncover unmet customer needs, speak, and write, and build relationships.

So when I told my career story to Unity's CEO and pitched him on my vision for this new job, I told him the story of how I developed those skills, and how that leveling up journey inevitably led me here, to this new role.

That's the bottom line here: when job crafting propels us into the pursuit of new opportunities, we craft new stories. And in these stories, our *skills* are the heroes, not our job titles. When we write our résumés, we'll tell the stories of our skills. When we answer interview questions, we'll tell the stories of our skills. And when we eventually move into new roles, it will be because of our skills.

This is the mechanism by which customer service reps become account managers. It's the mechanism by which teachers become engineers and engineers become teachers. When making these pivots, we tell stories about the skills we built through job crafting. And when we tell the stories of our skills, career transformations look inevitable.

All this talk has obviously led us back, deep into the realm of Phase 3 job hunting. Which means that our second cycle through the loop is almost entirely complete. There's just one piece left to tackle: community.

20

Community Loop: Bosses

20.1 Everything Old Is New (Again)

We know the refrain by now: job crafting is both a loop phase of its own and a kind of arrow, propelling us through our next cycle of the Core Career Loop. It's learning, earning, and advancement all at once.

Given that job crafting contains all the other loop phases, it'll naturally require that we work with all the community members we've met before: our mentors, coaches, sponsors, and peers. And, because job crafting also represents a loop phase of its own, it'll simultaneously bring in new community members: bosses.

Although our whole community will play a role, these bosses will wield the most power during job crafting, which is why the fourth phase of the Community Loop is named for them (see Figure 20.1).

20.2 No Dead Mentors (Again)

In Chapter 11, we established that the population size of a career looper's community should always trend upward. As we progress from phase to phase, we never want to leave anyone behind. Sure, people come and

Figure 20.1 Community Loop

go from our communities because that's how life works, but we never outgrow the elemental roles they play. We never stop benefitting from mentors or coaches or sponsors or peers.

During job crafting, I'd take that assertion a step further. It's not just that we continue benefiting from having these folks in our lives—we actually *need* them during Phase 4. *All* of them.

20.2.1 Mentors

In Phase 1 of the Community Loop, we turned to mentors for holistic guidance. They helped us make sense of who we were and what we were meant to do. Now that we're in Phase 4, we arguably need them more than ever.

When we invest in a particular professional path, identifying with it, leveling up toward it, grinding to get a job in it, it often becomes difficult to disentangle ourselves from it. It can be easy to forget that we once chose that path. That we can choose to leave it behind. That we can choose a new path if we want to.

Other times, we might struggle with the opposite problem. We might become unreasonably dissatisfied with our work. We might come to believe that our current professional path has unique hardships and that the grass will be greener elsewhere—when, in fact, the things that make our work unpleasant aren't unique to this job or this company or this profession.

In Phase 4, our mentors help us make sense of the work lives we find ourselves in. If we're stuck, they help us unstick—help us rediscover a sense of gravitational pull and open us up to the possibility that the pull might be leading us elsewhere. If we're eager to go, our mentors can level set, drawing on their own experience to help us judge just how big a change we ought to make.

In a nutshell, they do what they did before. They offer perspective. They help us broaden our vision of what's possible. They help us clarify our passions, skills, mission, and financial needs. They motivate, inspire, and guide our job crafting efforts with concern not just for our careers but also for our lives.

20.2.2   Coaches

Once our mentors help us figure out what kind of professional growth we want to pursue during job crafting, we turn to coaches for help, just as we did during Phase 2. Coaches get down to brass tacks, helping us achieve specific goals and overcome specific challenges.

We can turn to coaches for help on specific problems. How much should I charge to photograph weddings? Why does my website keep redirecting to a 404 page? If I clone carnivorous dinosaurs and build a theme park around them, what might go wrong?

Coaches can also help us more broadly by structuring our job crafting journeys, thinking through the little quests and mile markers that lead to growth.

20.2.3   Sponsors

Sponsors help us achieve the final outcomes that we're pursuing through job crafting. If our goal is to move into a new job on a new team at a new company, then we'll need sponsors just as we did in Phase 3. They'll introduce us to helpful new connections and sing our praises to hiring managers.

If our goal is to permanently change our job description, to change our job title, or to secure a promotion, sponsors will do similar work, championing our cause to internal leaders who have the power to decide our fates. And just as we'll continue to rely on mentors, coaches, and sponsors during job crafting, we'll continue to rely on peers as well.

20.2.4 Peers

Everything our peers contributed during Phases 1–3 they contribute again now. As we suss out which new professional path to take, we turn to these peers for insight. Our friends can tell us about what they do, why they do it, how they feel about it, and whether they think we'd like it. They can introduce us to *their* friends, who'll do the same. And they can act as peer mentors, too. It's not uncommon for a friend to reflect back to us, *It really sounds like you hate this about your job. It really sounds like you love that about your job. I wonder whether you'd like this other profession more?*

And once we find a new professional path to pursue, our peers help us level up. They can keep us accountable, checking in to find out whether we've made progress. They can inspire us with their own job crafting efforts. And they can even become coaches, offering guidance in their own areas of expertise.

Then, when it comes time to seek out new jobs, we turn to our peers again—especially our weak ties. These folks will make the most valuable introductions, finding us the best-fit job openings, and recommending us for roles.

And, as we've seen throughout this book, these peers can come from anywhere. The internet has become one of the most powerful tools for making connections like these. And there are the old-school connection-building forums as well. Community spaces like neighborhood gardens and sports leagues. Professional organizations, either for our current profession or our future profession. And, best of all, connections made by mutual friends. (*Hey, you two should get coffee.*)

When pursuing these peer relationships, it's important to note that location matters. A lot. Many industries have official or unofficial hubs. And some big, metropolitan cities like New York, London, and Shanghai are hubs for just about everything. You can build a successful career from anywhere, but living in a hub dramatically increases the likelihood that you'll meet peers who'll open doors to your field of interest.

I grew up in Waukesha, Wisconsin, the dead center of the American Midwest. When the big arcade moved into town, it wasn't big, and it wasn't really an arcade either. It was six games in a movie theater. People didn't ever come to Waukesha and people never really left. In my career, I've stumbled my way from an FCC internship to an internet-building startup to a leadership role at an industry-leading tech titan with offices in more than 20 countries across the globe. None of that ever would've happened if I'd stayed in Waukesha, Wisconsin.

Big towns aren't better than small towns. Coastal cities aren't better than landlocked ones. And careers with brand names and global reach certainly aren't better than careers built close to our roots. What matters are our values. Passion, skills, mission, sustainability.

If our values root us in Waukesha, Wisconsin, then that's where we should stay. If our values are hubbed elsewhere, then we should take those geographic realities seriously. If we want to work in tech, we should seriously consider tech hubs like New York and the Bay Area. If we want to work in film, we should head for Hollywood.

There will be times in our lives when moves like these won't be possible. Finances, family obligations, and other factors might keep us anchored outside of industry hubs. Fortunately, there's never been a better time to live far away from our dreams—remote work and long-distance networking have created so many new ways to access opportunity. But I'd be remiss not to emphasize that one peer in the right place can open more doors than 20 peers anywhere else.

20.3   Now, Bosses

Phase 4 calls on every community member we've met until now: mentors, coaches, sponsors, and peers. And it also introduces new players as well: bosses. Job crafting is defined by the fact that it takes place *on the job*. For that reason, our bosses and other managers will play central roles in determining the scope, timeline, and direction of our job crafting efforts.

These folks have enormous power in Phase 4, which they can use for good or for evil. When our bosses support us, they can help us align our job crafting efforts with the needs of the business—an offering that clarifies which skills of interest deserve the most focus. And they can do more than that, too.

Once they've helped us identify a business purpose for job crafting, our bosses have the authority to take stale responsibilities off our plate, creating new growth-oriented responsibilities to replace them. Should we want to seriously reshape our job descriptions, alter our job titles, or pursue promotions, our bosses can then become champions for us, sponsoring our causes behind locked doors with other company leaders.

But what they can give, bosses can also take a way. The wrong manager can hold us back at least as much as the right manager can support us. There are the passively unhelpful bosses: the ones who withhold constructive feedback—leaving us unaware of our growth needs—and the ones who simply don't know how to mentor or coach us.

And then there are the actively unhelpful bosses, who make concerted efforts to suppress our job crafting efforts. They refuse our requests for new responsibilities, insist that we focus on stale tasks, and trap us in dead-end roles. Sometimes, this pernicious behavior is instinctual, born of an old-school, stay-in-your-lane sensibility, or of a toxic relationship to power. Other times, bosses behave this way strategically, in an ironic effort to reduce turnover. (If you can't ever grow, then you can't ever leave!)

There are two things we can do to head this behavior off before it happens, and two things we can do once we realize we're stuck with a bad boss.

First, preemptive strategies. In Chapter 15, Mona Mourshed warned us about the gap between opportunities and *quality* opportunities. Before taking any job, she recommended that we ask three questions:

1. How long do people stay on this team?
2. Are people like me thriving on this team?
3. What professional development opportunities does this team provide?

Asking these questions before accepting offers should help us predict whether we'll be able to job craft from within the company. If it seems like people leave quickly, people like us aren't thriving, or this employer doesn't offer compelling professional development opportunities, then we're dealing with a low-quality offer. It's possible that this company's managers are mortal enemies to job crafters everywhere. If we have the wherewithal to decline, we should.

Once we're on the job, we can also try heading off these problems by being hyper-communicative. The more we tell our bosses about what we want to do, why it matters to us, how we think it can work, and how we think it'll help the company, the more likely we are to find support. That goes both for encouraging a boss to actively engage in our growth and discouraging them from blocking us.

Then, if our boss does prove difficult—or even just inept—we've got two major modes of recourse. First, we can go to other company leaders for mentorship, coaching, and sponsorship. We'll find this tactic especially helpful in cases where the problem is capability: if our boss just doesn't have the skill to mentor or coach us, no problem. We can look elsewhere!

If our boss actively tries to block our job crafting efforts, then it's possible that another leader might be able to change their minds or counteract their efforts. But more likely, this will be an indicator that we need to resort to our fourth option. In option number four, we make sure we've saved our game. Then we quit and start a new game somewhere else.

Next time we go looking for a job, we'll know to look out for great bosses.

20.4   Great Bosses

This all leads us to the fifth and final part of this book, which will begin in Chapter 21. In Part V, we'll go beyond the loop, offering bosses guidance on how they too must adapt to meet this new world—hiring, managing, and promoting in ways that account for contemporary career paths.

Even if you're not anyone's boss, I encourage you to stick with this book through Part V. Reading about the world from your boss's perspective can give you a huge leg up. It's through that kind of study that we learn to identify healthy workplaces and quality managers. We learn what managers ought to be giving us—so we know what to ask for if we aren't getting it. And we get the inside scoop on factors that contribute to hiring and promoting decisions.

And then, of course, I especially encourage managers, recruiters, and other kinds of senior leaders to read on. In Part V, we'll learn how to do the following:

• Hire for adaptability and long-term outcomes.
• Encourage and support job crafting for better retention.

- Prepare for the career-looping behaviors that modern employees bring to the workplace.
- Discard antiquated management styles in favor of new approaches.

Employees and employers alike will walk away from Part V understanding not just how careers are changing but also how the relationships, teams, and businesses around them are changing, too.

Part V

Beyond the Loop: Hiring, Managing, and Promoting

For more than a century, leaders took a pseudo-scientific approach to management. We estimated our needs, articulated those estimates with bizarre precision, then searched for the candidates whose prior experience most identically matched our estimations. Once we had employees onboard, we rewarded those who hit our arbitrary targets and punished those who failed.

That approach won't work in the new economy. Employees just don't put up with it anymore—they have too much freedom and too much choice. Meanwhile, today's market requires employee flexibility and ingenuity that cannot be achieved through rigid, old-school management.

To win in the modern market and adapt to the expectations of career-looping employees, today's leaders need a new approach.

How are hiring, managing, and promoting changing in the new economy?

21

How Managers
Learned to Lead

21.1 Taylor, the Man of Steel

Faster! Cheaper! More more more!

It was 1898, and the United States was bursting at its seams. Utah
had just become the 45th state, rushing in right after Wyoming, Idaho,
and the Dakotas joined up. Railroads were crisscrossing the continent,
connecting the nation. Where railroads went, industry followed. And
where industry went, steel followed.

Steel to keep the trains on track. Steel to launch newfangled sky-
scrapers into the heavens. Steel to expand urban centers. Steel to build
new hubs of industry.

Ten years earlier, in 1880, the country had been consuming about a
million tons of steel per year. Now, in 1898, that number was *10* million.[1]
Ten times more steel meant ten times more industry. Ten times more
construction. Ten times more steam chasing after ten times more trains,
from coast to coast.

Andrew Carnegie and the other titans of steel raced to keep pace,
even as new furnaces opened with the hope of putting them out of business. One of these competitors, the Bethlehem Steel Company, would

someday grow to be the second largest steelmaker in the country. But in 1898, they were new and scrappy, and they needed to get efficient quick.

To help, they brought in a consultant, Frederick Winslow Taylor. Taylor promised to find every inch of wasted time, every morsel of wasted resource, and eliminate, eliminate, eliminate. He would put the rush in *steel rush*.

So Taylor headed to Bethlehem, where he, his notepad, and his trusty stopwatch measured the efficiency of steelworkers. The time management critic Oliver Burkeman explains what Taylor "discovered" there:

> The Bethlehem workers, Taylor calculated, were shifting about 12.5 tons of iron per man per day—but predictably, when he offered a group of "large, powerful Hungarians" some extra cash to work as fast as they could for an hour, he found that they performed much better. Extrapolating to a full work day, and guesstimating time for breaks, Taylor concluded, with his trademark blend of self-confidence and woolly maths, that every man ought to be shifting 50 tons per day—four times their usual amount.[2]

Until now, no one had ever thought to study work this way. Terms like *efficiency* and *productivity* weren't yet in vogue. Nor was the idea that work expectations ought to be calculated, measured, or predicted so microscopically. But a new economy was demanding a new approach.

Taylor promised to get industry up to date with a system that he'd eventually come to call *scientific management*. He'd developed it as an apprentice, as a foreman, and eventually as a chief engineer. Scientific management, he explained, was all about "knowing exactly what you want men to do, and then seeing that they do it in the best and cheapest way."[3]

The bosses, he said, should calculate precisely what needs to be done, what *can* be done, and what they'd be willing to pay to get it all handled. Then they'd turn that information over to their workers, whom they'd consider to be interchangeable cogs in their larger machines.

As a manager, Taylor argued, you wanted to find yourself the best, quickest cogs, and push them as hard as they could go. When a cog slowed down, that was no problem really. You'd just switch it out for another.

Meanwhile, Taylor assumed that these cogs would pursue their own efficiencies. They wouldn't want to work. They wouldn't care about the company or its mission. They'd only care about making as much money as they could for as little work as possible. In Taylor's words, the manager's job was to counteract this "natural instinct and tendency of men to take it easy."[4]

To this end, Taylor's system called for every laborer to be given "A LARGE DAILY TASK" (caps his), which "should be circumscribed carefully and completely, and should not be easy to accomplish."

"When [the worker] fails," Taylor wrote, "he should be sure that sooner or later he will be the loser by it."[5]

21.2 The Loser

Taylor's system caught on like wildfire (and burned like it, too). Henry Ford called on Taylor to help create his new assembly lines.[6] Taylor's system spread to France and Canada.[7] Many credit Taylor for catalyzing today's personal efficiency craze. And to this day, consultants and senior executives everywhere pride themselves on their abilities to push for more, more, more productivity.

In today's brave new world of digitization and hybrid work, Taylor's ghost continues pushing, now with the dangerous overreach of "people analytics"—the data-driven study of employee potential, performance, behavior, and attitudes. At its best, people analytics helps companies adapt to the wants and needs of their employees. It helps hiring managers and bosses make "evidence-based, talent-centric, and meritocratic" decisions—which is to say decisions less governed by bias.[8] And all of that's terrific.

But the most Taylor-haunted, analytics-driven managers risk reducing every employee to a handful of charts and numbers. A person becomes keywords on a résumé. Keystrokes per minute.

As remote work's gone normative, unchecked analytics have gone Big Brother, taking screenshots of employee terminals, tracking movements, predicting behavior.[9]

Somehow, what gets lost in all this precision is the impact.

Looking back at the history, Taylor's reforms sometimes produced short-term gains. But many gains dropped off quickly when workers burned out and abandoned ship. Often, laborers unionized and went on strike, refusing to work until sanity was restored—an outcome that cost employers more than it saved them.

In 1912, an investigation by the US government found that the system was so injurious to both body and morale that they banned its use in government settings.[10] And although many write and speak fondly of Taylor's work at Bethlehem Steel, few mention how things turned out there.

In 1901, Bethlehem Steel fired Taylor. They'd tried his scientific system, sunk oodles of cash into it, and hadn't gotten any more productive as a result.

21.3 Relating as Humans

Despite the shortcomings of scientific management, it took until the 1920s and 1930s for a new approach to emerge. A group of researchers studied working conditions at a Western Electric factory, and, after nearly a decade of inquiry, they reached a radical series of conclusions:

> A great deal of attention has been given to the economic function [of a company]. Scientific controls have been introduced to further [its] economic purposes. . . . Much of this advance has gone on in the name of efficiency . . . [but] nothing comparable to this advance has gone on in the development of . . . co-operation, that is, for getting individuals and groups of individuals working together effectively and with satisfaction to themselves.[11]

Their research revealed that scientific management had entirely neglected to address the social or emotional well-being of workers. And that oversight was hurting both businesses and the people who kept them running.

Workers were not interchangeable parts, these researchers explained. Workers were devoted teams, made up of unique individuals, each "bringing to the work situation a different background of personal and social experiences." Both the group and its individuals would have to be managed with care, accounting for their unique wants, needs, capabilities, and offerings.

In their sharpest condemnation, the Western Electric researchers wrote that, to scientific management, "man is essentially an economic being carrying around with him a few noneconomic appendages." This attitude could no longer be tolerated.

Their research spurred on decades of innovation in management—a paradigm shift that became known as the *human relations movement*.

21.4   From Humans to People

Thirty years later, the MIT scholar Douglas McGregor launched management theory forward again in a book written just four years before his death. It was his central question, really, that changed everything. A question that it took until 1960 for someone to ask. In his book's introduction, McGregor wrote, "What are your assumptions (implicit as well as explicit) about the most effective way to manage people?"

McGregor demonstrated that, although the human relations movement had changed management rhetoric in meaningful ways, the implicit assumptions of scientific management had lived on. He called this bundle of assumptions *theory X*, and suggested that it contained three core tenets, quoted here:

- The average human being has an inherent dislike of work and will avoid it if he can . . .
- Because of this human characteristic of dislike of work, most people must be coerced, controlled, directed, threatened with punishment to get them to put forth adequate effort . . .
- The average human being prefers to be directed, wishes to avoid responsibility, has relatively little ambition, wants security above all.[12]

McGregor then went on to suggest that another theory was possible: *theory Y*. Theory Y stated that people can actually enjoy work and responsibility given the right conditions. That workers could find motivation in the pride and satisfaction of their work. That employers might not actually need to exert "external control and the threat of punishment." And that most people would bring "imagination, ingenuity, and creativity" to their work if given the chance.[13]

Believe it or not, these were radical ideas at the time, and they inspired a new trend toward democratic, so-called participatory management, where workers could finally contribute creatively, take responsibility, and enjoy doing it. In the purest application of participatory management, employees took responsibility for solving client problems, designing their own jobs, setting organizational goals, and even leading organizational changes.[14]

In the present day, theory Y has continued to inspire new management movements. Today, business leaders everywhere are building "people-centric organizations," where employees are seen not merely as a company's most valuable tools, but as its most basic genetic material. These organizations aim to craft the entire employee experience with care—from hire to retire. They draw on data and analytics, yes. But they pair those analytics with human judgment and direct efforts toward the improvement of working conditions. They pursue more flexibility, more coaching. Less rigidity, less authoritarianism. And, ultimately, they aim to foster senses of well-being and purpose for every employee.

21.5   Managing Career Loopers

Today's managers can no longer afford to think mechanistically. People are not machinery. It's no longer enough to simply hire the person with the best specs, tell them what to do, and promote them when they do it. With this approach, we miss out on the unique gifts that each person has to offer, and we risk driving direct reports to burnout and exit.

Instead, today's managers must take a more human approach. They must look beyond the specs when hiring. They must empower their direct reports. They must account for the creative, innovative powers of their employees. And they must guide those employees onward toward growth.

It's not just career loopers who must evolve to meet the moment. With the evolution of the Core Career Loop must come an evolution in how leaders lead. In the final chapters of this book, we'll talk through the practical means by which business leaders can achieve all this as they hire, manage, and promote.

And these chapters aren't just for managers either. Here, in Part V, employees and individual contributors—career loopers themselves—will learn what their managers are thinking and wrestling with. That knowledge is power. It'll help us better understand the following:

- How to identify healthy, promising workplaces and managers.
- What to ask managers for if we aren't already getting it.
- What managers are looking for when hiring and promoting.

Today's people-centric organizations demand more of us in some ways, but they offer more, too. As employees, they require us to bring our curiosity, our ingenuity, and our fail-forward determination to work every day. In return, they give employees the power to make demands—demands for more opportunity, more flexibility, and more stewardship.

Notes

1. "A Brief History of the American Steel Industry." National Material Company, January 24, 2018. https://www.nationalmaterial.com/brief-history-american-steel-industry/.
2. Burkeman, Oliver. "Why Time Management Is Ruining Our Lives." *The Guardian*, December 22, 2016. https://www.theguardian.com/technology/2016/dec/22/why-time-management-is-ruining-our-lives.
3. Taylor, Frederick Winslow. *Shop Management* (Harper & Brothers Publishers, 1911). https://www.gutenberg.org/cache/epub/6464/pg6464-images.html.
4. Reshef, Yonatan. "Frederick Winslow Taylor (1856 - 1915) Principles of Scientific Management." Stanford.edu, accessed September 21, 2024. https://web.stanford.edu/class/sts175/NewFiles/Taylorism#:~:text=According%20to%20Taylor%2C%20%22the%20natural,was%20one%20reason%20to%20soldier.
5. Taylor, *Shop Management*.
6. "A Science Odyssey: People and Discoveries: Ford Installs First Moving Assembly Line." PBS, accessed September 22, 2024. https://www.pbs.org/wgbh/aso/databank/entries/dt13as.html.
7. "The Development of Scientific Management by Frederick Taylor." Creative Safety Supply, accessed September 22, 2024. https://www.creativesafetysupply.com/articles/the-development-of-scientific-management-by-frederick-taylor/.
8. Chamorro-Premuzic, Tomas, and Ian Bailie. "Tech Is Transforming People Analytics. Is That a Good Thing?" *Harvard Business Review*, 21 (October 2020). https://hbr.org/2020/10/tech-is-transforming-people-analytics-is-that-a-good-thing.
9. Chamorro-Premuzic and Bailie, "Tech Is Transforming People Analytics."
10. Frey, John P. *Scientific Management and Labor* (1900): 3. https://archive.org/details/scientificmanage00frey/page/n3/mode/2up?q=us+government.
11. Roethlisberger, F. J., and William J. Dickson, ed. *Management and the Worker*, Vol. V (Routledge, 2005), 397.
12. McGregor, Douglas. *The Human Side of Enterprise: Annotated Edition*, ed. Joel Cutcher-Gershenfeld (McGraw-Hill, 2006), 82.

13. McGregor, *The Human Side of Enterprise: Annotated Edition.*

14. Gama, Joao. "Participative Management: The Elements, Characteristics and Impediments." Medium, October 17, 2020. https://medium.com/@joao_gama/participative-management-the-elements-characteristics-and-impediments-dc8d892b9416#:~:text=Participation%20as%20a%20management%20style%20was%20suggested%20in%20the%20classical,better%20(Crane%2C%201979).

22

Hiring Career Loopers

22.1 In Good Company

It took about three and a half centuries for the word *company* to become synonymous with *business institution*. The word has its roots in 12th-century Old French, where *compagnie* meant something like "friendship and society." This, in turn, was derived from the Latin roots *com* and *panis*, which combined to suggest "people who eat bread together."[1]

In the near millennium since humanity first spoke of creating a company, I worry that many of us have forgotten these roots. A company's roots are in its society. In its people. Without those people, a company's just a mission statement. A bank statement. An empty building. It's *people* who make it run, who give it value. It's *people* who fill buildings, fill bank accounts, and put missions into action.

Leading a company requires that we think critically about our people. And that thinking begins with hiring. Who do we want on our team? Who do we want to break bread with? And can we look past the keywords and stats and biases to see the real people who want to join *us?*

Today, many employers, recruiters, and hiring managers continue to hire the same way that folks hired generations ago. In the rush to fill vacancies, these decision-makers fall back on methods that haven't evolved to account for contemporary business challenges or contemporary applicant pools.

And when employers like these don't keep up, they risk losing out. In particular, employers who don't modernize and adapt will end up looking

- In the wrong place
- For the wrong things

In this chapter, we'll talk about the new hiring strategies that solve for these problems. For employers, recruiters, and hiring managers, this chapter will offer guidance on how we can adapt to win in the new economy. Meanwhile, for career loopers, this chapter will reveal the qualities that today's and tomorrow's employers look for in job applicants.

22.2   Problem 1: Looking in the Wrong Place

Throughout this book, we've discussed the importance of networking. We've said over and over that growth and opportunities come to us via relationships. We've explored an entire loop built on that concept—the Community Loop.

But this principle has a dark side. From the employer perspective, hiring exclusively from within our own networks hurts us, hurts others, and hurts the business.

It's the old-school tradition. You hire the people you know. And if you can't hire them, you hire their children. But we can expect three big misses with this approach: we miss great employees, we miss great innovations, and we miss great transformations.

22.2.1   *Missing Great Employees*

In Chapter 18, we met Anuja Dharkar, Unity's global head of education. She brings special insight to management both because of her own experience hiring and managing global teams and because of her work here at Unity. She helps us teach interactive tech skills worldwide while partnering with employers to ensure that skilled creators find their ways into jobs.

She explains that when we, as leaders, hire only from within our own personal networks, "We miss what other people are able to do." We miss out on all the great hires out there who happen not to come from our circles, happen not to have gone to our schools, happen not to have worked in our fields.

To drive home this point, she often tells the story of one of her proudest hires, who came to Unity via an experimental internship program:

> We would never have found him if we didn't open ourselves up. He had no experience in anything tech-related. He worked at Home Depot before working with us at Unity. And he's amazing at his job. Amazing. And I don't think we would have found him if we'd said, "We're just gonna stick with the people we know."

22.2.2   Missing Great Innovations

Another problem with hiring only from within our own networks is that we can't truly diversify our teams. And if we don't diversify, we miss out on great innovation opportunities.

When I talk about diversity here, I'm talking about diversity of social identities like race and gender. And I'm also talking about a broader diversity of lived experience. Where have people worked? What disciplines have they studied? What industries have they worked in? What challenges have they faced?

Diverse hiring doesn't just help advance the cause of social equity. It also helps drive better business outcomes. And when we don't hire diversely, business suffers.

If my team looks just like everyone else's teams, then it's probably going to arrive at similar conclusions. That means less innovation. If everyone on my team shares similar experiences and backgrounds, then we're probably not going to challenge each other's assumptions. That means lower quality.

These wouldn't have been problems back in the day, when most of us worked for incumbents, and incumbents were safe to rest on their laurels. But in today's economy, every company, no matter how well established, must innovate or die. Excel or die. We need one-of-a-kind teams that arrive at novel solutions and challenge each other's assumptions, driving us to build better.

22.2.3 Missing Great Transformations

Life isn't just about business outcomes. As employers, recruiters, and hiring managers, we have the unique opportunity to, as Anuja puts it, "Change people's lives forever." And we can do that by looking past our own networks, creating opportunities for people who won't get opportunities elsewhere.

James Stone—the Black IT specialist turned police officer turned documentary photographer turned tech leader—explains how past employers transformed his life by hiring outside their own networks:

> I have no formal education, and there's been a fair amount of difficulty with my skin color. The only reason I'm here is because other people took a chance. And yeah, alright, I've put in the time and the work, and that's really important. But some doors just don't open when people like me are knocking on them.
>
> I'm unbelievably thankful for the people out there who are willing to do something different. They're not following the traditional norms. They're willing to see somebody who doesn't fit any of that and go, "Do you know what? I'll take a chance on them."

When we stick to old-school hiring practices, just hiring from within our own networks, we risk missing out on great employees. We miss their great innovations. We miss the opportunity to facilitate great transformations for others.

Plus, that's not the only way that old-school practices send us careening off in the wrong direction.

22.3 Problem 2: Looking for the Wrong Things

We've met Lyle Maxson a few times throughout this book (Chapters 5 and 10). He's the games-for-good tech leader who's on our employer advisory board, which advocates for better hiring practices across the games industry.

Lyle explains that his biggest problem with old-school hiring managers is that "they typically just hire people based off of technical skill, not based off of mission alignment, or their community involvement, or their own personal practice." For Lyle, "personal practice" is the process by which we develop durable skills like emotional intelligence, resilience, and adaptability. Lyle argues that we should all be hiring for this latter group of skills.

As we've seen throughout this book and will continue to see throughout this chapter, durable skills are vital for success in the new economy. In particular, Anuja says, what matters most isn't what people know, but how well they can adapt. After all, given an economy where technological tools and industry boundaries are constantly changing, the power to change with them goes a lot further than the power to master any single, short-lived paradigm.

Lyle adds that the products and services that companies offer inevitably reflect the people who created them. When creators have invested in their own personal development, their values carry over into their work product. Speaking specifically about how this phenomenon plays out in tech, Lyle says:

> If we think of technology as a mirror, then the developers themselves need to mirror what they're building in a good way. . . . Typically, when we think of developers, we think of unhealthy people, slouched over, with poor sleep schedules, poor diets. And if those are the people that are building our technologies, then I think we're in trouble. That's a systemic problem.

If we want to make great products, then we need to hire great people—not just people who took the right courses in college.

22.4   Five Tactics for Better Hires

When employers don't challenge their intrinsic and extrinsic assumptions about hiring, they end up looking in the wrong places, for the wrong things. They end up missing opportunities to innovate, excel, and transform. They often end up hiring technical specialists who aren't well equipped for success in the new economy.

The good news is that plenty of people-centric organizations have already begun implementing better hiring practices, and we can follow their leads. Their practices are better designed to capitalize on the capabilities and offerings of contemporary career loopers, and they're better designed to drive business wins in the contemporary marketplace.

In this book, we'll address five of these modern hiring tactics in particular:

1. Redefining job requirements
2. Prioritizing adaptability
3. Accounting for durable skills
4. Staying on mission
5. Decentering bias

22.4.1 Redefining Job Requirements

"The definition of insanity," says the old adage, "is doing the same thing over and over, expecting a different result." We look for candidates with the right school, the right degree, the right work history, and, miraculously, we get them! And then we end up having to replace them.

Every manager has seen evidence that some people with the right credentials do low-quality work. So why do we keep assuming that the "right credentials" matter?

In fact, we know from Core Career Loop Phases 1 and 4 that people's values change often. There's a pretty strong likelihood that someone with years and years of experience in one area should really be moving on to something else. As Anuja points out, "A person may come with a lot of experience, but they may not be happy to be in the same position anymore. You never know where they're coming from." There's good reason to be suspicious of deep, long-term specialization.

Meanwhile, many of us have also seen employees with no formal experience excel when given the chance. Anuja says that these hires sometimes prove even better than their more traditional counterparts. "Someone who doesn't have the on-paper skills and knowledge for the job, but could do it anyway is usually the most interesting candidate," she says. Anuja explains that these folks have had to come by the necessary capabilities circuitously, and their outsider perspectives will likely give them an innovative edge over other candidates.

This isn't to say that we should hire folks with zero relevant experience. It's to say that we should expand our ideas about what's relevant. We should look past job titles and pedigree—which don't correlate well to success—and ensure that our search criteria more accurately reflect the job's true skill demands.

22.4.2   *Prioritizing Adaptability*

In the modern economy, the only constant is change. Technologies change, industries change, economies change. Tools change, demands change, clients change. Our own companies change. Given this fluctuating state of affairs, one of the most important qualities in any contemporary employee is the capacity to adapt to change and thrive under new conditions.

The importance of adaptability far exceeds the importance of technical mastery. An adaptable candidate can master new technical skills on the job, and roll with the punches when those technical skills inevitably fall out of relevance. But a long-time specialist with one particular bundle of technical skills might not have the same capacity to adapt.

Put more simply, all adaptation experts can develop technical skills, but not all technical experts can adapt. As employers, we want to hire a talent base that can move into new roles as they're created, not a talent base that's locked into the technical skills of the moment.

Résumés and interviews might offer indicators of adaptability, but the best way to test for it during recruiting is with performance tasks, which actually simulate the work that needs to be done. If we want to find adaptable candidates, then we shouldn't just assess their *output* on these tasks. We should also assess their methods. Did they try to solve the problem on their own, or did they get curious about the insights of others and crowdsource for help? Did they go with the first idea that hit them, or did they iterate and experiment and challenge assumptions? Did they try to attack the problem from a novel perspective, or did they just take it head on?

Then, when making our hiring decisions, we should choose candidates who exhibit the most adaptable methodologies, not necessarily the best immediate results.

22.4.3   *Accounting for Durable Skills*

Let's zoom out. We just spoke about the fact that things change quickly in the contemporary economy, and we need to hire folks who can adapt to all that change. True adaptability requires more than just the willingness to roll with the punches and think outside the box. True adaptability requires a wider suite of durable skills.

Think about our discussion of durable skills during Phase 2. These include things like emotional intelligence, communication, and collaboration. Employees who have large durable skill sets will be able to evolve as the company evolves, as the competitive landscape evolves, as the economy evolves. These employees will remain resilient storytellers and compassionate teammates no matter what tools they're using or what roles they're moving into.

22.4.4 Staying on Mission

Lyle adds that, along with durable skills, he also looks for mission alignment:

> A lot of my colleagues focus on the technical skills, and you either have them or you don't. That creates a lot of tension within a company, because you don't really know how long people are gonna stay with you, and how committed they are. Especially in a hybrid work world where you don't actually know how much people are working.
>
> In my companies, we don't have to worry about that. We have basically 100% retention with our employees, and it's because they're attached to the mission. They feel a sense of community with the people that they're working with. They understand the mission and why they're connected to it, and their place in it too, and how they can offer value.

Lyle observes that technical experts with no mission alignment tend to come and go more quickly, and give less to the team while they're onboard. Meanwhile, employees whose personal missions align with the company's tend to stick around and carry the organization further.

22.4.5 Decentering Bias

To achieve all of this—to find and hire candidates who have the core capabilities to excel at the job, who are adaptable, who are durable, and who are truly aligned on mission—we need to decenter bias.

I say *decenter* rather than *eliminate* because, as Anuja puts it, "Bias is inherent. We all have implicit bias within us." Rather than set the impossible goal of eliminating this bias altogether, we need to get better at recognizing bias when it arises. We need to notice when the judgments we make about people are disconnected from their actual capacity to perform well. And when we notice those things, we need to pivot.

Anuja elaborates:

> How do I react when I see a candidate? Whether it's the name I read, whether it's the person I look at, whether it's the mannerisms in the way they speak. I have to figure out whether my reaction is tied to their ability, or whether my reaction is just a reaction—and so probably tied to a bias.

Although bias arises all the time, and rears its head in all kinds of places, there are a few starter tactics that employers can use to decenter bias and emphasize capability during hiring.

- **Forget cultural fit.** The more diverse our team is, the less we're going to feel an immediate sense of cultural fit. We can still build a unified team culture, but it should emerge organically based on team membership. It shouldn't be engineered to suit personal preference.
- **Look past our own networks.** Recruiting from our own networks biases outcomes because our networks inevitably reflect our own identities and experiences.
- **Think twice about post-secondary degree requirements.** The skills needed for many jobs aren't actually taught in degree programs, and these programs aren't the only way to skill up. Meanwhile, requiring these degrees reduces diversity in our candidate pools, because higher education is unequally accessible and distributed. Degree requirements also lower the size of our pools in general: only a third of adult US citizens have a four-year degree.[2]

22.5   Recruiting Loopers

Contemporary career loopers move through many professions over the course of their careers, driven in large part by deep senses of passion and mission. And because their professions change so often, the priorities and methods of these career loopers differ considerably from old-school job seekers.

In particular, today's strongest candidates put adaptability and durability first. They build technical skills—sure—but only as temporary tools for solving immediate problems, not as core capabilities. When new technical skills are needed, contemporary career loopers learn quickly, often developing these new skills independently, without the help of degree programs.

As employers, recruiters, and hiring managers we need to recognize how top talent is changing and rethink our search terms to match. If we keep searching for candidates the way we used to, prioritizing the people in our own networks, optimizing for the best technical skills match and the most name brand pedigree, we're going to miss out. We're going to miss the opportunity to bring on great candidates with unusual backgrounds. We're going to miss the opportunity to build diverse, innovative teams. And we're going to miss the opportunity to transform the lives of others. Ultimately, teams built with old-school recruiting techniques won't survive in the new economy, where tools, technologies, and markets change at a moment's notice.

We need to redefine what makes a candidate "qualified," decentering bias while focusing on adaptability and other durable skills. And if we want to reduce turnover, we need to hire for mission alignment as well. Ultimately, it's the adaptable, mission-aligned employees who will stick with us. They're the ones who will stay devoted to our teams, growing on the job and delivering wins—just so long as we know how to manage them.

Notes

1. "Company." Etymonline, accessed September 22, 2024. https://www.etym online.com/word/company.
2. US Census Bureau. "Census Bureau Releases New Educational Attainment Data." Census.gov, February 16, 2023. https://www.census.gov/newsroom/press-releases/2023/educational-attainment-data.html.

23

Managing Career Loopers

23.1 Taylor's Ghost

Remember Frederick Winslow Taylor's gospel of scientific management? His system was essentially designed to calculate how much iron you could get a steelworker to carry per day without killing them. It obviously wasn't a great approach, and management theory's come a long way since then. But Taylor's ghost continues to haunt managers everywhere.

In contemporary applications of Taylorism, a manager's job is to ensure that their team hits or exceeds their targets. The manager tells employees what to do, and the employees do it. If a manager catches their employees "taking it easy," those employees get punished. If employees don't hit their targets, those employees get punished.

And employees who *do* hit their targets? They get bumped up into leadership roles. Boom. Managed!

23.2 A Few Problems with Taylorism

As previously discussed, historical evidence suggests that Taylor's system might never have worked. But regardless of whether it worked in the 1890s, it certainly doesn't work in today's economy. For one thing, direct reports just don't put up with this stuff anymore. They have so much choice and flexibility—if employees don't feel empowered, they pack up and leave.

What's more, Taylor's system isn't actually suited to creating value in the contemporary economy. It was designed to move iron from Point A to Point B. It was designed to keep furnaces hot and keep factories churning. But those aren't the problems of today's economy. Today, we need employees to solve problems creatively and make good decisions— especially in ambiguous conditions where there are no known solutions.

The upshot: we need to train employees to make strong decisions, and we need to build environments where they feel valued and free to grow. So, in contemporary management, leaders need to make five key changes relative to old-school techniques.

1. Be a coach, not a boss.
2. Motivate employees.
3. Track emotional wellness.
4. Democratize insight.
5. Lead toward growth.

23.3   Change 1: Be A Coach, Not a Boss

Historically, Taylor-possessed folks have thought of management as an authoritarian role: it's about telling people what to do. But contemporary leaders take a different approach. They conceive of themselves as coaches, not bosses.

"Management has become about cultivating talent," says Anuja Dharkar. "How do you help your people find what makes them happy professionally as well as personally? And how do you help bring out the ways that person could become really impactful?"

We might think of these as two distinct areas where managers offer coaching: (1) holistic personal improvement and (2) business impact. In part, we offer our direct reports guidance on life and durable skills. We help them develop the tenacity and mental fitness to overcome failure. We help them learn to manage their own anxieties. Communicate better. Balance work and life better. In a way, we become nonexpert therapists.

This is a huge part of the compensation that we offer career loopers. More than salary, more than equity, we offer employees skills that they can take with them anywhere. Simultaneously, it's our job to help every employee channel their abilities, insights, and growth toward delivering business wins.

23.4   Change 2: Motivate Employees

In Part II of this book, we talked about intrinsic and extrinsic motivators. We said that intrinsic motivations come from within—passion, curiosity, and mission, for example. Meanwhile extrinsic motivators come from others—money and praise and trophies.

Taylor's system of scientific management only ever addressed extrinsic motivation: if people carried less stuff, they'd make less money. If people carried more stuff, they'd make more money. And, in the modern-day expression of Taylorism, those who score highest on key metrics get senior titles and teams to manage—regardless of whether these high scorers have any interest in management.

When managing contemporary career loopers, extrinsic motivators like titles and money do still matter. But they're not all that matter.

As a manager, Anuja often needs to "change a low performer into a high performer." And she does that by offering both intrinsic and extrinsic reinforcement:

> I try to tease out: What is the work that you are intrinsically interested in doing? I might ask, what interests you in a job? Or if you could do anything else you wanted to do, what would that be? What gets you up in the morning? What makes you feel good about the work that you do? And can it align with what we need?
>
> And secondly, what are you externally motivated by? Is it money? Is it a title? Is it praise? And how do we turn you into a better performer by meshing together your intrinsic passion and extrinsic motivation?

23.5   Change 3: Track Emotional Wellness

Old-school scientific management assumed that people could deliver the same quantity of work product every day. But the reality, of course, is that work product fluctuates. People's lives affect their work. If we, as managers, know about our employees' lives, we can not only create a kinder, more caring work environment but also tailor our expectations, behavior, and requests to people's real-time emotional states.

For this reason, Lyle Maxson says that it's important to check in with our teams regularly about their lives and emotional wellness.

> Outside of just work check-ins, actual *life* check-ins are really important. We do it all the time. We do a check in for every single meeting. It's usually 5 to 10 minutes where we're going around with everyone in the meeting and just seeing where they're at.
>
> Doing that before starting a meeting is so important because then you know how to speak to people. If you know somebody is just dealing with a death in the family, you can speak to them differently and not demand as much or just be softer with them.

And, of course, the inverse is true, too. If you know that someone's feeling good and energized, then you know that today is the day to onboard them for a new project or get them brainstorming about a new initiative.

23.6   Change 4: Democratize Insight

In Chapter 22, we established that colliding perspectives generate innovation. That's a big part of why we diversified our search pool and our final hiring selections. But it's not enough to simply hire for diverse perspectives. Once we're managing our new hires, we need to preach and practice the central philosophy here: that great ideas can come from anywhere.

I'm a big believer that the higher up we get in the chain of the command, the less we know. Partly, that's about proximity to the customer: my direct reports work more closely with our customers than I do, and their direct reports work even more closely still. It's also about age: junior team members are nearly always going to be more tapped into the cultural zeitgeist.

And then there's the fact that today's career loopers, by necessity, are walking around with so many more skills than I am. What used to be five separate people is now one person. You'll get individual early-career employees who can already code, design, project manage, market, and so on. That's the nature of career looping: it encourages today's workforce to develop a huge breadth of skill.

For all these reasons, contemporary managers need to encourage every direct report to speak up—even, and perhaps most especially, the junior ones. Some starter tactics for achieving this:

- **Broadcast your receptivity.** Assure team members that their opinions are valued and that there will be no negative consequences for expressing their thoughts. Listen actively and avoid dismissive language or behavior.

- **Ask open-ended questions.** Move beyond questions that require a simple yes or no answer. Solicit long-form input without signaling expectations for what a "right answer" sounds like.

- **Yes-and employees.** When team members do speak up, acknowledge their input, reflect back what they said, and build on their offerings.

- **Choose their insights over yours.** Demonstrate taking employees' ideas regularly instead of your own.

- **Digitize brainstorming.** Don't just ask for insight during synchronous meetings. Soliciting digital contributions gives people space to digest and reflect.

23.7 Change 5: Lead Toward Growth

During Phase 4 of the loop, we saw how important it is for every individual to continue growing on the job, whether they're an individual contributor, a manager, or a C-suiter. And we saw that one of the best things a job crafter can do is approach their manager directly about growth opportunities.

Well, now that we're in management, it's time to consider our role in helping direct reports grow on the job. Rather than waiting for employees to come to us, we should go to them. We should ask what they want to learn, and then help them find ways to do just that. More specifically, Anuja recommends asking the following questions:

- Where do you want to be?
- What skills do you feel like you're lacking?
- How can we find a way to give you that experience without disrupting or overloading them?

Along the way, we can also share our insights with them, letting them know what kinds of skills and behaviors might help them get promoted or connected to other job opportunities. Then, if they're interested, we can work with them to create opportunities for developing in those directions.

Across all of this guidance, we want to be sure never to take job crafting for granted. We have to reward direct reports who pursue growth and help employees incorporate new skills into their roles in meaningful ways so that they aren't simply doing three people's jobs for the salary of one.

Ultimately, these efforts should help us put employees on track for promotion.

24

Promoting Career Loopers

24.1 Promotion

In the old school of management, promotions were a carrot, promised to anyone who hit their targets at work. If an employee did what was asked of them, they'd get a title bump. Then, if they kept doing what was asked of them, we'd give them a team to manage.

This was a bad strategy. Senior roles are not trophies. They're difficult jobs, requiring skills that might or might not have any relationship to the skills demanded by junior roles. And management? Management is an entirely distinct discipline of its own. Distributing leadership roles as thank-yous for great technical work risks exposing us to toxicity and mismanagement.

In this chapter, we're going to talk through how contemporary leaders approach promotion, rethinking the promotion-as-carrot model by addressing these issues:

- Whom to promote
- Candidate sponsorship

- External considerations
- Alternatives to promotion

Along the way, career loopers will learn what it takes to earn promotions on contemporary teams.

24.2 Whom to Promote

Senior roles and management roles require more than just deep technical skills. They require a variety of durable skills, chief among them, skills in leadership and communication.

Although poorly coached candidates often focus on technical development, the promotion panels that I've been part of usually don't debate technical ability. They debate whether candidates listen well when interacting with teammates. They debate whether candidates give others the space to solve problems and grow. In short, they debate whether candidates exhibit the management skills and behaviors that we discussed in Chapter 23.

Anuja adds that promotion decisions often "come back to adaptability. Changes happen—organizational, economic, and technological. The capacity to adapt to that change is an important criterion for promotion."

If we take the demands of contemporary management seriously, then we should look at Chapter 23 and promote for the skills laid out there. It's not just about skill either. It's also about desire. Any promotion will only endure time and satisfy the candidate if they genuinely want to learn the skills required for their new role. The right promotion candidate will possess deep durable skills, a strong capacity for adaptation, and an enthusiastic desire to grow into leadership.

24.3 Candidate Sponsorship

As managers, it's not just our job to identify someone who should get promoted. We have to become their sponsor. At first, they're going to need a sponsor to advocate for their promotion. Then, down the road, once they've secured a promotion, the candidate's going to need us to legitimize and explain that promotion.

Former peers won't understand why this candidate was promoted. They won't understand the candidate's new role. And they won't know how to treat them or learn from them. It's our job as managers to cascade that information down through the team and regularly reinforce that messaging until it takes hold.

If we don't sponsor our direct reports for promotion, then other company leaders won't notice them or take action. And if we don't launch a sustained campaign to reinforce the promotion post facto, then automatic team dynamics will take over. The host will reject the graft, and the promotion won't ever take.

Without long-term sponsorship, expect politics and exits down the road. With strong sponsorship, expect a successful promotion and long-term growth for the individual, the team, and the business as a whole.

24.4   External Considerations

As managers, it's our responsibility to coach promotion candidates on two major external factors that will influence their promotions.

24.4.1   Other Stakeholders

Besides us, a host of other stakeholders will weigh in on the promotion decision. These can include the candidate's future peers as well as other, more senior members of the team. We need to team up with our candidates in order to win all these people over and secure the promotion.

24.4.2   *Business Needs*

Sometimes a direct report would make a great director of engineering, but the company just doesn't need another director of engineering right now. To find success, we have to work together with the candidate to prove that this promotion will serve the business.

24.5   **Alternatives to Promotion**

During promotion, always do a double-check. As the candidate's manager and sponsor, it's our responsibility to make sure that—of all the things we could possibly do for this person—promotion is the one thing that will serve them best.

Again, this is where old-school attitudes about promotion can lead us astray. If, like previous generations, we see promotion as a thank-you for a job well done, and we've got a hard-working direct report, then promotion might feel like the obvious next step. But contemporary managers appreciate that senior roles are more than just trophies. They're entirely different jobs, with different responsibilities.

However successful an employee's been in their current role, they might have a skill gap keeping them from promotion readiness. In those cases, it's our job to ensure that the employee knows what they need to do in order to demonstrate growth.

Meanwhile, we have to remember that not every employee's professional path will point them toward leadership. We've already said that new roles confer new responsibilities. And that principle comes with a corollary: new roles also take old responsibilities away.

If an engineer becomes a director of engineering, they, ironically, won't get to spend as much time engineering. So if we've got a kickass engineer reporting to us, and their professional path is leading them toward growing into an even more kickass engineer, then promoting them to that director role won't actually serve their long-term growth. Admittedly, this does sometimes mean that the best next step for one of our direct reports might be on someone else's team, or even at someone else's company.

I've had to make this call many times throughout my career, supporting people exiting the company because we knew that their best next opportunity wasn't a promotion to leadership on my team, but a promotion to even cooler independent contributor opportunity on someone else's.

Anuja sums this up well:

> Many managers are like, "Well, if I've got a really strong person on my team, I'm never letting them go. I've got to do whatever I can to keep them on the team."
>
> But, the shift for modern managers is to accept that that's not their responsibility. Their responsibility is to ask, "How do you help that person get to where they want to go?" *That* is managing. Helping them find their opportunity. That could be on your team, or not.
>
> You have to accept the risk that you've invested and put time into a person that will leave. It's hard, but it's the thing to do if you really want to cultivate strong people who are going to go off and make an impact in the world.

24.6   Beyond This Loop

If we look at the Community Loop discussed throughout this book, we'll see that our direct reports are looking for all kinds of supporters in their careers besides great bosses. They need mentors. They need coaches. They need sponsors.

Our job, as managers, is to fill as many of those roles for our direct reports as we can. It's our job to help guide them for as long as they're with us. That might be for one cycle of the loop or for many. But it almost certainly won't be for their entire careers.

We help them find their professional paths on our teams. We help them level up. And we help them pursue their next opportunities, whether on our teams or elsewhere. We help them loop and loop and loop, until, someday, they loop away from us.

Yoda put it best: "We are what they grow beyond."

Conclusion

To folks from previous generations, today's economy looks like a horror game—just one jump scare after another. You're walking along . . . minding your own business . . . and *BAM!* New tech flying at you! *BAM!* Evil robots stealing your job! *BAM!* Undead startups axing your industry to bits!

It's the stuff of nightmares! One minute, you think you're gonna have a linear career—first you learn a bunch of stuff in school, then you earn a bunch of money at work. And then one day at the office, these Cylons and Daleks and Droidekas show up from out of nowhere and blast it all to bits.

Of course, normies are gonna hate these jump scares. But gamers? Gamers don't jump, because gamers know where the scares are. And when you know where the scares are, they aren't really scares at all. They're *thrills*.

As gamers, we don't expect linearity. We don't expect things to go as planned. We expect thrills. We expect things to keep on changing. More specifically, we expect things to change in *cycles*: first the change comes, then we master it, then we earn our reward. Repeat. Change, triumph, reward. Change, triumph, reward.

And as gamers, we don't just *expect* these cycles of change. We *crave* these cycles of change. It's these cycles that make things fun. They're what give the game of work its challenge. Without these cycles, there couldn't be play.

And it's not just about fun either. For us, all that change and all that disruption don't spell danger. They spell possibility.

If we get to keep respawning and leveling up—if we get to keep growing throughout our careers—then we aren't stuck with our starting stats. We aren't limited by our degrees or our schools or our inherited family networks. We have the opportunity to master new technologies, acquire new skills, and build new communities. We have the opportunity to keep learning more, keep earning more, and keep advancing.

Learn, Earn, Advance

As in any game, we navigate this cycle of growth in a loop—in this case, the Core Career Loop.

Phase 1: Choose Quest

We choose a profession to pursue.

Phase 2: Level Up

We learn the skills necessary to work in that profession.

Phase 3: Job Hunt

We hunt down a job in that profession.

Phase 4: Job Craft

We use that job as a springboard toward further growth, beginning the cycle again.

Along the way, we find that gaming hasn't only prepared us to navigate loops in general. It's also given us the key skills necessary to master this particular loop.

When Phase 1 challenges us to make hard choices, we find that we're master decision-makers. Contemporary choice-driven games have already trained us to explore vast worlds, weigh competing values, and carve out unique paths.

Then, when the time comes to build new skills in Phase 2, we do so naturally. We could go back to school, but, as gamers, that's not our only option. Games have trained us to learn independently, seeking out optimized challenges, embracing failure, and, ultimately, raking in the high scores. As *Elden Ring* creator Hidetaka Miyazaki explained, games are, at their core, the medium of "hardship and accomplishment," "risk and reward."[1] For us, leveling up isn't a hassle. It's an addictive hobby.

With the necessary skills built, we don't just grind for jobs in Phase 3—we hack the grind, too. We use a host of independent and community-based strategies to bypass the norm of sending out tens, or even hundreds, of résumés. We're still diligent, but we focus our diligence. We target-lock on a handful of specific employers, and we use every narrative and team-based tool at our disposal to win a quality offer.

Finally, once we're on the job, we draw on our experience of emergent play to work subversively. We break and bend and rewrite the rules of the game while we play it. We reinvent ourselves on the job, and we begin the loop again.

From Player to Creator

Throughout this book, we've heard from lots of game developers who've mastered the loop. There was James Stone, the officer-photographer-developer-tech leader. There was Stacey Haffner, who beat the NBA at its own game. There was Ray Graham, who worked at EA and 2k and Ubisoft before becoming a games industry mentor. There was Joy Horvath. There was Andrew Connell. There was Steven Christian.

Across the decades I've spent at the intersection of games, education, and workforce development, I've learned that there's only one group of people who are better prepared than gamers for career looping in the new economy. And that's game *creators*. Most especially—*indie* game creators.

When it comes to Phase 1 decision-making, these folks have unparalleled experience. Like many other kinds of creators, they research tools and techniques, weigh pros and cons, and, when they have to, they follow their guts. But there's more to it than that.

Contemporary games are, among other things, a medium of choice. So these creators don't just need to understand their own decision-making processes; they need to understand the decision-making processes of others. As they craft branching narratives and intuitive mechanics, creators study why people make the decisions they make, and then they engineer better choices for them.

Meanwhile, an indie developer's capacity for leveling up in Phase 2 is unrivaled. Today's indies need to become tech wizzes, designers, writers, artists, musicians, marketers. They become project managers and producers and fundraisers. They acquire some of the deepest, broadest skill sets on the market, and, in the process, they learn to level up quickly, preparing them for any challenge they face.

When Phase 3 comes around, these creators are, of course, expert storytellers, better positioned than anyone to craft interactive application narratives. And when it comes time to job craft in Phase 4, game developers are uniquely prepared to design their own systems and their own rules—to hack and mod and iterate.

Along the way, creators develop some of the most important durable skills: adaptability, resilience, and flexibility. And these skills don't just prepare creators to go into the games industry. Our research shows that Unity creators commonly go on to about two dozen other industries and professions, where their game development skills serve them well. Engineering and animation. Aerospace, automotive, and transportation. Architecture and construction. Health, education, finance, defense.

So for any gamers who are interested, I strongly encourage you to make the leap from player to creator. It's never been easier than it is now.

At Unity, our tech teams work every day to make game development tools more accessible and more intuitive. And the education team is constantly rethinking, reworking, and reinventing the way we teach game development skills. We've built tons and tons and *tons* of free resources with both techies and non-techies in mind.

If you're one of those non-techies and you try it out—if you find yourself baffled or stuck, *tell us.* If there's anything standing between you and learning to develop in Unity, we want to hear about it.

I believe that game development has an extraordinary power to transform each of our careers. And I've devoted my own career to making sure that everyone has that opportunity.

Dear Leaders

If you're an institutional leader reading this, I hope you'll take the same lessons to heart. I hope you'll walk away from this book appreciating that whether they're being played or being created, games have an extraordinary capacity to prepare us for success in the new economy—both as students and as team members. And I hope you'll walk away with a new perspective on which skills really matter.

We're going to need to see transformation in educational institutions of all kinds. From primary schools to universities. From vocational programs to bootcamps. These programs need to evolve, graduating more durable, more adaptable alumni, who are better prepared to navigate cyclical careers.

Meanwhile, employers and industry leaders, I encourage you to rethink old-school hiring practices. Let's look beyond personal networks, beyond finite technical skills, and let's focus on building more diverse teams that are better equipped to adapt and innovate.

To the leaders in education access and workforce development, I send thanks and encouragement. You're the ones who are going to help this generation of job seekers bridge the gap between old-school, traditional, linear education and the cyclical realities of the modern market.

For leaders of all kinds, it's a difficult road ahead. As a group, we skew older. Many of us were born into a more stable, less disrupted world. My advice: we should be looking to our youngers. To them, chaos isn't scary. Chaos is a ladder. Every challenge is an opportunity to level up, to create a new opportunity, and to reap new rewards.

So even as they look to us for mentorship, coaching, sponsorship, and leadership, we should be looking to them as role models for the skills and mentalities that will move the needle in the new economy.

Looping Back to Community

Mentorship. Coaching. Sponsorship. Leadership. Ultimately it's our communities that will determine what each of us achieves. Without the help of our peers and our elders, our friends and our family, work acquaintances and weak ties and total strangers, none of us will get anywhere at all.

Life is, as it always has been, a multiplayer game. We need our guilds and our clans to help guide us. Our communities help us see our own values and make strong choices. They help us stay accountable and level up. They open doors and sing our praises. And, when the time comes, they wave us goodbye and send us off on our next great adventures.

If you're looking to jump-start your Community Loop, check out CareerGameLoop.com, where we, as gamers and career loopers, are pursuing new professions together. When we join this platform, each of us commits to asking for help when we need it, and to giving help when we can—offering to chat, to give pointers, to make introductions.

Come join us. Let us help you find your gravitational pull, figure out your little quests, tell your job story, and craft your way to a new role. Come share your progress. Come mentor and coach and sponsor others.

Along the way, you'll find downloadable workbooks, as well as templates for the following:

- Professional Pathfinder
- Networking emails

- Job story outlines
- Portfolios
- And lots more

Press X to Jump

Everyone knows that jump scares are scariest when we're playing alone. When we build our careers together, we become all the more adaptable, durable, and resilient. And the scares turn to thrills.

The thrill of learning. The thrill of earning. The thrill of opportunity.

I've said it before, and I'll say it again: we have never been so free to choose our own paths, so at liberty to pivot, or so empowered to adapt.

In the new economy, we don't need special social or economic privileges, and we don't need inherited family networks to thrive. All we need are the right tools, a good map, and a keen sense of adventure.

Let the games begin.

Note

1. Nightingale, Ed. "Elden Ring Creator Hidetaka Miyazaki on Originating the Soulslike Genre." Eurogamer, February 21, 2024. https://www.euro gamer.net/elden-ring-creator-hidetaka-miyazaki-on-originating-the-soulslike-genre.

Index